Focus on PRONUNCIATION 3

THIRD EDITION

Linda Lane

American Language Program
Columbia University

Focus on Pronunciation 3, Third Edition

Pearson Education, 10 Bank Street, White Plains, NY 10606

Staff credits: The people who made up the *Focus on Pronunciation 3, Third Edition* team, representing editorial, production, design, and manufacturing, are Dave Dickey, Nancy Flaggman, Ann France, Maria Pia Marrella, Lise Minovitz, Liza Pleva, Mary Perrotta Rich, Robert Ruvo, and Lynn Sobotta.

Cover image: Shutterstock.com
Text composition: ElectraGraphics, Inc.
Text font: 10/12 New Aster
Illustrations: Gary Torrisi and Jill Wood

Library of Congress Cataloging-in-Publication Data

Lane, Linda (Linda L.)
  Focus on pronunciation : [v.] 1 / Linda Lane. — 3rd ed.
      p. cm.
  ISBN 0-13-231493-2 (v. 1) — ISBN 0-13-231494-0 (v. 2) — ISBN 0-13-231500-9 (v. 3)   1.   English language—Pronunciation—Problems, exercises, etc.   2.   English language—Textbooks for foreign speakers.   I. Title.
  PE1137.L22 2012
  428.3'4—dc23

                                                              2011047246

ISBN 10: 0-13-231500-9
ISBN 13: 978-0-13-231500-5

Printed in the United States of America

2 3 4 5 6 7 8 9 10—V011—17 16 15 14 13

CONTENTS

INTRODUCTION

Focus on Pronunciation 3 is a comprehensive course that helps high-intermediate to advanced students speak English more clearly, confidently, and accurately. The course covers important topics from all aspects of pronunciation—sounds, stress, rhythm, and intonation.

The vowel and consonant sounds presented are those that occur frequently in English and that students recognize as new or difficult. Stress, rhythm, or intonation topics focus on pronunciation features that are important for clear English communication and that students can easily notice.

Each unit ends with Communication Practice about a theme (for example, gift giving or brain food). As such, the activities and practice provide students with opportunities to improve their pronunciation and communication skills in context.

ORGANIZATION OF *FOCUS ON PRONUNCIATION 3*

Focus on Pronunciation 3 is divided into five parts: Vowels; Consonants; Syllables and Stress within Words; Rhythm; and Intonation. Each unit deals with specific pronunciation points and has the following organization:

STEP 1   PRESENTATION

This section introduces, explains, and provides information about the pronunciation point. It may show how sounds are made or present other useful information. This is often achieved through the use of diagrams or illustrations. Pronunciation explanations are student friendly and easy to understand.

STEP 2   FOCUSED PRACTICE

This section consists of controlled classroom activities that allow students to develop skill and proficiency with the pronunciation point.

STEP 3   COMMUNICATION PRACTICE

This section provides communicative practice activities that focus on a theme. The activities are more open-ended and they ensure student involvement through the use of games and interactive tasks. When students are engaged in the communicative activities, they should be encouraged to keep in mind these global features of clear speaking:

- Speak slowly.
- Speak loudly enough.
- Pay attention to the ends of words.
- Use your voice to speak expressively.

NEW!   NATURAL ENGLISH

New to this edition, the Natural English box in each unit highlights ways to speak English more naturally. In some cases, the Natural English box reviews or "pulls in" another important aspect of pronunciation that is not the focus of the current unit. Students might, for example, be reminded to group words together in a consonant or vowel unit in order to make their English more understandable to others. Additionally, the Natural English box may highlight the pronunciation of useful expressions (such as the use of *me too* for agreement).

STEP 4   EXTENDED PRACTICE

This section consists of recorded homework activities. Accuracy Practice reviews key controlled exercises within the unit and serves as a warm-up for Fluency Practice, a freer speaking task that deals with the content of the unit. Students who have access to a computer can record their voices and review their pronunciation. The teacher can also listen to these recordings and provide feedback. Directions for how to make and send electronic files are at the back of the Student Book.

AUDIO PROGRAM

The **Classroom Audio CDs** have the recordings for all the pronunciation and listening exercises in the Student Book.

The **Student Audio CD-ROM** in the back of the book has all the recordings needed to complete the Accuracy Practice exercises in MP3 format.

KEY TO ICONS

🎧 —material recorded as part of the Classroom Audio CDs

🎧 —material recorded as part of the Student Audio CD-ROM in the Student Book

🎤 —material for students to record and give to the teacher

PLANNING A SYLLABUS

The units in *Focus on Pronunciation 3* can be used in any order. Teachers can "skip around"—for example, teaching the overview unit for Vowels, then a specific vowel unit, then the overview for Rhythm, then a specific unit dealing with rhythm, and so on. Teachers who adopt this approach could also cover all the overview units at the beginning of the course and then skip around within the sections. The units can also be taught in order, first covering vowels, then consonants, and so on.

GENERAL REFERENCES

Most students have difficulty with English vowels and with stress, rhythm, and intonation, regardless of their native language background. With the exception of a few consonants (for example, the first sound in *think*), consonant difficulty depends more on the native language. The following references provide information on pronunciation problems related to native language:

Avery, Peter and S. Ehrlich. *Teaching American English Pronunciation*. Oxford: Oxford University Press, 1992.

Lane, Linda. *Tips for Teaching Pronunciation*. Pearson Longman, 2010.

Swan, M. and Smith, B. *Learner English, 2nd Ed.* Cambridge, UK: Cambridge University Press, 2001.

The following research influenced the content and approach of this book:

Avery, Peter and S. Ehrlich. *Teaching American English Pronunciation*. Oxford: Oxford University Press, 1992.

Celce-Murcia, Marianne, D. M. Brinton and J. M. Goodwin. *Teaching Pronunciation: A Reference for Teachers of English to Speakers of Other Languages*. Cambridge: Cambridge University Press, 1996.

Lane, Linda. *Tips for Teaching Pronunciation*. Pearson Longman, 2010.

ABOUT THE AUTHOR / ACKNOWLEDGMENTS

Linda Lane is a senior faculty member in the American Language Program of Columbia University. In addition to the *Focus on Pronunciation* series, she is also the author of *Tips for Teaching Pronunciation,* Pearson, 2010. She served as director of the Columbia University Humanities Media Center for 10 years and coordinated Columbia's TESOL Certificate Program for another 10 years, teaching classes in Applied Phonetics and Pronunciation Teaching and Introduction to Second Language Acquisition. She received her EdD in Applied Linguistics from Teachers College, Columbia University, her MA in Linguistics from Yale University, and her BS in Mathematics from the University of Washington, Seattle.

I am indebted to a number of people whose support, patience, and good humor made this book possible. I am grateful for the help and suggestions of my editors at Pearson: Lise Minovitz, Lynn Sobotta, and Robert Ruvo.

I would like to thank the reviewers who offered suggestions that shaped the new edition: Ashkhen Strack, Tunxis Community College, Farmington, CT; Victor Matthews, Assumption College, Lampang, Thailand; Judy Gilbert, Columbia University, New York, NY; Joanna Ghosh, University of Pennsylvania, Philadelphia, PA.

In addition, I would like to thank those reviewers whose insights shaped the previous edition: Dr. John Milbury-Steen, Temple University, Philadelphia, PA; Michele McMenamin, Rutgers University, Piscataway, NJ; Gwendolyn Kane, Rutgers University, Piscataway, NJ; William Crawford, Georgetown University, Washington, D.C.; Linda Wells, University of Washington, Seattle, WA; Tara Narcross, Columbus State Community College, Columbus, OH; Robert Baldwin, UCLA, Los Angeles, CA; Mary Di Stefano Diaz, Broward Community College, Davie, FL; Barbara Smith-Palinkas, University of South Florida, Tampa, FL; Susan Jamieson, Bellevue Community College, Bellevue, WA; Andrea Toth, City College of San Francisco, San Francisco, CA; Fernando Barboza, ICPNA, Lima, Peru; Adrianne P. Ochoa, Georgia State University, Atlanta, GA; Greg Jewell, Drexel University, Philadelphia, PA; Cindy Chang, University of Washington, Seattle, WA; Emily Rosales, Université du Québec à Montréal/École de Langues, Montréal, QC, Canada.

My colleagues at the American Language Program at Columbia University have always been an inspiration and source of generous support.

For the encouragement and patience of my family, Mile, Martha, Sonia, and Luke, and of my dear friend Mary Jerome, whom I miss every day, I am also deeply grateful.

Finally, I want to thank my students—for teaching me how they learn pronunciation, for wanting to improve their pronunciation, and for showing me how to help them.

–Linda Lane

VOWELS

STEP 1 PRESENTATION

There are 14 vowel sounds in American English: 11 vowels and 3 complex vowels. Vowels are produced by movements of the tongue up and down, and front and back. Movements of the middle of the tongue (not the tip) produce vowel sounds. Listen to the vowels and sample words.

The Vowels of English

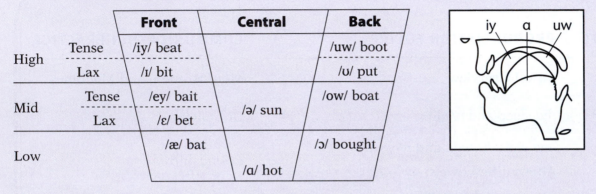

		Front	Central	Back
High	Tense	/iy/ beat		/uw/ boot
	Lax	/ɪ/ bit		/ʊ/ put
Mid	Tense	/ey/ bait	/ə/ sun	/ow/ boat
	Lax	/ɛ/ bet		
Low		/æ/ bat	/ɑ/ hot	/ɔ/ bought

The columns show whether the tongue is toward the front, center, or back of the mouth.

The rows show whether the tongue is high, in the middle, or low in the mouth.

The drawing on the right shows the approximate positions for three of the vowels.

Complex Vowels

There are three complex vowels:

/aw/ how   /ay/ high   /oy/ boy

Tense and Lax Vowels

Tense and lax vowel pairs, such as *feet-fit*, are difficult for many students. Tense vowels are pronounced with more muscle tension. With lax vowels, the muscles of the mouth are more relaxed.

1. **Tense vowels: /iy/ s**ee**, /ey/ p**ay**, /ow/ gr**ow**, /uw/ sh**oe
    Many languages have vowels that are similar to these vowels.
    In English, the tense vowels are not *pure* vowels—they end in /y/ or /w/.

2. **Lax vowels: /ɪ/** thin**, /ɛ/** br**ea**d**, /ʊ/** g**oo**d
    These are new vowels for many students.

Joining Vowels to Vowels

When a vowel that ends in /y/ or /w/ is followed by another vowel, join the vowels together with /y/ or /w/.

grow up   go^w on   lay-offs   three^y animals

STEP 2 FOCUSED PRACTICE

EXERCISE 1: Feeling Sounds

PAIRS: Do the vowel experiments with your partner.

1. **Front and Back Vowels.** The vowel in *he* /iy/ is a front vowel; the vowel in *who* /uw/ is a back vowel.

   Say /iy-uw-iy-uw/ (the vowels in *he* and *who*).

   Concentrate on the middle of your tongue—feel it move from front to back (it may be easier to feel the movement if you close your eyes as you speak).

   Say /ey-ow-ey-ow/ (the vowels in *day* and *go*).

   What happens to your lips when you move from front vowels (/iy/ or /ey/) to back vowels (/uw/ or /ow/)?

2. **High and Low Vowels.** The vowel in *be* /iy/ is a high vowel. The vowel in *hot* /ɑ/ is a low vowel.

   Say /iy-ɑ-iy-ɑ/ (the vowels in *be* and *hot*).

   Feel the tongue moving up and down (or, feel your jaw opening and closing).

   What happens to your lips when you move from /iy/ to /ɑ/?

EXERCISE 2: Tense and Lax Vowels

Look at the diagrams of the vowel pairs. For the lax vowels, the mouth looks more relaxed because the lips are less spread and less rounded. The muscles inside the mouth are also more relaxed.

Tense	Lax		Tense	Lax		Tense	Lax
/iy/	/ɪ/		/ey/	/ɛ/		/uw/	/ʊ/
he'd	hid		age	edge		Luke	look

A | *Listen and repeat the words. Say the tense vowel first. Then let your tongue drop a little to the center of your mouth and say the lax vowel. Keep your lips relaxed for the lax vowel.*

	Tense	Lax		Tense	Lax		Tense	Lax
1.	**a.** /iy/	**b.** /ɪ/	5.	**a.** /ey/	**b.** /ɛ/	9.	**a.** /uw/	**b.** /ʊ/
2.	**a.** each	**b.** itch	6.	**a.** wait	**b.** wet	10.	**a.** Luke	**b.** look
3.	**a.** leave	**b.** live	7.	**a.** paper	**b.** pepper	11.	**a.** who'd	**b.** hood
4.	**a.** sleep	**b.** slip	8.	**a.** faints	**b.** fence	12.	**a.** stewed[1]	**b.** stood

B | *Listen again and circle the words you hear.*

C | *PAIRS: Say a word from Part A. Pronounce the vowel carefully so your partner can tell you which word you said.*

---

[1] stewed: *meat and vegetables cooked slowly in liquid*

EXERCISE 3: Words with /ɛ/, /æ/, /ə/, and /ɑ/

Look at the mouth diagrams for the vowels.

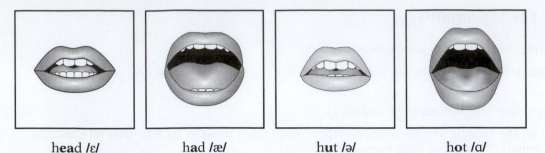

head /ɛ/   had /æ/   hut /ə/   hot /ɑ/

The vowels in *head, had, hut,* and *hot* are difficult for many students. These vowels are pronounced in the front or center of the mouth, with the tongue in the middle of the mouth or low in the mouth.

- The lips are spread for the vowels in *head* and *had*.
- The lips are not spread for the vowels in *hut* and *hot*.
- The mouth is open for the vowels in *had* and *hot*.
- The mouth is more closed for the vowels in *head* and *hut*.

A | *Listen and repeat the words.*

	/ɛ/	/æ/		/ə/	/ɑ/		/æ/	/ɑ/
1.	**a.** pet	**b.** pat	**4.**	**a.** once	**b.** wants	**7.**	**a.** lack	**b.** lock
2.	**a.** men	**b.** man	**5.**	**a.** luck	**b.** lock	**8.**	**a.** impassible	**b.** impossible
3.	**a.** said	**b.** sad	**6.**	**a.** nut	**b.** not	**9.**	**a.** black	**b.** block

B | *Listen again and circle the words you hear.*

C | *PAIRS: Say a word from Part A. Use the diagrams in Exercise 3 to help you. Pronounce the vowel carefully so your partner can tell you which word you said.*

EXERCISE 4: Fill in the Grid

PAIRS: Each of you has a grid that is partially complete. Don't show your grid to your partner. Take turns asking each other for missing words. Pronounce the vowels in the words carefully. When you finish, compare your grids. They should be the same. Student A's grid is on page 253. Student B's grid is on page 259.

MEN, WOMEN, AND MACHINES

EXERCISE 5: Watson

A | *Listen and repeat. Make sure you understand the words.*

artificial intelligence	tournament
contestant	clue
Jeopardy	in-depth
quiz show	trivia
challenge	diagnose

B | *Listen to the recording and then answer the questions.*

1. What kind of system did Ferruci set out to build?
2. What challenges does a quiz show like *Jeopardy* present for computers?
3. What kind of system does Professor Chase want? How will it be different from the Watson designed for *Jeopardy*?
4. Do you think computers will ever be as intelligent as humans?

C | *GROUPS: Compare your answers.*

EXERCISE 6: Robots

People used to think of robots as "futuristic." Today, however, robots are becoming more and more common in industry and perhaps will one day be in our homes.

A | *Listen and repeat the sentences. Join words together.*

1. Industri^{y}al robots have replaced a lot of factory workers and caused layoffs.*

2. I'd be happy to have a robot do^w all my cleaning.

3. I'd rather be^y alone than have a robot companion.

4. My father had robotic surgery.

5. There's a robot soccer tournament on TV tonight.

6. There are a lot of employment opportunities for roboticists.

---

*Natural English

Join two vowel sounds inside a word with /y/ or /w/. The letter *y* or *w* is usually not written inside the word.

industri^{y}al

sci^{y}ence

influ^{w}ence

B | *GROUPS: The sentences in Part A mention possible or actual uses of robots as well as opinions about robots. What are the uses? What are the opinions? How would you feel about having a robot in your home? What would you want it to do?*

STEP 4   EXTENDED PRACTICE

Accuracy Practice   *Listen again to Exercises 2A and 3A on pages 3 and 4. Then record the words.*

Fluency Practice   *What are the advantages of robots? What are the disadvantages? Record your answers to the questions.*

UNIT 2 /iy/ sl__eep and /ɪ/ sl__ip

STEP 1 PRESENTATION

The Vowels

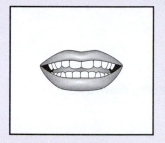

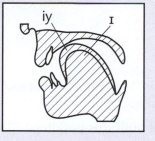

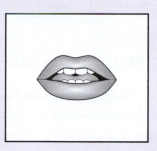

sleep /iy/

slip /ɪ/

Spread your lips.

Most languages have a pure vowel similar to /iy/.

In English, /iy/ is not a pure vowel: It ends in a /y/ sound.

Don't spread your lips.

Drop your tongue down from its position for /iy/.

/ɪ/ is a "lax" (relaxed) vowel.

/ɪ/ is a new vowel for most students.

Notes

Joining /iy/ to Following Vowels: When /iy/ is followed by another vowel, use /y/ to join the two vowels together. The vowels are in different syllables.

radi^yo   be^y open

Spellings for /iy/		Spellings for /ɪ/	
Common		**Common**	
ee	three, freeze	*i*	six, picture
e . . . e (silent e)	these, complete	*y*	gym, system
e	me, even, recent		
ea	tea, leaf		
ie	piece, believe		
Other		**Other**	
ey	key, donkey	*e*	English, pretty
ei	receive, ceiling	*ui*	build, guilty
i	ski, machine	*u*	busy, business
eo	people	*o*	women

7

STEP 2 FOCUSED PRACTICE

EXERCISE 1: Phrases with /iy/

🎧 *Listen and repeat the phrases and sentences. When /iy/ is followed by another vowel, use /y/ to join the vowels together. (The letter **y** has been added to help you.)*

1. a d**ee**p sl**ee**p
2. a w**ee**k at the b**ea**ch
3. Pl**ea**se k**ee**p it.
4. Let's m**ee**t at the mus**e**ᵞum.
5. It s**ee**ms **ea**sy.
6. Did you s**ee**ᵞ it?
7. When will the m**ee**ting b**e**ᵞ over?
8. Don't l**ea**ve the k**ey** in the door.

EXERCISE 2: Phrases with /ɪ/

🎧 *Listen and repeat the phrases and sentences. When you say /ɪ/, let your tongue drop down a little from the /iy/ position and don't spread your lips.*

1. s**i**x s**i**ck w**o**men
2. g**i**ft-g**i**ving traditions
3. **i**n the m**i**ddle
4. **i**n a m**i**nute
5. B**i**ll b**ui**lt this b**ui**lding.
6. a sl**i**ppery h**i**ll
7. My ch**i**n **i**tches.
8. b**u**sy b**u**sinessmen

EXERCISE 3: Listen for Differences

🎧 **A** | *Listen and repeat the phrases and sentences.*

1. a. sleep a lot
   b. slip a lot
2. a. Heat it.
   b. Hit it.

3. a. good feet
   b. good fit
4. a. I've got a bad feeling.
   b. I've got a bad filling.[1]

5. a. the son's reason
   b. The sun's risen.
6. a. cheap containers
   b. chip containers

🎧 **B** | *Listen again and circle the phrases or sentences you hear.*

C | *PAIRS: Say a phrase or sentence from Part A. Pronounce the vowels carefully so your partner can tell you which phrase or sentence you said.*

EXERCISE 4: Differences in Meaning

🎧 **A** | *Listen to the sentences and responses.*

Sentences	Responses
1. a. He has to <u>live</u> there.	That's too bad. It's a terrible neighborhood.
b. He has to <u>leave</u> there.	That's too bad. He seemed so happy at that job.
2. a. He has a <u>sheep</u>.	I've heard they make good pets.
b. He has a <u>ship</u>.	I thought he was afraid of the water.

---

[1] filling: *dental work that fills a decayed spot in a tooth*

3. a. <u>Fill</u> the glass.   With water?

    b. <u>Feel</u> the glass.   It's very smooth.

4. a. He got the <u>least</u> of the winners.   Really? He deserved to get the most!

    b. He got the <u>list</u> of the winners.   Is my name on it?

B | *PAIRS: Say a sentence. Pronounce the underlined word carefully so your partner can say the correct response.*

EXERCISE 5: Fill in the Grid

PAIRS: Each of you has a grid that is partially complete. Don't show your grid to your partner. Take turns asking each other for missing words. Pronounce the vowels in the words carefully. When you finish, compare your grids. They should be the same. Student A's grid is on page 253. Student B's grid is on page 259.

STEP 3 COMMUNICATION PRACTICE

GIFT GIVING

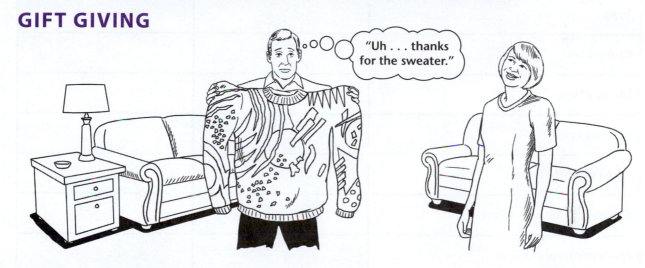

"Uh . . . thanks for the sweater."

EXERCISE 6: A Gift for Him

A | *Listen to the recording and complete the sentences with the words you hear. The missing words have /ɪ/ or /iy/ sounds.*

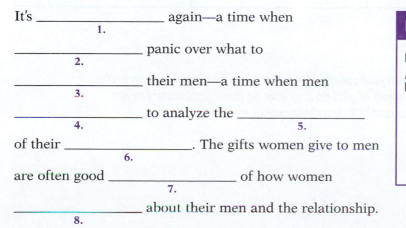

It's _____ again—a time when
1.

_____ panic over what to
2.

_____ their men—a time when men
3.

_____ to analyze the _____
4.   5.

of their _____. The gifts women give to men
6.

are often good _____ of how women
7.

_____ about their men and the relationship.
8.

Natural English

Pronounce the plural *women* as /wɪmən/. The plural is written with the letter *o*, but there is no *o* sound.

Women panic over what to give their men.

Women have a hard time deciding what gifts to give men.

B | PAIRS: *Compare your answers from Part A on page 9. Then practice reading the passage to each other. Pronounce the vowels carefully.*

EXERCISE 7: Good Gift or Bad Gift?

The 12 gifts in this chart are gifts that women have given to the special men in their lives. According to a website for men, six of the gifts are "good gifts," and six are "bad gifts."

PAIRS: Which gifts do you think are "good gifts" and which are "bad gifts"? What makes them good or bad? (You can check your answers on page 11.)

Gifts for Men	Good or Bad?	Reasons
Tickets to see his favorite team play		
A tie		
Something he can use for his favorite hobby		
Tools		
Opera tickets		
Silver cuff links		
A picture of her		
Race-car driving lessons		
A book from the best-seller list		
An electric razor		
White socks		
A sweater		

EXERCISE 8: Your Turn

GROUPS: Describe the gift-giving traditions in your country: On what occasions do people give gifts (for example, birthdays or holidays)? What types of gifts do they give on these occasions? Do you ever have trouble deciding what to give a person? Discuss these questions in your group.

EXERCISE 7: Good gifts and (reasons): Tickets to see his favorite sports team (she pays attention to his needs); a gift he can use for his favorite hobby (she wants him to enjoy himself); silver cuff links (they're classy); race-car driving lessons (she wants to add excitement to his life); a book from the best-seller list (she thinks he's intellectual); a sweater (a symbol of style and warmth). **Bad gifts and (reasons):** Ties (very "cliché"); tools (she wants him to do some work for her); opera tickets (they're a present for herself); a picture of her (she thinks too much of herself); electric razor (boring); white socks (she has no fashion sense and/or she doesn't care).

4. Do you think he or she liked it?

3. What is the last gift you gave to this person?

2. What do you usually give him or her?

1. Is it easy or difficult to find this person a gift? Why?

for each of the three people.

Fluency Practice *Think of three people you give gifts to. Record your answers to the questions*

and sentences.

Accuracy Practice *Listen again to Exercises 1, 2, and 3A on page 8. Then record the phrases*

STEP 4 EXTENDED PRACTICE

/ey/ w<u>ai</u>t, /ɛ/ w<u>e</u>t, and /ɪ/ w<u>i</u>t; Alternating Vowels: /iy/ ~ /ɛ/

STEP 1 PRESENTATION

The Vowels

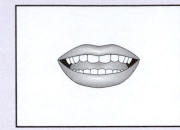

late /ey/

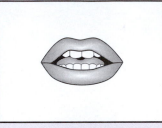

let /ɛ/

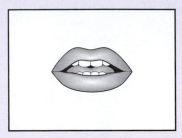

lit /ɪ/

Spread your lips.

/ey/ ends in a /y/ sound.

Start with /ey/. Let your tongue drop down a little.

Spread your lips just a little.

Relax your tongue, your lips, and your cheeks. /ɛ/ is a lax vowel.

Start with /iy/, the vowel in *eat*. Let your tongue drop down a little.

Don't spread your lips.

The tongue is a little higher in the mouth for /ɪ/ than for /ɛ/. /ɪ/ is a lax vowel.

Notes

1. **Joining /ey/ to a Following Vowel:** When another vowel follows /ey/, use /y/ to join the two vowels together. The vowels are in different syllables.

    weigh^yit   say it   formula^yic

2. **Alternating Vowels:** In some related words, the stressed vowel alternates between /iy/ and /ɛ/.

    m**e**ter ~ m**e**tric   k**ee**p ~ k**e**pt

Spellings for /ey/		Spellings for /ɛ/		Spellings for /ɪ/
Common		**Common**		See Unit 2.
a . . . e (silent *e*)	taste, plate	*e*	tennis, seven, left	
a	paper, baby			
ai	wait, praise			
ay	pay, stay			
Other		**Other**		
eigh	weigh, eight	*ea*	dead, breakfast	
ea	break, great	*a*	many, any	
ey	they, obey	*ai*	said, again	
ei	vein	*ay*	says	
		ie	friend	

EXERCISE 1: Phrases with /ey/, /ɛ/, and /ɪ/

🎧 *Listen and repeat the phrases. The bold letters are pronounced /ey/, /ɛ/, or /ɪ/. Join final consonants to following vowels. Join /ey/ to following vowels.*

/ey/	/ɛ/	/ɪ/
1. take a train	4. my best friend	7. single women
2. explain our mistakes	5. wet weather	8. Which wish?
3. stay out late	6. credit card debt	9. busy businessmen

EXERCISE 2: Listen for Differences

🎧 **A** | *Listen and repeat the phrases and sentences.*

1. a. Rake it.	3. a. I spilled milk.	5. a. a better butter
b. Wreck it.	b. I spelled "milk."	b. a bitter butter
2. a. Savor it.[1]	4. a. a trained setter.[3]	6. a. the age of the universe
b. Sever it.[2]	b. a trendsetter[4]	b. the edge of the universe

🎧 **B** | *Listen again and circle the phrases and sentences you hear.*

C | *PAIRS: Say a phrase or sentence from Part A. Pronounce the vowels carefully so your partner can tell you which phrase or sentence you said.*

EXERCISE 3: Differences in Meaning

🎧 **A** | *Listen to the sentences and responses.*

Sentences	Responses
1. a. He can't write with the <u>pain</u>.	Maybe he should see a doctor.
b. He can't write with the <u>pen</u>.	Is it out of ink?
2. a. We're going to have a little <u>test</u> now.	I wish I'd studied last night.
b. We're going to have a little <u>taste</u> now.	Oh, good. I love chocolate.
3. a. He has a lot of <u>debts</u>.	Credit cards can be very dangerous.
b. He has a lot of <u>dates</u>.	I wish my social life were as active!
4. a. Let's <u>weight</u> the branches down.	I'll put these rocks on them.
b. Let's <u>wet</u> the branches down.	They do look awfully dry.

B | *PAIRS: Say a sentence. Pronounce the underlined word carefully so your partner can say the correct response.*

---

[1] savor: *to enjoy something (usually a taste)*; [2] sever: *to cut*; [3] setter: *breed of dog*; [4] trendsetter: *someone who creates (or sets) new trends or styles*

EXERCISE 4: Alternating Vowels

In some related words, the stressed vowel alternates between /iy/ and /ɛ/. The vowel in the more basic word is usually /iy/.

 **A |** *Listen and repeat the words.*

	/iy/		/ɛ/			/iy/		/ɛ/
1.	**a.** meter	**b.** metric		**5.**	**a.** serene	**b.** serenity
2.	**a.** sleep	**b.** slept		**6.**	**a.** deceive	**b.** deception
3.	**a.** sincere	**b.** sincerity		**7.**	**a.** receive	**b.** reception
4.	**a.** brief	**b.** brevity				

B | *PAIRS: Pronounce the word pairs and decide whether the bold letters are alternating vowels or the same vowel. Write **A** if the letters are alternating vowels. Write **S** if the letters are the same vowel.*

1. please—pleasant ___A___

2. reason—reasonable _____

3. discreet—discretion _____

4. delete—deletion _____

5. please—pleasure _____

6. compete—competitive _____

7. secret—secretive _____

8. heal—health _____

STEP 3   COMMUNICATION PRACTICE

FRIENDSHIP

EXERCISE 5: Quotations about Friendship

 **A |** *Listen to the recording and complete the sentences with the words you hear.*

1. A real _____ is one who walks _____ _____ others walk out.

2. A friend is someone who believes in you _____ you have ceased to believe _____ _____.

3. Lots of people want to ride with you in the limo,[1] but what you want is someone who will

_____ the bus with you _____ the limo _____

down.

4. When it hurts to look back, and you're _____ to look _____, you

can look beside you, and your _____ friend will be _____.

5. _____ and your friends feel superior. Succeed and _____ feel

_____.

6. The statistics on sanity are that one out of _____ four _____ is

suffering from some form of _____ _____. _____

of your three best friends. If _____ OK, _____ it's you.

7. Everywhere is nowhere. When a person _____ all his or her time in foreign

travel, the person _____ up having many _____, but no friends.

Natural English

Want and *to* are often blended into one word, *wanna*. In infinitives, *to* has a very short pronunciation, /tə/, and often joins closely to the following verb.

Lots of people *wanna* ride with you in the limo.

It hurts *tə* look back on the past.

B | *PAIRS: Compare your answers from Part A. Then say the quotations. Which quotes do you think are meant to be humorous? Which ones are serious?*

EXERCISE 6: Friends

A | *Listen and repeat. Make sure you understand the words.*

   1. network   **2.** sounding board   **3.** tangible   **4.** coping   **5.** buffer

B | *Listen to the recording and take notes on the types of support friends provide.*

Type of Support	Examples
1.	
2.	
3.	

---

[1] limo: *short for* limousine

C | *Now listen to three people describe how their friends helped them. What type(s) of support do the friends provide?*

1. Mary _____

2. Joe _____

3. Beth _____

EXERCISE 7: Your Turn

GROUPS: Discuss the questions.

1. Of the three types of support mentioned in the recording, which type do you think is most important in friendships? Why?
2. Do you have friends who provide all three types of support?
3. Do you think some types of support are more likely to be provided by family rather than friends? Why?
4. How do social networks increase/decrease the kinds of support friends can give each other?

STEP 4 EXTENDED PRACTICE

Accuracy Practice *Listen again to Exercises 1 and 2A on page 13. Then record the phrases and sentences.*

Fluency Practice *Think of a good friend of yours. Then record your answers to the questions.*

1. How long have you been friends? What do you like to do together?
2. How do you and your friend help each other?

/æ/ m<u>a</u>n and /ɛ/ m<u>e</u>n; Alternating Vowels: /ey/ ~ /æ/

STEP 1 PRESENTATION

The Vowels

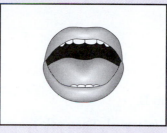

man /æ/

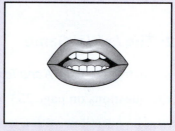

men /ɛ/

Open your mouth and spread your lips.

The tip of your tongue is behind the lower teeth, pushing down and slightly forward.

Your mouth is less open and more relaxed for /ɛ/ than for /æ/.

Notes

Alternating Vowels: In some related words, the stressed vowel alternates between /ey/ and /æ/.

sane → sanity

stable → establish

Spellings for /æ/		Spellings for /ɛ/	
Common		**Common**	
a	that, glasses	*e*	tennis, seven, left
Other		**Other**	
au	laugh, **au**nt	*ea*	d**ea**d, br**ea**kfast
ai	pl**ai**d	*a*	m**a**ny, **a**ny
		ai	s**ai**d, ag**ai**n
		ay	s**ay**s
		ie	fr**ie**nd

EXERCISE 1: Phrases with /æ/ and /ɛ/

🎧 *Listen and repeat the phrases.*

/æ/	/ɛ/
1. a bad example	**5.** precious metals
2. a ham sandwich	**6.** deli menu
3. natural reaction	**7.** heavy schedule
4. fast food	**8.** heaven and hell

EXERCISE 2: The /æ/-/ɛ/ Game

Play this game in two teams—Team A and Team B.

Team A: Ask the questions on page 253 to the players on Team B.

Team B: Answer the questions with a word that has an /æ/ or /ɛ/ vowel. Then ask Team A the questions on page 259. Give points for correct answers, correctly pronounced.

> **EXAMPLE:**
> **TEAM A:** What's another way of saying *50 percent*?
> **TEAM B:** Half.

EXERCISE 3: Sentences Full of Sounds

🎧 **A |** *Listen and repeat the sentences. Group words together and pronounce the vowels carefully.*

1. Ten tan tennis players attempted to take the champion's racket.
2. The cook blended a breakfast drink of bananas and bran in the black blender, but it was too bland to drink.
3. The experts expended a lot of energy creating a plan for the bridge expansion.

B | *PAIRS: Practice the sentences. Then choose one of the sentences and say it to the class. Speak as smoothly as you can.*

EXERCISE 4: Alternating Vowels

In some related words, the stressed vowel alternates between /ey/ and /æ/. The vowel in the more basic word is usually /ey/.

🎧 **A |** *Listen and repeat the words.*

	/ey/	/æ/		/ey/	/æ/
1.	sane	sanity	**5.**	nature	natural
2.	shade	shadow	**6.**	nation	national
3.	grateful	gratitude	**7.**	grain	granular
4.	depraved	depravity	**8.**	exclaim	exclamatory

B | PAIRS: Pronounce the word pairs. Write **A** if the bold letters are alternating vowels. Write **S** if the letters are the same vowel.

1. gr**a**ve—gr**a**vity __A__
2. sp**a**ce—sp**a**tial _____
3. f**a**me—f**a**mous _____
4. st**a**te—st**a**tic _____
5. br**a**ve—br**a**very _____
6. gr**a**de—gr**a**dual _____

7. b**a**the—b**a**th _____
8. st**a**tion—st**a**tionary _____
9. c**a**ve—c**a**vity _____
10. expl**a**in—expl**a**natory _____
11. esc**a**pe—esc**a**pist _____
12. beh**a**ve—beh**a**vior _____

STEP 3   COMMUNICATION PRACTICE

STAYING HEALTHY

EXERCISE 5: The Cost of Health

A | Listen to the conversation. The bold letters are pronounced /æ/ or /ɛ/.

ARTURO: Do you want to stop for pizza?
ROSANNA: No thanks. I'm trying to stay away from f**a**st food. I've started cooking.
ARTURO: I'm impr**e**ssed. Cooking takes a lot of time.
ROSANNA: Y**ea**h. There's grocery shopping, washing v**e**getables, chopping[1]—it's a lot of work.
ARTURO: Y**ea**h, but it's worth it. Home cooking is h**ea**lthier and probably cheaper.
ROSANNA: I don't think it's cheaper. I sp**e**nd a lot of money at the grocery store.

Natural English

The words in the phrase *a lot of* are often pronounced together as a single word, when the next word begins with a consonant: *alotta*.

   alotta time

   alotta work

B | PAIRS: Practice the conversation in Part A. Then talk about how often you eat home-cooked meals.

---
[1] chopping: *cutting into pieces*

EXERCISE 6: Lighten Up, Brooklyn

A | *Listen and repeat. Make sure you understand the words and phrases. The bold letters are pronounced /æ/, /ɛ/ or /ey/.*

ch**a**llenge	pit n**ei**ghbor ag**ai**nst n**ei**ghbor	coll**e**ctive
c**a**mp**ai**gn	shr**u**nk	

B | *Listen to the recording and fill in the information.*

Weight-loss goal _____   Winners' weight loss _____

Length of diet _____   Winners' prize _____

Number of winners _____   Total participant weight loss _____

EXERCISE 7: Your Turn

Health organizations are increasingly concerned about the growing number of overweight people in the world. The causes for this problem are complex, involving lifestyle, diet, education, standard of living, and genetics.

A | *The list below shows some of the reasons why people are overweight or obese. Check (✓) the three that you think are most responsible for these problems. The bold letters are pronounced /æ/ or /ɛ/.*

1. eating too much f**a**t _____

2. taking in too m**a**ny calories _____

3. eating too much sugar _____

4. eating too much f**a**st food _____

5. lack of **e**xercise _____

6. watching too much TV _____

7. sp**e**nding too much time online _____

8. lack of information _____

9. gen**e**tic prop**e**nsity _____

10. poverty/w**ea**lth _____

11. longer hours of work _____

12. Other _____

B | *GROUPS: Compare your answers. Are they the same? Talk about your choices and listen while others explain their opinions. Then look at the list again. Would you check the same three causes now?*

STEP 4   EXTENDED PRACTICE

Accuracy Practice *Listen again to Exercise 1 on page 18. Then record the phrases.*

Fluency Practice *Record the reasons you think that excess weight and obesity are becoming a global health problem.*

UNIT 5 /ɑ/ l<u>o</u>ck and /ə/ l<u>u</u>ck; Reduction of Unstressed Vowels

STEP 1 PRESENTATION

The Vowels

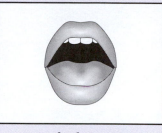

lock /ɑ/

Your mouth is open.
The tip of your tongue rests in the bottom of your mouth.
Your lips are not rounded.

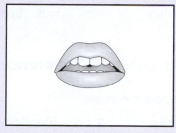

luck /ə/

Your tongue rests in the center of your mouth.
Your lips should be relaxed and open only a little.

/ə/: The Most Common Vowel

1. Most unstressed vowels are pronounced /ə/, making it the most common vowel in English.

    əgó (ago)   əccúr (occur)   ópən (open)   əbándən (abandon)

2. /ə/ is the "hesitation" sound of English, usually written *uh*.

    It's . . . uh /ə/ . . . uh /ə/ . . . it's . . . uh /ə/ . . . I'm sure it's here somewhere.

Spellings for /ɑ/		Spellings for stressed /ə/	
Common		(As an unstressed vowel sound, /ə/ can be spelled with any vowel letter.)	
o	block, pr<u>o</u>bably	**Common**	
a	f<u>a</u>ther, start	*u*	bus, husband
		o	money, come
Other		**Other**	
ua	g<u>ua</u>rd	*ou*	country, young
ow	kn<u>ow</u>ledge	*oo*	bl<u>oo</u>d, fl<u>oo</u>d
		oe	d<u>oe</u>s, d<u>oe</u>sn't
		a	wh<u>a</u>t, w<u>a</u>s

STEP 2 FOCUSED PRACTICE

EXERCISE 1: Phrases with /ɑ/ and /ə/

🎧 *Listen and repeat the phrases. The bold letters are pronounced /ɑ/ or /ə/. Your mouth should be open for /ɑ/ and nearly closed for /ə/.*

/ɑ/

1. modern technology
2. odd jobs
3. the heart of the problem
4. popular policy

/ə/

5. enough money
6. corrupt government
7. once a month
8. brotherly love

EXERCISE 2: Listen for Differences

🎧 **A |** *Listen and repeat the words.*

1. a. soccer
   b. succor[1]
2. a. body
   b. buddy

3. a. blonder
   b. blunder[2]
4. a. collar[3]
   b. color

5. a. hog[4]
   b. hug
6. a. wants
   b. once

🎧 **B |** *Listen again and circle the words you hear.*

EXERCISE 3: Sounds and Spelling

🎧 **A |** *Listen to the word pairs. Write S if the bold vowel sounds are the same. Write D if the bold vowel sounds are different. Then circle the words that have the /ə/ sound.*

1. done, bone __D__
2. love, move _____
3. monkey, donkey _____
4. what, hat _____
5. does, poet _____
6. honey, lunch _____

7. other, nothing _____
8. blood, food _____
9. couple, flood _____
10. touch, duck _____
11. once, young _____
12. cousin, cough _____

B | *PAIRS: Compare your answers. Then practice the words.*

---

[1] succor: *help;* [2] blunder: *mistake;* [3] *Some people pronounce* collar *with the /ɔ/ vowel;* [4] hog: *large pig*

EXERCISE 4: Unstressed Vowels

The words below have been "respelled" to show how the unstressed vowels are pronounced. Listen and repeat the words. Then write the correct spelling of the word in the blank.

1. pəséssəv

   _____possessive_____

2. ənnóuncemənt

   _____

3. hóstəl

   _____

4. státəs

   _____

5. pəllútəd

   _____

6. bənánə

   _____

7. cəmmánd

   _____

8. əppéarənce

   _____

9. təníght

   _____

STEP 3   COMMUNICATION PRACTICE

THE LOVE OF MONEY

EXERCISE 5: The Witch of Wall Street

A | *Listen and repeat. Make sure you understand the words and phrases.*

1. notorious
2. miser
3. inherited
4. amputated
5. died of a stroke
6. allegedly

B | *Listen to the recording. As you listen, count the number of times you hear the word* money.

I heard *money* _____ times.

> ### Natural English
>
> The first vowel in *money* is pronounced /ə/. Don't use an /a/ or an /ow/ sound when you say *money*.
>
> money /məniy/

C | PAIRS: Answer the questions about the recording in Part B. Use the word **money** in your answers.

1. What happened when Mrs. Green's father died?

   _____

2. Why did Mrs. Green's son have to have his leg amputated?

   _____

3. Why didn't Mrs. Green use hot water?

   _____

4. What do you think happened to Mrs. Green's money when she died?

   _____

EXERCISE 6: Your Turn: The Value of Money

We use money to buy things we want and need, such as food or clothes or a car. But we also use it to obtain intangibles[1], such as independence, power, status, or security.

A | PAIRS: Each of you has statements from three people who use money to obtain one of the intangibles listed in the box. Read a statement aloud. Your partner will decide which intangible the statement refers to. Do you agree? Could it refer to another intangible as well? Student A's statements are on page 253. Student B's statements are on page 259.

love/friendship	power	status
loyalty	security	independence

B | PAIRS: If you had all the money you wanted, what would you do with it? Explain.

STEP 4 EXTENDED PRACTICE

Accuracy Practice Listen again to Exercises 1 and 2A on page 22. Then record the phrases and words.

Fluency Practice Record your answers to the questions.

1. How important is money to you?
2. If you suddenly had a lot of money, do you think it would change you? How?

---

[1] intangibles: *a quality or feeling that cannot be clearly felt or described*

Review: /ɛ/ h<u>ea</u>d, /æ/ h<u>a</u>d, /ə/ h<u>u</u>t, and /ɑ/ h<u>o</u>t

STEP 1 PRESENTATION

The Vowels

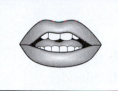

head /ɛ/

Spread your lips a little.
Your mouth is almost closed.

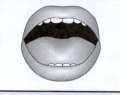

had /æ/

Spread your lips.
Your mouth is open.

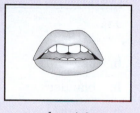

hut /ə/

Relax your lips.
Your mouth is almost closed.

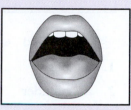

hot /ɑ/

Relax your lips.
Your mouth is open.

Notes

Reductions of /æ/ and /ɑ/: The vowels /æ/ and /ɑ/ are reduced to /ə/ in some common words.

- *-man* and *-men* are pronounced /mən/ in words such as *fireman/firemen, chairman/chairmen,* and *policeman/policemen.*

- *-body* sounds like *buddy* in *somebody, nobody, everybody,* and *anybody.*

- *Can* is pronounced /kən/ before a verb: *Shekən dance.* (She can dance.)

Spellings for /ɛ/	Spellings for of /æ/	Spellings for /ə/ and /ɑ/
See Unit 3.	See Unit 4.	See Unit 5.

STEP 2 FOCUSED PRACTICE

EXERCISE 1: Words with /ɛ/, /æ/, /ə/, and /ɑ/

🎧 **A** | *Listen and repeat the words.*

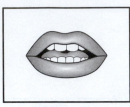 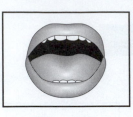 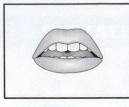 

/ɛ/ head	/æ/ had	/ə/ cup	/ɑ/ cop
1. a. beg	**b.** bag	**c.** bug	**d.** bog[1]
2. a. blender	**b.** blander[2]	**c.** blunder[3]	**d.** blonder
3. a. peppy[4]	**b.** pappy[5]	**c.** puppy	**d.** poppy[6]
4. a. leg	**b.** lag[7]	**c.** lug[8]	**d.** log

🎧 **B** | *Listen again and circle the words you hear.*

EXERCISE 2: Listen for Differences

🎧 **A** | *Listen and repeat the words.*

1. a. cut		**3. a.** net		**5. a.** lock	
b. cat		**b.** Nat/gnat*		**b.** luck	
c. cot		**c.** not/knot		**c.** lack	
2. a. ten		**4. a.** pet		**6. a.** suck	
b. tan		**b.** pot		**b.** sack	
c. ton		**c.** putt*		**c.** sock	

B | *PAIRS: What vowel sounds do the words in Part A have? Write the words on one of the lines below.*

/ɛ/ (bed) _____

/ə/ (but) _____

/æ/ (bad) _____

/ɑ/ (hot) _____

---

[1] bog: *land almost below water—marshland;* [2] blander: *comparative of* bland—*plain;* [3] blunder: *mistake;* [4] peppy: *energetic;* [5] pappy: *daddy (dialect);* [6] poppy: *large red flower;* [7] lag: *to follow behind;* [8] lug: *to carry something heavy;* [8] gnat: *small, flying insects;* [9] putt: *a short golf stroke to get the ball in the hole*

EXERCISE 3: Fill in the Grid

PAIRS: Each of you has a grid that is partially complete. Don't show your grid to your partner. Take turns asking each other for missing words. Pronounce the vowels in the words carefully. When you finish, compare your grids. They should be the same. Student A's grid is on page 254. Student B's grid is on page 259.

EXERCISE 4: Differences in Meaning

A | *Listen to the sentences and responses.*

	Sentences	Responses
1. **a.**	There's a small red <u>bug</u> on the table.	It's a ladybug.
b.	There's a small red <u>bag</u> on the table.	It's a present—open it!
2. **a.**	What shall I do with this <u>poppy</u>?	Put it in a vase.
b.	What shall I do with this <u>puppy</u>?	Feed it.
3. **a.**	Bring me the green <u>cup</u>.	I'm drinking out of it.
b.	Bring me the green <u>cap</u>.	It's too small for your head.
4. **a.**	This is a new <u>cut</u>.	Playing with knives again?
b.	This is a new <u>cot</u>.	Is it comfortable?

B | *PAIRS: Say a sentence. Pronounce the underlined word carefully so your partner can say the correct response.*

EXERCISE 5: Conversations

A | *Listen to the conversation. The capitalized words are heavily stressed. The vowels in* can, *-man/-men, and* -body *are reduced.*

1. **A:** Who's outSIDE?

   B: NObody. It's just the WIND.

   A: It SOUNDS like somebody's at the DOOR.

   B: NO. It's NObody.

   A: NO. I can HEAR somebody at the DOOR. Go CHECK.

   B: Go BACK to sleep. There's NObody at the DOOR.

2. **A:** I THINK we're LOST. Let's STOP and ask for diRECtions.

   B: There's nobody aROUND. Maybe we can find a GAS station and ask somebody THERE.

   A: Everything seems to be CLOSED. I guess everybody in this TOWN goes to BED early.

   B: If you start SPEEDing, I'm SURE we'll find a poLICEman. THEN we can ask for diRECtions.

B | *PAIRS: Practice the conversations. Take turns.*

HAPPINESS

EXERCISE 6: The Study of Happiness

🎧 **A |** *Listen to the recording. Complete the sentences with the words you hear. The missing words have /ɛ/, /æ/, /ə/, or /ɑ/ sounds.*

Modern _____ has focused on the _____ and treatment of
1.   2.

_____ or emotional _____, such as _____. Recently,
3.   4.   5.

however, an older trend has reemerged: The investigation of people who are _____
6.

and the conditions that allow them to stay happy.

There are two _____ definitions of happiness. Happiness is sometimes defined
7.

as the _____ between _____ and pain over a period of time. This
8.   9.

type of happiness varies with our day-to-day experiences. On one day, we may feel

_____ or _____ because of a fight with a close _____.
10.   11.   12.

The _____ day we may feel good because we got a good grade on an important
13.

_____. A second definition reflects a person's general level of satisfaction with life.
14.

Research suggests that people return to this level despite the _____ and downs of
15.

daily life.

B | *PAIRS: Compare your answers.*

EXERCISE 7: Happiness Research

A | *Scientists have investigated the influence that genetics, age, income, marriage, children, and social ties[1] have on happiness. Read each statement below. Then write whether you think each statement is **T** (True) or **F** (False).*

_____ 1. **Genetics:** The role of genetics in happiness is probably small.

_____ 2. **Age:** People who are 20 to 30, or 40 to 50 years old are happier than people who are 70 to 80 years old.*

_____ 3. **Income:** People who don't have enough money to meet their basic needs are unhappier than upper-middle-class and wealthy people.

_____ 4. **Marriage:** Married people are happier than unmarried people.

_____ 5. **Children:** People with children are happier than those without.

_____ 6. **Social ties:** Happiness spreads quickly through networks of close relationships.

---

*Natural English

Pronounce plural endings in expressions for age groups. Notice which words are plural in the following examples.

They're 20 to 30 year olds. (say "twenty to thirty year olds")

They're people in their twenties.

They're people who are 20 to 30 years old.

They're 20 to 30-year-old females.

B | *PAIRS: Check your answers to the statements in Part A. Student A has the half of the answers on page 254. Student B has the other half on page 260. Read the answers to each other and correct the false statements.*

---

[1] social ties: *connections between people*

EXERCISE 8: Your Turn

A | *Many conditions¹ affect how happy we feel. Listen and repeat the conditions. The bold letters are pronounced /ɛ/, /æ/, /ə/, or /ɑ/. Then check (✓) the four conditions that you think are most important.*

Conditions that Affect Happiness

Money	☐
Suc**c**ess at work	☐
Job satisfaction	☐
Marriage and f**a**mily	☐
Fr**ie**nds	☐
Good h**ea**lth	☐
Positive outlook	☐
Human rights	☐
Gen**e**tics	☐

B | *GROUPS: Compare your checklists. Explain why you think some conditions are more important than others.*

STEP 4 EXTENDED PRACTICE

Accuracy Practice *Listen again to Exercise 1A on page 26. Then record the words.*

Fluency Practice *Record your answers to the questions.*

1. How much does your level of happiness vary from day to day?
2. How much control do you feel you have over your level of happiness?

---

¹ conditions: *the situation or environment in which someone lives or something happens*

STEP 1 PRESENTATION

/r/ after Vowels

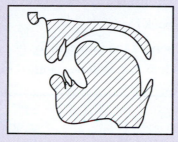

Turn the tip of your tongue up and slightly back.

Important Vowel + *r* Combinations

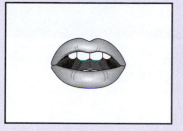

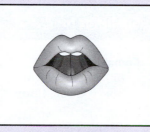

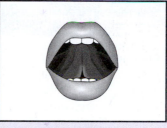

| h**er** /ər/ | **or** /or/ | ha**rd** /ɑr/ |

h**er** /ər/

The mouth is almost closed.

The lips are slightly rounded.

Turn the tip of your tongue up and back.

or /or/

The lips are rounded.

Turn the tip of your tongue up and back.

ha**rd** /ɑr/

The mouth is open.

The lips are not rounded.

Turn the tip of your tongue up and back.

(continued on next page)

The Complex Sound in *world* and *girl*: /ərl/ or /ərəl/

/r/   +   /l/

w**orl**d

Your mouth is almost closed and your lips are a little rounded.

Turn the tip of your tongue up and back for /r/.

The tip of the tongue then touches behind the top teeth for /l/.

If this sound is difficult, pronounce it as two syllables, joined together: /wə́rəl/, /gə́rəl/.

Notes

Dialects: There are some dialects of American English that drop /r/ after vowels ("*r*-less" dialects), but most dialects pronounce it. Your English will be clearer if you learn to pronounce /r/ after vowels.

Spellings for /ər/	Spellings for /or/	Spellings for /ɑr/
Common	**Common**	**Common**
er **her**, s**er**ve	*or* st**or**e, w**or**e	*ar* st**ar**t, h**ar**d
ir f**ir**st, b**ir**d	*oor* d**oor**, fl**oor**	
ur h**ur**t, ch**ur**ch		
Other	**Other**	**Other**
wor + consonant, **wor**k, **wor**d	*our* f**our**	*war* + consonant **war**, **war**n
our j**our**ney		*ear* h**ear**t
ear **ear**th, h**ear**d		*uar* g**uar**d

EXERCISE 1: Words with Vowel + *r*

🎧 *Listen and repeat. Turn the tip of your tongue up and back to make /r/. Then choose a word from each set and say it to the class.*

/ər/	/ɑr/	/ɪr/	/ɛr/
1. were	4. hard	7. hear	10. hair
2. first	5. far	8. fear	11. fair
3. heard	6. heart	9. near	12. wear

/or/	/ayər/	/awər/	/(y)ʊr/
13. tore	16. tire	19. hour	22. tour
14. pour	17. fire	20. tower	23. cure
15. war	18. hire	21. sour	24. pure

EXERCISE 2: Listen for Differences

🎧 **A** | *Listen and repeat the words.*

1. a. ear	3. a. tore	5. a. heard	7. a. were
b. air	b. tour	b. hard	b. war
2. a. far	4. a. bird	6. a. heart	8. a. stir
b. fur	b. beard	b. hurt	b. steer

🎧 **B** | *Listen again and circle the words you hear.*

C | *PAIRS: Say a word from Part A. Your partner will tell you which word you said.*

EXERCISE 3: Sounds and Spelling

🎧 **A** | *Listen to the word pairs. Write **S** if the bold vowel sounds are the same. Write **D** if the bold vowel sounds are different.*

1. f**ur**ious, f**ur**riest ___D___

2. acc**or**d, aw**ar**d _____

3. f**ie**rce, f**ir**st _____

4. j**our**ney, ch**ur**ch _____

5. b**ear**d, b**ir**d _____

6. w**eir**d, w**ear**y _____

7. reg**ar**d, rew**ar**d _____

8. h**eir**, **air** _____

9. b**ir**thday, w**or**thy _____

10. ch**ar**ming, w**ar**ming _____

B | *PAIRS: Say the word pairs. Take turns.*

EXERCISE 4: The Complex Sound in *world*

🎧 *Listen and repeat the words. The bold letters can be pronounced as two syllables: /ə́rəl/.*

1. w**orl**d
2. g**irl**
3. c**url**
4. wh**irl**
5. p**earl**
6. tw**irl**
7. the best in the w**orl**d
8. the whole w**orl**d
9. w**orl**d leaders
10. w**orl**dwide
11. W**orl**d War II
12. c**url**y hair
13. p**earl** earrings
14. g**irl**friend
15. g**irl**s' dormitory

EXERCISE 5: *Work* and *Walk*

🎧 **A |** *Listen and repeat. When you say* **walk**, *your mouth should be open. You can pronounce* **walk** *with the vowel in* **father**. *The* **l** *in* **walk** *is not pronounced.*

1. walk
2. take a walk
3. You can talk the talk, but can you walk the walk?
4. walk on eggshells
5. walk a thin line
6. all walks of life
7. work
8. a workaholic
9. Things will work out.
10. the works
11. went like clockwork
12. a work of art

🎧 **B |** *Listen. Complete the sentences with idioms and expressions.*

1. **A:** What would you like on your sundae? We have chocolate sauce, caramel sauce, strawberry sauce, peanuts, and whipped cream.

   B: Give me everything. I want _____ _____.

2. The new supervisor can _____ _____ _____, but can she _____ _____ _____? She's saying all the right things, but I don't know if she'll be able to make any real changes.

3. In New York City, there are people from _____ _____ _____ _____: On the same street, you can see CEOs and homeless people, older people and younger people, artists and businessmen.

4. I never know whether you're going to be happy or angry, whether I've done something right or wrong. I always feel like I'm _____ _____ _____ with you.

5. The day _____ _____ _____. I wasn't late for anything, and I finished everything I needed to do.

6. He's been in tough spots and always manages to come out better than before. Things will _____ _____ for him.

C | *PAIRS: Compare your answers. Then practice the sentences. What do you think the idioms and expressions in Part B mean? (You can check your answers on page 36.)*

STEP 3   COMMUNICATION PRACTICE

FIRST PLACE

Mount Everest   Mount Kilimanjaro   Mount Whitney

EXERCISE 6: First in the World

PAIRS: These things hold first place in the world in their category. With a partner, decide what the category is for each thing. (You can check your answers on page 36.) Then write a sentence including a superlative and the phrase in the world. *Practice reading the sentences to each other. Pronounce* world *carefully.*

1. Mount Everest   *Mount Everest is the tallest mountain in the world.*
   _____

2. the Burj Khalifa in Dubai _____

3. the whale _____

4. China _____

5. the Nile River _____

6. the cheetah _____

7. the Pacific Ocean _____

Natural English

The article *the* is usually used with superlatives. Be sure to pronounce the *th* in *the* correctly: Put the tip of your tongue between your teeth.

   the tallest mountain

   one of *the* highest buildings

   She ate *the* most.

EXERCISE 7: *Jeopardy*: Firsts

Jeopardy is a game where the answers are known and you have to think of the questions.

PAIRS: Take turns with your partner as **host** (the person who has the answers or clues) and **contestant** (the person who must provide the question). The category for this game is Firsts: People or places that were the first in some way. *Student A's answers are on page 254. Student B's answers are on page 260.*

Here's how to play:

- The contestant chooses the number of points to risk in the category *Firsts*. The higher the amount, the greater the difficulty.
- The host reads the answer (the information) for that amount. (Be sure to pronounce *first* carefully.)
- The contestant has to say a question that makes sense for the answer the host just read.
- If the question is correct, the contestant earns the points assigned to that answer. If the question is incorrect, the contestant loses that number of points.

EXAMPLE:

STUDENT A (CONTESTANT):	I'll take *Firsts* for 100.
STUDENT B (HOST):	This country was the first to have a population of one billion people.
STUDENT A:	What is China?
STUDENT B:	That's correct! You win 100 points.

STEP 4   EXTENDED PRACTICE

Accuracy Practice *Listen again to Exercises 1, 2A, and 4 on pages 33 and 34. Then record the words and phrases.*

Fluency Practice *Record your answers to the questions using complete sentences. Pronounce words such as* **first** *and* **world** *carefully.*

1. What are three important problems facing the world today?

2. What leader has had a positive impact on the world? Why?

3. What leader has had a negative impact on the world? Why?

EXERCISE 6: 1. Mount Everest is the tallest mountain in the world. 2. The Burj Khalifa in Dubai is the tallest building in the world (as of 2011). 3. The whale is the biggest animal/mammal in the world. 4. China is the most populous country in the world. 5. The Nile River is the longest river in the world. 6. The cheetah is the fastest animal in the world. 7. The Pacific Ocean is the biggest/largest body of water in the world.

EXERCISE 5B: 1. *the works:* Everything; 2. *talk the talk, walk the walk:* Say the right things, then do what you say you'll do; 3. *all walks of life:* All types of people; 4. *walking on eggshells:* Having to be overly careful about what you say or do so you don't offend someone; 5. *went like clockwork:* Function/perform smoothly, without problems; 6. *work out:* Be successful.

36   UNIT 7

/ow/ b<u>oa</u>t, /ɔ/ b<u>ou</u>ght, and /ɑ/ p<u>o</u>t; Alternating Vowels: /ow/ ~ /ɑ/; Dialects

STEP 1 PRESENTATION

The Vowels

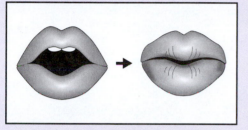

b<u>oa</u>t /ow/

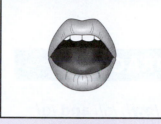

b<u>ou</u>ght /ɔ/

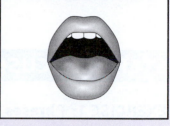

p<u>o</u>t /ɑ/

Start with your lips rounded. Continue rounding to make /ow/.

In many languages this vowel is a pure vowel /o/. In English, it ends with /w/.

Your mouth is open.

Your lips are slightly rounded.

This vowel is pronounced in the back of the mouth.

Your mouth is open.

Your lips are not rounded.

Your tongue is in the low center of the mouth.

Notes

1. **Joining /ow/ to Vowels:** When /ow/ is followed by another vowel, use /w/ to join the two sounds together. The two vowels are in different syllables.

   po^wetry   I have no^w idea.

2. **Alternating Vowels:** In some related words, the stressed vowel alternates between /ow/ and /ɑ/.

   kn<u>o</u>w ~ kn<u>o</u>wledge   diagn<u>o</u>sis ~ diagn<u>o</u>stic

3. **Dialects:** In British English, /ɔ/ has more of an *o* sound than in American English. In American English, it has more of an /ɑ/ sound. Many Americans from the West and Midwest, however, do not use the /ɔ/ vowel. In these dialects, words such as *bought* and *loss* are pronounced with /ɑ/, the vowel in *father*. If you have difficulty pronouncing /ɔ/, you can substitute /ɑ/.

(continued on next page)

Spellings for /ow/		Spellings for /ɔ/		Spellings for /ɑ/
Common		**Common**		See Unit 5.
o . . . e (silent *e*)	j**o**ke, expl**o**de	*au*	p**au**se, f**au**lt	
o	f**o**cus, **o**pen	*aw*	l**aw**, d**aw**n	
oa	r**oa**d, b**oa**t	*a* (before *l*)	f**a**ll, c**a**ll	
ow	gr**ow**, kn**ow**	*o*	l**o**ss, str**o**ng	
Other		**Other**		
oe	t**oe**, J**oe**	*ough*	b**ough**t, th**ough**t	
ough	d**ough**, alth**ough**	*oa*	br**oa**d	
ew	s**ew**			

STEP 2   FOCUSED PRACTICE

EXERCISE 1: Phrases with /ow/, /ɔ/, and /ɑ/

🎧 *Listen and repeat the phrases.*

/ow/	**/ɔ/**	**/ɑ/**
1. **o**ld cl**o**thes	5. an **aw**ful l**o**ss	9. t**o**p j**o**bs
2. f**o**cus on g**oa**ls	6. a l**o**ng w**a**lk	10. a l**o**t of kn**o**wledge
3. the wh**o**le sh**o**w	7. a l**o**st c**au**se	11. st**o**cks and b**o**nds
4. I supp**o**se s**o**.	8. a c**au**tious **o**ffer	12. a m**o**del ec**o**nomy

EXERCISE 2: Joining Words

🎧 **A |** *In these words and phrases, /ow/ is followed by another vowel. Listen to how the syllables and words join together. Then repeat the words and phrases.*

1. po^wet

2. co^werce[1]

3. go^wout

4. I know it.

5. a show-off

6. ko^wala

7. There's no^wanswer.

8. co^woperation

9. grow up

B | *PAIRS: Find words or phrases from Part A to complete the sentences. Practice saying the sentences.*

1. The phone's ringing, but _____.

2. Shakespeare was a playwright and a _____.

3. _____ bears are native to Australia.

---

[1] coerce: *to force*

EXERCISE 3: Dialect Differences

In the Northeast, some people pronounce *bought* and *pot* with different vowels. In the Midwest and West, most people pronounce both words with the vowel in *pot* /ɑ/.

🎧 *Listen to the difference in the pronunciation of these words. A person from Portland, Oregon, might use the first pronunciation (/ɑ/). A person from New York might use the second pronunciation (/ɔ/).*

1. thought
2. sorry
3. law
4. dawn
5. hall
6. long
7. caught
8. pause

EXERCISE 4: Differences in Meaning

🎧 **A** | *Listen to the sentences and responses.*

Sentences	Responses
1. a. I dropped the <u>ball</u>.	Did it bounce?
b. I dropped the <u>bowl</u>.	Did it break?
2. a. What a beautiful <u>fall</u>!	Yes, the trees are spectacular.
b. What a beautiful <u>foal</u>![1]	Yes. Its mother is beautiful, too.
3. a. Why did he <u>sock</u>[2] the pillow?	It's part of his anger management therapy.
b. Why did he <u>soak</u> the pillow?	It was an accident—he spilled some water.
4. a. Why were you <u>cold</u>?	I left my coat at home.
b. Why were you <u>called</u>?	They want to interview me.
5. a. The <u>low</u> building is beautiful.	Yes. The architect thought a tall building wouldn't look right in the countryside.
b. The <u>law</u> building is beautiful.	Yes. And several famous judges have taught classes in this building.

B | *PAIRS: Say a sentence. Pronounce the underlined word carefully so your partner can say the correct response.*

EXERCISE 5: Alternating Vowels

In some related words, the stressed vowel alternates between /ow/ and /ɑ/. The vowel in the more basic word is usually /ow/.

🎧 **A** | *Listen and repeat the words.*

/ow/	/ɑ/
1. j<u>o</u>ke	j<u>o</u>cular
2. ev<u>o</u>ke	ev<u>o</u>cative
3. verb<u>o</u>se	verb<u>o</u>sity
4. c<u>o</u>de	c<u>o</u>dify

---

[1] foal: *a baby horse;* [2] sock: *to hit (slang)*

B | *PAIRS: Pronounce the word pairs. Write **A** if the bold letters are alternating vowels. Write **S** if the letters are the same vowel.*

1. s**o**lo—s**o**litude ___A___

2. gr**ow**—gr**ow**th ____

3. h**o**ly—h**o**liday ____

4. er**o**de—er**o**sion ____

5. prom**o**te—prom**o**tion ____

6. cl**o**thing—cl**o**th ____

7. **o**men—**o**minous ____

8. expl**o**re—expl**o**ratory ____

9. kn**ow**—kn**ow**ledge ____

10. teleph**o**ne—teleph**o**nic ____

STEP 3   COMMUNICATION PRACTICE

LEAVING HOME

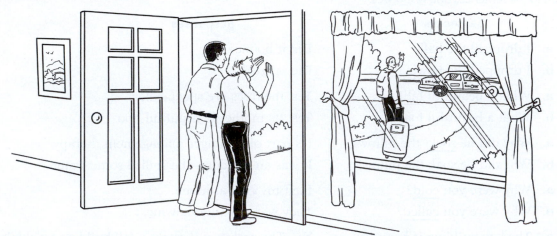

EXERCISE 6: When Should Kids Leave Home?

A | *Listen to the conversation. The bold letters are pronounced /oʊ/, /ɔ/, or /ɑ/.*

MARIA: I read that some people in Italy are c**a**lling for a l**aw** to make gr**ow**n children leave h**o**me by the age of 18.

AL: That's prep**o**sterous. Eighteen-year-**o**lds aren't **o**ld enough to move out. Why are they doing that?

MARIA: There was a legal case that made the wh**o**le country angry. A judge ruled that a 60-year-**o**ld f**a**ther had to keep giving his d**au**ghter an allowance.[1] And she didn't have a j**o**b.

AL: But a l**aw**suit? It makes you wonder what kind of relationship the f**a**ther and d**au**ghter had. Maybe the d**au**ghter couldn't find a j**o**b.

MARIA: Maybe. I think it's harder for kids to leave h**o**me than it was before.

AL: I d**o**n't think it was ever very easy. I think the wh**o**le pr**o**blem is that we expect things to be easy now.

Natural English

Use the article *the* before *whole* when it's used as an adjective. The letter *w* in *whole* is silent (like the *w* in *who* and *whose*). Use *whole* before singular countable nouns.

the whole country

the whole problem

the whole world

---

[1] allowance: *money you are given regularly or for a specific purpose*

B | PAIRS: Practice the conversation in Part A. Then discuss the Italian case. What do you think about the judge's ruling? Do you think 18-year-olds are old enough to live independently? Why or why not?

EXERCISE 7: Your Turn

A | Listen to the phrases in the left column. Then match each phrase with a definition in the right column. (You can check your answers below.)

Phrases	Definitions
_____ **1.** Boomerang kids (Australia)	**a.** kids who stay at home when they should be independent
_____ **2.** Kippers (Britain)	**b.** kids who leave home in their early 20s then move back later
_____ **3.** Big babies (Italy, translation of *bamboccioni*)	**c.** single children in their late 20s, living at home because it's more comfortable to do so
_____ **4.** Parasite singles (Japan, *parasaito shinguru*)	**d.** kids who spend their parent's retirement savings

B | Why do young people in your country leave home? Check (✔) the reasons below.

Young people leave home to . . .

go to school ☐

get a job ☐

be independent ☐

get married ☐

C | GROUPS: Compare your answers. Then share the term(s) people use in your country to describe children who continue to live at home or return home (such as boomerang kids).

STEP 4   EXTENDED PRACTICE

Accuracy Practice Listen again to Exercises 1 and 2A on page 38. Then record the words and phrases.

Fluency Practice Record your answers to the questions.

1. Do you think it's more difficult for young people to leave home and begin living independently now than in the past? Explain your answer.

2. If you live on your own now, when did you move out? What problems did you experience when you first began living on your own? If you're still living with your family, do you feel pressure to leave home? Explain.

EXERCISE 7A: 1. b 2. d 3. a 4. c

/uw/ cool, /ʊ/ could, and /yuw/ cute; Alternating Vowels: /uw/ or /yuw/ ~ /ə/; The Sequence /wʊ/: woman

The Vowels

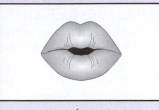

cool /uw/

Start with your lips rounded and continue rounding to make /uw/.

/uw/ ends in a /w/.

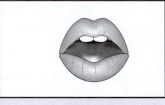

could /ʊ/

Your lips are less rounded.

Your tongue drops a little toward the center of your mouth for /ʊ/ compared with /uw/.

Notes

1. **Alternating Vowels:** In some related words, the stressed vowel alternates between /uw/ (or /yuw/) and /ə/.

    assume ~ assumption   deduce ~ deduction

2. **Words with /wʊ/ or /ʊ/:** A few words can be pronounced with /uw/ or /ʊ/.

    roof   hoof   root

3. **The Sequence /wʊ/:** Some students have trouble pronouncing /w/ when the next sound is /ʊ/. Their pronunciation of *woman* may sound like *'oman*. If this is a problem for you, try these tips:

    • Start with your lips very rounded. Unround them a little (unrounding creates the beginning /w/ sound).

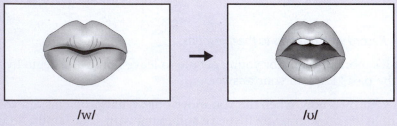

/w/   →   /ʊ/

    • Say two /u/ sounds together. Stress the second /u/: uúman (*woman*), uúd (*wood*).
    • Stretch a rubber band as you say the first part of *woman*.

4. **Spelling, Sounds, and Grammar:** The first sound in words such as *union* or *united* is the consonant /y/. Use the article *a* with these words. (Compare *a union* versus *an umbrella*).

Spellings for /uw/		Spellings for /yuw/	Spellings for /ʊ/	
Common		**Common**	**Common**	
oo	balloon, boot	*u* human, cute	*oo*	good, book
oo . . . e (silent *e*)	choose, loose		*u*	pull, push
u	student, truth			
Other			**Other**	
o	do, move		*ou*	could, should
ou	group, soup		*o*	woman, wolf
ough	through			
ew	flew, new			
ui	suit, juice			

STEP 2   FOCUSED PRACTICE

EXERCISE 1:   Phrases with /uw/ or /yuw/, /ʊ/, and /wʊ/

🎧 *Listen and repeat the phrases.*

/uw/ or /yuw/	/ʊ/	/wʊ/
1. cool as a cucumber[1]	6. good books	11. I wouldn't care.
2. consumer reviews	7. sugar cookies	12. a tall woman
3. a booth for two	8. push or pull	13. a wool sweater
4. fruit and vegetables	9. a good butcher	14. in the woods
5. future news	10. good-looking	15. a wild wolf

EXERCISE 2:   Listen for Differences

🎧 **A |** *Listen and repeat the words.*

1.	a. Luke	4.	a. wooed[2]	7.	a. suit
	b. look		b. wood/would		b. soot[3]
2.	a. pool	5.	a. stewed	8.	a. shooed[4]
	b. pull		b. stood		b. should
3.	a. fool	6.	a. who'd	9.	a. cooed[5]
	b. full		b. hood		b. could

🎧 **B |** *Listen again and circle the words you hear.*

---

[1] cool as a cucumber: *calm in times of stress;* [2] woo: *to win the affections of someone;* [3] soot: *black dust left after burning;* [4] shoo: *to make someone leave, to wave someone away;* [5] coo: *to make soft, loving noises*

EXERCISE 3: Alternating Vowels

In some related words, the vowel alternates between /uw/ (or /yuw/) and /ə/. The vowel in the more basic word is usually /uw/ (or /yuw/).

A | *Listen and repeat the words.*

	/uw/ or /yuw/	**/ə/**
1.	a. res**u**me	b. res**u**mption
2.	a. cons**u**me	b. cons**u**mption
3.	a. n**u**merous	b. n**u**mber
4.	a. sed**u**ce	b. sed**u**ction
5.	a. p**u**nitive	b. p**u**nish
6.	a. introd**u**ce	b. introd**u**ction

B | *PAIRS: Pronounce the word pairs. Write* **A** *if the bold letters are alternating vowels. Write* **S** *if the letters are the same vowel.*

1. st**u**pid—st**u**pefy ___S___

2. ass**u**me—ass**u**mption _____

3. red**u**ce—red**u**ction _____

4. all**u**de—all**u**sion _____

5. st**u**dent—st**u**dy _____

6. m**u**tate—m**u**tant _____

7. imm**u**ne—imm**u**nity _____

8. prod**u**ce—prod**u**ction _____

EXERCISE 4: Phrases and Idioms

A | *Listen to the phrases and definitions. The bold letters are pronounced /uw/, /yuw/, or /ʊ/.*

	Phrases		**Definitions**
__e__	1. l**oo**k up to (someone)	a.	be in someone's situation
_____	2. l**o**se my shirt	b.	**u**se influence to avoid r**u**les or regulations
_____	3. be in your sh**oe**s	c.	survive
_____	4. p**u**t up with	d.	tolerate
_____	5. p**u**ll thr**ough**	e.	admire or respect someone
_____	6. p**u**ll strings	f.	l**o**se all your money
_____	7. f**oo**d for thought	g.	cooperate, **u**nite during bad times
_____	8. p**u**ll together	h.	something that makes y**ou** think or reconsider
_____	9. p**u**t off	i.	postpone

B | *Match each phrase in the left column with its definition in the right column. Then compare your answers with a partner. (You can also check your answers on page 47.)*

C | PAIRS: Complete the sentences with idioms from Part A. Then practice the conversations with a partner.

1. **A:** I can't _____ _____ _____ my r**oo**mmate any longer. She's

   just t**oo** p**u**shy. Can you help me get another r**oo**m?

   B: In the middle of the semester? Well, maybe. I have a friend wh**o** works in the housing

   office. Maybe I c**oul**d _____ some _____ for y**ou**.

2. **A:** I borrowed a lot of money to buy that stock. If the price keeps falling, I'm going to

   _____ _____ _____.

   B: Don't worry. You always buy risky stocks, and in the end, you d**o** all right. You'll

   _____ _____.

3. **A:** After my dad got sick, we decided we had to _____ _____ and help the

   family. My mom got a second job, and my sister came home every day after school to take

   care of my dad. I think I sh**oul**d _____ _____ college for a year so I can

   help out, t**oo**.

   B: I think that's a g**oo**d idea. If I _____ _____ _____

   _____, I'd stay at home and help out t**oo**.

EXERCISE 5: Sounds and Spelling

The vowel /uw/ occurs in more words than /ʊ/. The letters *oo* are usual spellings for both /uw/ and /ʊ/. The words in Part A are common words in which *oo* is pronounced /ʊ/. If you learn these, you can assume that most other *oo* spellings are pronounced /uw/.

A | Listen and repeat the words. All of the oo spellings are pronounced /ʊ/.

1. good	5. book	9. stood	13. foot
2. took	6. cookie	10. wood	14. wool
3. hood	7. soot	11. brook	15. crooked[1]
4. cook	8. hook	12. look	16. shook

B | Listen to the words. The oo spellings are pronounced /uw/ or /ʊ/.

1. school	3. shook	5. food	7. room	9. book
2. proof	4. fool	6. wool	8. shoot	10. foot

C | PAIRS: Write the words from Part B on the correct lines below.

/uw/ words: _____

/ʊ/ words: _____

---

[1] crooked: *not straight*

BRAIN FOOD

EXERCISE 6: Food Categories

A | *Write five foods in each category below.*

Vegetables*	Fruits	Grains, Cereals	Meat	Dairy Products

---

*Natural English

Pronounce the word *vegetable* as a three-syllable word, not a four-syllable word: *vétchtable*.

five servings of "vetchtables"

fruit and "vetchtables"

B | *GROUPS: Compare your lists from Part A. Which types of foods do nutritionists recommend that we eat more of? Less? What are some other food categories?*

EXERCISE 7: Big Brains

A | *Listen and repeat. Make sure you understand the words.*

1. ancestors
2. roots
3. digestion
4. scarce
5. barbeque
6. SAT test

B | *PAIRS: Listen to the recording and then answer the questions.*

1. What did our human ancestors probably eat originally?
2. What were the disadvantages to this diet?
3. Why do scientists believe our ancestors began eating meat?
4. What happened when our ancestors began eating meat?
5. Describe the advantages of eating cooked food over raw food.

EXERCISE 8: Your Turn

A | *Read the statements in the chart. Are they true or false about your country? Write **T** (True) or **F** (False).*

Most people in my country . . .	True or False
eat more fruit and vegetables than meat.	
eat more meat than fruit and vegetables.	
eat more fish than meat.	
eat more carbohydrates, such as rice or bread, than meat.	

B | *GROUPS: Compare your charts.*

STEP 4   EXTENDED PRACTICE

Accuracy Practice *Listen again to Exercises 1 and 2A on page 43. Then record the phrases and words.*

Fluency Practice *Record your answers to the questions.*

1. Describe your favorite food(s).
2. Do you think you should be eating more or less of particular foods? Explain.

EXERCISE 4B: 1. e 2. f 3. a 4. d 5. c 6. b 7. h 8. g 9. i

UNIT 10

/ay/ w<u>i</u>de, /aw/ h<u>ou</u>se, and /oy/ b<u>oy</u>;
Joining Vowels Together;
Alternating Vowels: /ay/ ~ /ɪ/

STEP 1   PRESENTATION

The vowels in *wide, house,* and *boy* are complex vowels that end in /w/ or /y/.

/ay/ w<u>i</u>de   /aw/ h<u>ou</u>se   /oy/ b<u>oy</u>

These vowels are also called the "pain" vowels because English speakers use each vowel as an expression of pain.

Ay!   Ow! /aw/   Oy!

Notes

1. **Joining Vowels Together:** When /ay/, /aw/, and /oy/ are followed by another vowel, use /y/ or /w/ to join the vowels together. The vowels are in different syllables.

   I^y agree.   sci^yence   now and then   a boy and girl

2. **Alternating Vowels:** In some related words, the stressed vowel alternates between /ay/ and /ɪ/.

   sign ~ signal   ride ~ ridden

3. **Specific Languages:** Chinese students may need to pronounce the last sound of /ay/ and /aw/ more strongly, especially when the vowels are followed by /n/ or /m/, as in *time* or *count* (in these words, the vowel sounds more like /ai/ or /au/). If this is a problem, concentrate on pronouncing the /y/ of /ay/ and the /w/ of /aw/ more strongly.

4. **Dialects:** Some Americans from the South pronounce /ay/ like a long /ɑ/: *eye* sounds more like *ah*; *time* sounds more like *Tom*.

Spellings for /ay/		Spellings for /aw/		Spellings for /oy/	
Common		**Common**		**Common**	
i . . . e (silent *e*)	time, invite	*ou*	surr**ou**nd, h**ou**se	*oi*	v**oi**ce, n**oi**se
i	Friday, m**i**nd	*ow*	cr**ow**d, all**ow**	*oy*	t**oy**, empl**oy**
igh	h**igh**, l**igh**t				
y	cr**y**, appl**y**				
ie	d**ie**, l**ie**				
Other		**Other**			
uy	b**uy**, g**uy**	*ough*	b**ough**, dr**ough**t		
eigh	h**eigh**t				
ai	**ai**sle				
ey	**ey**e				

EXERCISE 1: Phrases with Complex Vowels

🎧 *Listen and repeat the phrases.*

/ay/	/aw/	/oy/
1. science prizes	5. a crowded house	9. boys' toys
2. the right to privacy	6. a countdown	10. loyal employer
3. a bike ride	7. the town's boundary	11. spoiled boys
4. a tiny island	8. loud shouting	12. annoying noises

EXERCISE 2: Alternating Vowels

In some related words, the stressed vowel alternates between /ay/ and /ɪ/. The vowel in the more basic word is usually /ay/.

🎧 **A |** *Listen and repeat the words.*

	/ay/		/ɪ/
1.	a. collide	b.	collision
2.	a. decide	b.	decision
3.	a. crime	b.	criminal
4.	a. wise	b.	wisdom
5.	a. cycle	b.	cyclical
6.	a. hide	b.	hidden

B | *PAIRS: Pronounce the word pairs. Write **A** if the bold letters are alternating vowels. Write **S** if the letters are the same vowel.*

1. wide—width *A*
2. divide—division _____
3. guide—guidance _____
4. excite—excitement _____
5. divine—divinity _____
6. bite—bitten _____
7. bike—bicycle _____

8. style—stylist _____
9. wild—wilderness _____
10. type—typical _____
11. mild—mildness _____
12. precise—precision _____
13. line—linear _____
14. revise—revision _____

EXERCISE 3: Joining Vowels

🎧 **A** | *Listen and repeat the sentences and words. The underlined words in column A are joined together with /w/ or /y/. They have the same or nearly the same pronunciation as the underlined word(s) in column B.*

	A	**B**
1.	Say "aunts."	séance[1]
2.	Is she going to sue it?	suet?[2]
3.	Did you dye it?	diet?
4.	Go in there?	going there?
5.	Why are baskets sold here?	wire
6.	I didn't like her sow[3] or chicken.	sour chicken

B | *PAIRS: Practice the sentences and words.*

STEP 3 COMMUNICATION PRACTICE

SCIENCE QUESTIONS

EXERCISE 4: Why Are Tigers So Scary?

PAIRS: The questions below are some that children asked a scientist on a radio show. The scientist tried to answer all the questions. How would you answer them? (You can check the scientist's answers on page 51.)

1. Why are tigers so scary?
2. How does milk turn sour?
3. Do insects sneeze?
4. Why do people have eyebrows?
5. Does food taste the same to animals as it does to me?
6. Does sound travel in space?

> **Natural English**
>
> Information questions (questions that start with *who, what, how, why*, etc.) usually end in falling intonation:
>
> How does milk turn sour?
>
> *Yes / no* questions usually end in rising intonation:
>
> Does sound travel in space?

---

[1] séance: *a ritual to contact the dead;* [2] suet: *hard animal fat used for cooking;* [3] sow: *a female pig*

EXERCISE 5: Kids and Science

A | *Listen and repeat the words and phrases. The bold letters are pronounced /ay/ or /aw/.*

1. sn**ee**ze
2. c**ough**
3. **eye**br**ow**s
4. b**ou**ndless curi**o**sity
5. l**a**g

B | *Listen to the recording and then answer the questions.*

1. Describe the PISA (Program for International Student Assessment)
2. How did students from China do on the 2010 test? Students from the United States?
3. What did business leaders have to say about the U.S. scores?

C | *GROUPS: Compare your answers.*

EXERCISE 6: Your Turn

A | *PAIRS: The questions below are from educated adults who are not scientists. How are they different from the children's questions in Exercise 4? Do you think science will ever be able to answer them?*

1. What happened before the "Big Bang[1]"?
2. How are we going to cope with the world's growing population?
3. What is consciousness?

B | *Write three questions that you would like a scientist to answer.*

_____

_____

_____

STEP 4 EXTENDED PRACTICE

Accuracy Practice *Listen again to Exercises 1 and 3A on pages 49 and 50. Then record the phrases, sentences, and words.*

Fluency Practice *Record your answers to the questions.*

1. When you were in high school, what science courses did you have to take? Did you like them? Why or why not?

2. What were your favorite subjects?

---

[1] Big Bang: *The theory that the universe originated from a violent explosion of a small amount of matter*

EXERCISE 4: 1. Tigers are scary because they're big and have big teeth. They're the top predators in their habitat and have no real enemies except man. Would you be afraid of a tiger if it were the size of a cat? 2. Bacteria change the lactose in milk into a sour acid, lactic acid. 3. No. Insects don't sneeze or cough. Only animals that breathe like humans can sneeze or cough. Insects breathe through tiny holes in their skin. 4. Eyebrows haven't been studied very much. Because they stick out a little beyond the eyes, they might protect the eyes from falling things, such as dust. 5. That's a good question but I just don't know. We can't really know how food tastes to animals. 6. Not very much. Sound is produced when air gets pushed together. In space there isn't much air.

PART

II

CONSONANTS

(continued on next page)

Consonant Overview

STEP 1 PRESENTATION

There are 24 consonants in English. Listen to the words.

past /p/	pre**ss**ure /ʃ/
boat /b/	plea**su**re /ʒ/
take /t/	**ch**air /tʃ/
desk /d/	**j**azz /dʒ/
come /k/	**r**ight /r/
game /g/	**l**ight /l/
food /f/	**s**ome /m/
very /v/	**s**un /n/
thin /θ/	su**ng** /ŋ/
then /ð/	**y**es /y/
Sue /s/	**w**et /w/
zoo /z/	**h**ead /h/

The Mouth

Consonants are made by partially or completely blocking the flow of air through the mouth. For example, when you say *P*, your top and bottom lips press together, stopping the air briefly.

Look at the diagram of the mouth. The labeled parts are used to make consonants in English.

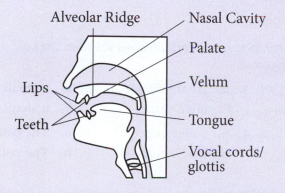

Alveolar Ridge Nasal Cavity

Palate

Velum

Lips

Teeth Tongue

Vocal cords/ glottis

EXERCISE 1: Awareness of Consonants

PAIRS: Try these "consonant experiments." They'll help you become aware of how consonants are produced.

1. Lips. Press your lips together and say *P*. What other consonant sounds are made with the lips? Write words with lip sounds on the line. Include words where the consonant is in the middle or at the end of the word.

   _____

2. Teeth. Put the tip of your tongue between your teeth and say, *thing*. Add other words with *th*, and write them on the lines. Include words where the consonant is in the middle or at the end of the word. Practice the words. Pronounce the *th* sound correctly.

   _____

EXERCISE 2: Voiced and Voiceless Sounds

Consonants can be voiced or voiceless. When the vocal cords vibrate, the sound is "voiced," like the /z/ in *zoo*. When the vocal cords don't vibrate, the sound is "voiceless," like the /s/ in *Sue*.

A | *Try this experiment.*

- Put your fingertips against the front side of your throat.
- Make a long /zzzzz/ and feel the vibration in your fingers; /z/ is a voiced sound.
- Make a long /sssss/ sound. There is no vibration because /s/ is a voiceless sound.
- Alternate between /z/ and /s/ and feel the voicing turn on and off /zzzsssszzzssszzzsss/.

B | *Listen and repeat. The bold consonant in the first phrase is voiceless. The bold consonant in the second phrase or sentence is voiced.*

1. **a.** hal**f** a glass
   b. ha**v**e a glass

2. **a.** an unusual ***H***
   b. an unusual a**ge**

3. **a.** great pri**c**es
   b. great pri**z**es

4. **a.** a new cu**p**
   b. a new cu**b**

5. **a.** a small lo**ck**
   b. a small lo**g**

6. **a.** The couple's we**t**.
   b. The couple's we**d**.

C | *PAIRS: Say a phrase or sentence. Pronounce the bold consonant carefully so your partner can tell you which phrase you said.*

EXERCISE 3: Difficult Consonants

A | *The consonants in the chart are difficult for many students.*

TH sounds	F and V	R	L
Put the tip of your tongue lightly between your teeth.	Touch your top teeth to your lower lip.	Start with the tip of the tongue turned up and back a little. Lower the tongue tip without touching the top of the mouth.	Touch the tip of the tongue behind the top teeth.

B | *Listen and repeat the words.*

1. **th**ing
2. heal**th**y
3. wi**th**

4. **f**act
5. **v**ery
6. gi**v**e

7. **r**ead
8. ar**r**ive
9. g**r**ass

10. **l**ead
11. a**l**ive
12. g**l**ass

EXERCISE 4: Fill in the Grid

PAIRS: Each of you has a grid that is partially complete. Don't show your grid to your partner. Take turns asking your partner for missing words. When you finish, compare your grids. They should be the same. Student A's grid is on page 254. Student B's grid is on page 260.

EXERCISE 5: Consonant Clusters

Consonant clusters are two or more consonant sounds pronounced together in a word. In English, they can occur at the beginning, in the middle, or at the end of words. Pronounce all the consonants in a cluster. Don't separate the consonants with a vowel sound.

A | *Listen and repeat the phrases.*

1. **a.** black stairway   **b.** back stairway
2. **a.** an expensive clone   **b.** an expensive cologne[1]
3. **a.** please restrain it   **b.** please restain[2] it
4. **a.** How many sports?   **b.** How many supports?
5. **a.** They dried it.   **b.** They deride[3] it.
6. **a.** a picture of water   **b.** a pitcher of water

B | *PAIRS: Say a phrase. Pronounce the consonants carefully so your partner can tell you which phrase you said.*

---

[1] cologne: *type of perfume;* [2] restain: *to stain (paint with a wood color) again;* [3] deride: *to make fun of*

THE BEAR IN THE CAR

EXERCISE 6: Don't Feed the Bears

 A | *Listen and repeat the words and phrases. Notice how the bold consonants are joined to the next sound.*

1. parked on a hill
2. half-eaten
3. get inside
4. woke up
5. ran away

6. started to honk
7. a comeback
8. garbage cans
9. livestock
10. limited hunting

Natural English

Join final consonants to following vowels clearly.

parked on a hill

half-eaten

Keep final consonants short when the next word starts with a consonant. Don't separate the two words.

garbage cans
livestock

B | *Listen to the recording and take notes.*

C | *PAIRS: Retell the story of the bear in the car. Why are wild bears making a comeback? You can use phrases from Part A or your own words.*

EXERCISE 7: Your Turn

GROUPS: Discuss the questions.

1. In your country, are wild animal populations growing, declining or both? Which animals?

2. Although human development has led to the extinction of some wild animals, other wild animal populations have grown. Do you think the comeback of certain wild animals, such as black bears in New Jersey, means that we don't have to worry so much about endangered animals? Explain your answer.

STEP 4 EXTENDED PRACTICE

Accuracy Practice *Listen again to Exercises 3B and 6A on pages 57 and 58. Then record the words and phrases.*

Fluency Practice *What are some endangered species? Where do they live? What human activities have threatened them? Record your answers to the questions.*

STEP 1 PRESENTATION

Beginning /p, t, k/ and Aspiration

1. At the beginning of a word, pronounce /p, t, k/ with aspiration, a strong puff of air (shown as "(").

    pʿan   tʿan   cʿan

    Try this: Hold a piece of paper so the bottom edge is about 2 inches (5 centimeters) from your mouth. Say, *Pʿan*.

    Aspirate the /p/: The puff of air should blow the paper away from your mouth.

2. Aspirate voiceless stops only when a stressed vowel follows.

    | **Aspiration:** | apʿárt | attʿáck | decʿáy |
    | **No aspiration:** | apple | attic | decadent |

Joining Final Consonants to Following Words

1. **Final consonant + vowel:** *fresh air*

    Join the consonant to the vowel clearly.

    atomic energy   keep it

2. **Final consonant + different consonant:** *stop⁾ sign*

    Pronounce the final consonant, but keep it short. Don't release (pronounce) it strongly (shown as ⁾). Don't add a vowel sound to separate the final and beginning consonants.

    stop⁾ sign   dot⁾ com

3. **Final consonant + same consonant:** *milk carton*

Pronounce one long consonant (shown as "⌒")—don't say the consonant twice.

black cat   bus stop

Pronounce one long consonant when the two consonants are similar (for example, /f/ and /v/ or /k/ and /g/).

safe vehicles   egg carton

STEP 2 FOCUSED PRACTICE

EXERCISE 1: Aspiration

A | *Listen and repeat the phrases. Aspirate the bold consonants.*

1. **p**olitical **p**arties	4. return the **t**ickets	7. **c**ompact **c**ars
2. ap**p**ly for the **p**osition	5. **t**ake your **t**ime	8. crowded **c**lasses
3. sup**p**ort the **p**resident	6. **t**ell the **t**ruth	9. a **q**uiet **c**ampus

B | *The consonants /p, t, k/ are only aspirated when a stressed vowel follows them. They are not aspirated after /s/ or when they end a word. Listen to the words and phrases. Place a stress mark (ˊ) over the stressed syllable. Then circle the bold letters that are aspirated sounds.*

1. **p**ópular **p**éople	6. **a**toms and a**t**omic energy
2. **p**urple **p**otatoes	7. open **c**ontainers
3. che**ck**ing ac**c**ount	8. bla**ck** **p**epper
4. **p**aper **p**roducts	9. ba**c**on and **t**omato sandwich
5. re**t**urned i**t**ems	10. a re**c**orded re**c**ord

EXERCISE 2: Differences in Meaning

The bold final consonants in the left column are short and not released (pronounced) strongly. The bold consonants in the right column begin a word or syllable and are longer and easier to hear. Listen and repeat the phrases.

	Unreleased		Released
1. a.	Mi**k**e Robial	b.	mi**c**robial
2. a.	migh**t** rain	b.	my **t**rain
3. a.	bi**k**e laws	b.	buy **c**laws
4. a.	great race	b.	gray **t**race[1]
5. a.	ma**k**e wrinkles	b.	May **C**rinkles
6. a.	Wol**f** Reebies	b.	wool **f**reebies[2]

[1] trace: *something that remains after a person or substance is removed;* [2] freebies: *free things (slang)*

EXERCISE 3: Joining Consonants

A | *In the left column, the bold consonants are the same, so they're pronounced as one long consonant. In the right column, the final consonants join clearly to the following vowels. Listen and repeat the phrases.*

One Long Consonant	Consonant + Vowel
1. a. like Coke	**b.** like oak[1]
2. a. white towel	**b.** white owl[2]
3. a. big Gabe	**b.** big Abe
4. a. both thighs[3]	**b.** both eyes
5. a. nice size	**b.** nice eyes

B | *PAIRS: Say a phrase. Join the words correctly so your partner can tell you which phrase you said.*

C | *Listen to the recording. Complete the sentences with phrases from Part A.*

1. That dog has _____ _____ and is a _____ _____.

2. Did you say you _____ _____ or _____ _____?

3. _____ _____ told _____ _____ the news.

4. There's a _____ _____ near the _____ _____.

EXERCISE 4: Final Voiced and Voiceless Consonants

A | *Vowels before voiced consonants are longer than vowels before voiceless consonants. In the left column, the vowels are before voiced consonants. In the right column, the vowels are before voiceless consonants. Listen to the words.*

Longer Vowel	Shorter Vowel
1. a. peas	**b.** peace
2. a. prove	**b.** proof
3. a. bags	**b.** backs
4. a. raised	**b.** raced
5. a. age	**b.** H
6. a. build	**b.** built

B | *PAIRS: Complete the sentence below with words from Part A. Pronounce the vowel and final consonant correctly so your partner knows which word you said first.*

Did you say "_____" or "_____"?

---

[1] oak: *a type of tree;* [2] owl: *a large night bird with big eyes;* [3] thigh: *the upper part of the leg*

THE HUMAN FOOTPRINT

EXERCISE 5: Hard Greens

Hard greens are environmentalists who propose unusual solutions to reduce the harmful effects of human activity on the environment.

A | *Listen and repeat. Make sure you understand the words and phrases. Notice how the bold consonants are pronounced.*

mainstrea**m** environmentalists	foo**t** print
promo**te** policies	wi**de** spread
clo**se** suburbs	sola**r** energy
pesticides	lar**ge** agribusinesses

B | *PAIRS: Listen to the recording and then answer the questions.*

1. What is the general solution proposed by hard greens to save the environment?

   _____

   _____

2. Why do hard greens support the growth of large cities?

   _____

   _____

3. How do hard greens feel about the use of pesticides? Organic farming?

   _____

   _____

EXERCISE 6: Making Inferences

A| *Read the statements below. If you think a hard green environmentalist would agree with a statement, write* **HG**. *If you think a soft green (mainstream environmentalist) would agree with the statement, write* **SG**. *If you think both hard and soft greens would agree with a statement, write* **both**.

1. The government should provide financial incentives to high-rise developers and people who live in them. _____

2. The government should increase subsidies on agricultural products to protect the small farmer. _____

3. Growth hormones fed to milk cows should be banned. _____

4. Nuclear energy plants should be closed. _____

5. Safety regulations at nuclear energy plants should be stricter. _____

6. National parks should prohibit snowmobiles because they disturb the wildlife. _____

Natural English

The letter *l* in *should* is silent. *Should* is usually stressed less than the verb that follows it.

The government shou*l*d provide incentives.

The government shou*l*d increase subsidies.

B| *PAIRS: Compare your answers from Part A. Then discuss which statements you agree with.*

STEP 4   EXTENDED PRACTICE

Accuracy Practice   *Listen again to Exercises 1A and 3A on pages 61 and 62. Then record the phrases.*

Fluency Practice   *Record your answers to the questions.*

1. What environmental problems does the area you live in face?

2. Is the basic position of hard greens reasonable and/or practical? Why or why not?

13 -ed Endings; Flapped /t/ and /d/

PRESENTATION

Past Tense -ed Ending

The past tense -ed ending is pronounced as a final syllable or a final consonant sound. The pronunciation depends on the last sound of the verb.

1. Pronounce the -ed ending as a new syllable (/əd/ or /ɪd/) when the base verb ends in /t/ or /d/.

   wait → We waited until 7:00 P.M.

2. Pronounce the -ed ending as /t/ or /d/ when the base verb ends in other sounds.

   a. Use /t/ when the base verb ends in /p, k, θ, f, s, ʃ, tʃ/.

      walk → They "walkt" (walked).

   b. Use /d/ when the base verb ends in a vowel sound or /b, g, ð, v, z, ʒ, dʒ, m, n, ŋ, r, l/.

      listen → He "listend" (listened) to me.

Notes

1. **Adjectives ending in -ed:** The pronunciation of most -ed adjectives follows the rules for the past tense ending.

   an interested person   a matched pair   a bruised arm

   In some adjectives, -ed is pronounced as a syllable, even though the base word doesn't end in /t/ or /d/. Many of these adjectives end in /k/ or /g/.

   naked   two-legged   wretched

2. **Adverbs ending in -edly:** In adverbs that end in -edly, -ed is usually pronounced as a syllable.

   supposedly   advisedly

3. **Flapped /t/ and /d/:** When /t/ and /d/ are preceded by a stressed vowel and followed by another vowel, they're "flapped" (written D). The tip of the tongue hits the top of the mouth very fast. You can also think of this sound as a "fast D." The flap is a voiced sound. It's a characteristic feature of American and Canadian English.

   If the flap is difficult for you to pronounce, you can say /t/ or /d/, but try to use the flap in the words *water* and *matter*.

Listen. The bold letters are flapped sounds.

   letter   rider   water   adding   data   middle

4. **Flaps and homophones:** The flap creates homophones, words that are pronounced the same but spelled differently. Most speakers of American English pronounce these pairs of words the same:

   latter—ladder   putting—pudding   liter—leader

EXERCISE 1: Past Tense

🎧 *Listen to the sentences. Underline the syllables in each bold verb and write the number of syllables in the blank. Then check (✓) the pronunciation of the -ed ending.*

	Syllables	/əd/ or /ɪd/	/t/	/d/
1. The glass **smashed** on the floor.	*1*	___	✓	___
2. He **invested** in the railroad.	___	___	___	___
3. I **offered** to help.	___	___	___	___
4. The flight was **delayed** by the storm.	___	___	___	___
5. We **finished** the race last.	___	___	___	___
6. She **persuaded** me to do it.	___	___	___	___

EXERCISE 2: Differences in Meaning

🎧 **A |** *Listen to the sentences and responses.*

Sentences	Responses
1. a. These people <u>paint</u> pictures on walls.	graffiti artists
b. These people <u>painted</u> pictures on walls.	prehistoric cave dwellers
2. a. These people <u>apply</u> to medical schools.	people who want to become doctors
b. These people <u>applied</u> to medical schools.	doctors
3. a. They <u>stop</u> at Waterloo.	the Waterloo trains
b. They <u>stopped</u> at Waterloo.	Napoleon's army
4. a. These people <u>cross</u> the ocean to find gold.	multinational mining companies
b. These people <u>crossed</u> the ocean to find gold.	16th-century Spaniards

B | *PAIRS: Say a sentence. Pronounce the underlined word carefully so your partner can say the correct response.*

EXERCISE 3: Adjective Endings

🎧 *Listen and repeat. The adjectives in the phrases end in -ed. As you listen, circle the adjectives in which -ed is pronounced as a syllable (/əd/ or /ɪd/).*

1. all dressed up
2. a two-legged animal
3. an unanswered challenge
4. a changed man
5. my beloved wife
6. a shocked public
7. wicked policies
8. a wrecked car

EXERCISE 4: Flapped /t/ and /d/

🎧 *The bold sounds in the sentences are flaps ("fast Ds"). Listen and repeat the sentences.*

1. Wha**t** are you doing?
2. Where's the wa**t**er me**t**er for the house?
3. I'd like a bi**t** of be**tt**er bu**tt**er.
4. What's the ma**tt**er with the la**dd**er?
5. They invi**t**ed us to come a**t** eight.
6. Ge**tt**ing a man on Mars will be a major accomplishment.

STEP 3   COMMUNICATION PRACTICE

TECHNOLOGICAL MILESTONES

EXERCISE 5: Technology Timeline

A | *The chart lists important advances in technology. Guess the chronology (order) of the advances. Write **1** next to the advance that was invented first and **6** next to the most recent advance. Then compare charts with a partner.*

Technology
_____ the steam engine
_____ the microchip
_____ the combustion engine
_____ the World Wide Web
_____ the personal computer
_____ the light bulb

B | PAIRS: Learn more about the advances in Part A by sharing information.

Student A: Look at the chart on page xx. Read the information aloud. Add *-ed* to the verbs in parentheses.

Student B: Look at the chart on page yy. Read the information aloud. Add *-ed* to the verbs in parentheses.

EXERCISE 6: Quotations

A | *Listen to the quotes. Then decide whether the **-ed** ending in the underlined words is pronounced as a final syllable (/əd/) or as a final sound (/d/).*

1. All of the biggest technological inventions <u>created</u> by man— the airplane, the automobile, the computer—say little about his intelligence, but speak volumes about his laziness.* (Mark Kennedy)

2. Technological progress has merely <u>provided</u> us with more efficient means for going backwards. (Aldous Huxley)

3. We've <u>arranged</u> a civilization in which most crucial[1] elements profoundly depend on science and technology. We've also arranged things so that almost no one understands science and technology. This is a prescription for disaster. (Carl Sagan)

4. Many people see technology as the problem behind the <u>so-called</u> digital divide.[2] Others see it as the solution. Technology is neither. It must operate in conjunction with[3] business, economic, political, and social systems. (Carly Fiorina)

5. Never before in history has innovation <u>offered</u> the promise of so much to so many in so short a time. (Bill Gates)

6. Globalization, as <u>defined</u> by rich people like us, is a very nice thing . . . you're talking about the Internet, you are talking about cell phones, you are talking about computers. This doesn't affect two-thirds of the people of the world. (Jimmy Carter)

> ***Natural English**
>
> The *-ed* ending of a word can change a final /t/ to a "flapped D" (a fast /d/).
>
> | | |
> |---|---|
> | creáte | creáDed |
> | invíte | invíDed |

B | PAIRS: Discuss the meanings of the quotes in Part A. Which quotations express a positive view of technology? Which ones do you agree with? Why do you think people worry about the effects of technology?

STEP 4   EXTENDED PRACTICE

Accuracy Practice *Listen again to Exercise 1 on page 66. Then record the sentences.*

Fluency Practice *Do you like to be the first to try a new technology or do you prefer to wait until you see how others feel about it? Explain your answer. Record your answers to the questions.*

---

[1] crucial: *very important;* [2] digital divide: *the fact that people in poorer countries have less access to advanced technology than people in richer countries;* [3] in conjunction with: *with*

STEP 1 PRESENTATION

The Consonants

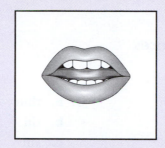

/θ/ **th**ink, /ð/ **th**ese

The tip of the tongue is between the teeth.

/θ/ is voiceless.

/ð/ is voiced.

Notes

Simplifications of the *TH* Sounds

1. When words ending in -*th* have an -*s* ending, the final -*th* is often dropped and the -*s* ending is lengthened.

   He brea<u>thes</u>. (say "he breazz" or "he breathes")

   the earth<u>'s</u> resources (say "the earsss resources" or "the earth's resources")

2. The plural *months* is almost always pronounced /mənts/.

3. *Clothes* is almost always pronounced like the verb *to close*.

Spellings for /θ/		Spellings for /ð/	
Common		**Common**	
th	**th**ink	*th*	**th**ese
Exceptions In the words *Thai* and *Thames*, the letters *th* are pronounced /t/.			

EXERCISE 1: Phrases with *TH* Sounds

🎧 *Listen and repeat the phrases.*

1. thirty-three thousand
2. those theaters
3. threatening weather
4. birth and death
5. Let's do something together.

6. mother and father
7. the fifth month
8. It's worth a thousand dollars.
9. my twentieth birthday
10. a thoughtful author

EXERCISE 2: Listen for Differences

🎧 **A |** *Listen and repeat the words.*

1. **a.** then
   b. den
   c. Zen[1]

2. **a.** author
   b. offer
   c. otter[2]

3. **a.** three
   b. tree
   c. free

4. **a.** bath
   b. bat
   c. bass[3]

5. **a.** writhe[4]
   b. rise
   c. ride

6. **a.** with
   b. wit[5]
   c. whiff[6]

7. **a.** thin
   b. tin
   c. sin

8. **a.** thinker
   b. sinker
   c. tinker[7]

9. **a.** soothe[8]
   b. suit
   c. Sue's

B | *PAIRS: Say a word. Pronounce the consonant carefully so your partner can tell you which word you said.*

EXERCISE 3: Sentences Full of Sounds

🎧 **A |** *Listen to the sentences. Then choose a sentence and say it to the class. Speak as smoothly as you can.*

1. Summer thunderstorms threaten the three thick but sick trees.
2. Someone should sing something soothing.
3. This theme seems thoroughly sorrowful.
4. Both boys were baffled[9] to see bass in the bathtub.
5. Either method is easier than those others.

---

[1] Zen: *a form of Buddhism;* [2] otter: *a mammal like a seal;* [3] bass: *a kind of fish;* [4] writhe: *to twist and turn as in pain;* [5] wit: *humor, intelligence;* [6] whiff: *smell;* [7] tinker: *to make small attempts to repair something;* [8] soothe: *to calm;* [9] baffled: *confused*

EXERCISE 4: The *TH* Game

Divide the class into two teams, A and B. Team A will start by asking questions, and Team B will answer. Then switch roles. All of the questions can be answered with a common TH word or phrase. The team that is answering questions receives a point for each correct answer, correctly pronounced. Team A's questions are on page 254; Team B's questions are on page 260.

> **EXAMPLE:**
> **TEAM A:** What's 10 + 3?
> **TEAM B:** Thirteen.

EXERCISE 5: Phrases and Idioms

A | Listen to the recording. Complete the phrases and idioms with the words you hear.

Phrases and Idioms	Definitions
1. _____ _____ and _____	in good times and bad times
2. back and _____	to and from
3. fall _____	fail to happen, not happen
4. It goes _____ saying	It's obvious.
5. make _____ most of _____ situation	find some good in a bad situation
6. on _____ whole	mostly
7. _____ a fit	lose control (usually in anger)
8. would _____	prefer

B | PAIRS: Compare your answers. Then choose one of the phrases or idioms to complete the sentences below. Practice the conversations.

1. **A:** Suzy works too hard. She's always tired.

   B: Yes, but it's her own business, so she says she'll stay with it _____

   _____ _____ _____.

2. **A:** When are you leaving for your vacation?

   B: Unfortunately, our plans have _____ _____, and we won't be going.

3. **A:** So you don't agree with the reorganization of the office?

   B: I wouldn't say that. _____ _____ _____, I think it's a good

   plan, but I think some of the details still need to be discussed.

LANGUAGE, THOUGHT, AND CULTURE

EXERCISE 6: Language and Thought

Speakers of different languages describe things in different ways. When we describe the location of an object, we choose a frame of reference. If you say that the car in the picture below is in front of the house, your frame of reference is another object—in this case, the house. If you say the car is to the left of the house, your frame of reference is yourself. If you describe the car as being to the southwest, you're using the cardinal directions north, south, east, and west. Research has shown that languages seem to have a preferred frame of reference.

A |*Look at the pictures and then read the sentences below. Which sentence would be the most natural to describe the picture in your language (properly translated)?*

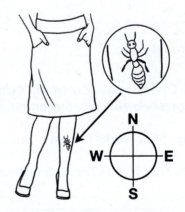

1. **a.** The car's to the southwest of the house.

    b. The car's in front of the house.

    c. The car's to the left of the house.

2. **a.** There's an ant on your southeast leg.

    b. There's an ant on your left leg.

B |*PAIRS: Compare your answers. Were they similar or different?*

EXERCISE 7: He Won't Speak Polish

Katrina and her husband Boris have been living in Chicago for four years. They plan to go back to Poland when Boris finishes medical school. Their three children, 13-year-old Peter, 7-year-old Katya, and 4-year old Ana, all have different attitudes toward their native language, Polish, and their second language, English.

A | *Listen to the conversation.*

KATRINA:	I think Peter's ashamed of us.
BORIS:	Why would you say that?
KATRINA:	He won't speak Polish to me anymore. Just English.
BORIS:	He's 13! He wants to be like all the other kids.
KATRINA:	Yeah. And their parents don't speak Polish.
BORIS:	It's just a stage. What does he use with Katya? She didn't used to want to speak English.
KATRINA:	She still doesn't. She misses Poland. She wants to go home. When Peter asks her a question in English, she answers him in Polish.
BORIS:	Well, there's no problem with Ana. She's happy to speak to anyone, in any language. With her, it's not an either-or kind of thing. *

> ***Natural English**
>
> The first vowel in *either* and *neither* can be pronounced /iy/ or /ay/ (the vowels in *see* or *my*). When *either-or* is used as an adjective, it describes a clear difference.
>
> It's not an *either-or* kind of thing.

B | *PAIRS: Practice the conversation. Then answer the questions.*

1. Do the ages of the three children influence their reactions to English and Polish? Explain.
2. What role does cultural identification play in their reactions?

EXERCISE 8: Your Turn

A | *People learn languages in different ways. What works well for you? Read the statements and check (✓) whether you agree, you're not sure, or you disagree.*

	Agree	Not Sure / Sometimes	Disagree
1. It's exciting to speak a new language.			
2. I feel frustrated when I speak English because I can't express myself as well as I can in my native language.			
3. I look for chances to speak English outside of class.			
4. I don't feel comfortable speaking because I make mistakes.			
5. The best way to learn a language is to live in a country where it's spoken.			
6. You need to study a language in a classroom in order to learn it.			
7. Some people are just good language learners—it's easy for them to learn new languages.			
8. I like to understand the grammar and have it explained.			
9. I don't try to learn new words—I pick them up through context.			

B | GROUPS: *Discuss your answers. When giving your opinion, start with the phrases* **I think that** . . . *or* **I don't think that** . . . .

STEP 4 EXTENDED PRACTICE

🎧 🎤 **Accuracy Practice** *Listen again to Exercises 1 and 2A on page 70. Then record the phrases and words.*

🎤 **Fluency Practice** *Record your answers to the questions. Pronounce words with* TH *carefully.*

1. What's the hardest part of learning English for you?

2. What sorts of things help you learn English? Television? The Internet? Conversation with a native speaker? Reading books? Making vocabulary lists?

UNIT 15 /p/ p̲ack, /b/ b̲ack, /f/ f̲an, /v/ v̲an, and /w/ w̲est

STEP 1 PRESENTATION

The Consonants

pack **/p/**, back **/b/**

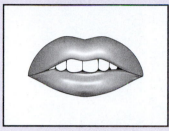

fan **/f/**, van **/v/**

west **/w/**

Press your lips together.

/p/ is voiceless.

/b/ is voiced.

The top teeth gently touch the lower lip.

/f/ is voiceless.

/v/ is voiced.

At the beginning of a word: Start with your lips tightly rounded, then unround.

Notes

1. **Woman and wood:** If you have difficulty pronouncing the beginning /w/ in words such as *woman* and *wood*, start with your lips tightly rounded and then unround them a little. Or try saying two /u/ sounds together. Stress the second /u/: uúman (*woman*), uúd (*wood*).

2. **Awful and apple:** Native speakers of Korean may confuse /p/ and /f/. For /p/, press your lips together firmly. For /f/, touch your top teeth to your bottom lip.

3. **Fine and vine:** Native speakers of Japanese should concentrate on /f/ and /v/. Touch your top teeth to your bottom lip.

4. **Berry and very:** Native speakers of Spanish may confuse /b/ and /v/. For /b/, press your lips firmly together. For /v/, touch your top teeth to your bottom lip.

5. **West and vest:** Native speakers of German, Russian, Turkish, and Chinese may confuse /w/ and /v/. For /w/, round your lips. For /v/, touch your top teeth to your bottom lip.

(continued on next page)

Spellings for /p/	Spellings for /b/	Spellings for /f/	Spellings for /v/	Spellings for /w/
Common *p* **p**ie, o**p**en *pp* a**pp**le, ha**pp**y	**Common** *b* **b**ag, a**b**le *bb* ro**bb**er	**Common** *f* **f**uel, li**f**e *ff* o**ff**, a**ff**ect	**Common** *v* **v**ote, lo**v**e	**Common** *w* **w**est, a**w**ay *wh*[1] **wh**at, **wh**ere
Silent Letters ~~p~~sychology, ~~p~~sychiatrist, ~~p~~sychic, ~~p~~neumonia, recei~~p~~t, cor~~p~~s, cu~~p~~board	**Silent Letters** clim~~b~~, thum~~b~~, lam~~b~~, com~~b~~, dou~~b~~t, de~~b~~t, su~~b~~tle	**Other** *ph* **ph**oto, **ph**one		**Other** *u* q**u**estion, q**u**it *o* **o**nce, **o**ne
				Silent Letters ~~w~~rite, ~~w~~rong, ans~~w~~er, s~~w~~ord, ~~w~~hole

STEP 2 FOCUSED PRACTICE

EXERCISE 1: Phrases with /p/, /b/, /f/, /v/, and /w/

Listen and repeat the phrases.

1. in the **f**irst **p**lace
2. a**b**andoned **f**armland
3. **p**retty **b**ad
4. **b**ox **o**ffice hits
5. a **v**ulnera**b**le **p**erson
6. **p**lenti**f**ul **f**ood
7. a **c**u**p** of **c**o**ff**ee
8. **Wh**at **w**ould you do?
9. **v**ery **w**et **w**eather
10. on **p**ur**p**ose
11. a **f**unny **w**oman
12. **b**io**f**uel **p**roduction

EXERCISE 2: Listen for Differences

A | *Listen and repeat the words.*

1. a. **b**ury
   b. **f**airy
   c. **w**ary

2. a. **p**et
   b. **v**et
   c. **w**et

3. a. **p**ine
   b. **v**ine
   c. **w**ine

4. a. **b**ite
   b. **f**ight
   c. **wh**ite

5. a. **p**ale
   b. **f**ail
   c. **wh**ale

6. a. a**b**oard
   b. a**ff**ord
   c. a**w**ard

B | *PAIRS: Choose a word and say it to your partner. Pronounce the consonant carefully so your partner can tell you which word you said.*

[1] In formal speaking, words spelled with *wh* may be pronounced /hw/: *when, where, white, while*

EXERCISE 3: Mouth Shapes

A | *PAIRS: Choose one of the numbered sets in Exercise 2A. Then face your partner and mouth (speak without sound) the words in any order you want. Your partner will look at the shape of your mouth to decide the order of the words. Exaggerate the mouth position.*

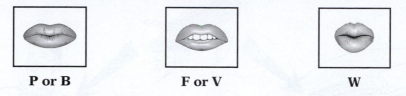

P or B **F or V** **W**

B | *PAIRS: Now say a word from Exercise 2A aloud to your partner. Your partner will tell you which word you said.*

EXERCISE 4: Conversations

A | *Listen to the recording and complete the phrases with the words you hear. Then compare your answers with a partner.*

1. _____ _____ _____

2. _____ abuse

3. variable _____

4. a _____ _____ flop

5. a _____ physicist

6. _____ _____

B | *PAIRS: Use the phrases from Part A to create short conversations below. Then practice them. Be sure to pronounce **p**, **b**, **f**, **v**, and **w** correctly.*

1. **A:** Who was Albert Einstein?

   B: _____

2. **A:** What's a term that means "hurting someone with words"?

   B: _____

3. **A:** How would you describe a "so-so" comedian?

   B: _____

4. **A:** What do you call a movie that people don't go to see?

   B: _____

5. **A:** What do Americans do every four years on the first Tuesday of November?

   B: _____

6. **A:** What do you call winds that change direction?

   B: _____

FOOD OR FUEL?

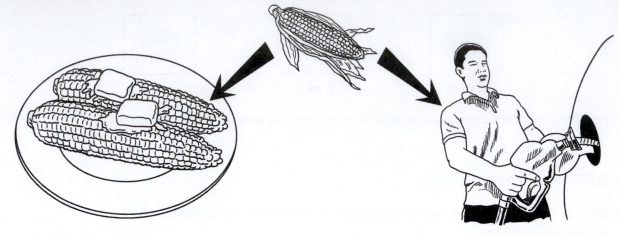

EXERCISE 5: Staple Foods

Staple foods keep the world alive. They're usually plant foods that make up the major part of a people's diet, supplying most of their energy and nutritional needs. They are inexpensive, plentiful[1], and can be stored for a long period of time.

GROUPS: Of the world's tens of thousands of plant foods, three supply most of the energy needs for over half the world's population. What do you think these three foods are? Add other staple foods to the list. What foods are staples in your country?

1. _____

2. _____

3. _____

Others: _____

EXERCISE 6: Abandoned Farmland

A | *Listen and repeat the words and phrases. Make sure you understand the meanings.*

   1. food riots   **2.** proponents   **3.** drawbacks

B | *PAIRS: Listen to the recording and then answer the questions.*

   1. What do some scientists propose to do with abandoned farmland?
   2. How much of the world's farmland has been abandoned?
   3. What do critics of the proposal say? How do the scientists answer these criticisms?
   4. What do you think of the proposal?
   5. Why do you think farmers abandon their land? List all the reasons you can think of.

   _____

---

[1] plentiful: *more than enough in amount or number*

Compounds are easy to recognize when the two parts of the compound are written together, as in *farmland*.

Many noun-noun phrases written as two separate words are also pronounced as compounds. The first word is stressed more heavily and pronounced on a higher pitch than the second.

fárm	stáple	plánt
lànd	fòods	fòods

EXERCISE 7: Benefits and Drawbacks of Biofuels

Many staple foods, such as corn, are used to make biofuels—substances produced from plants or other natural matter that can be used as fuel for cars, trucks, etc.

A | *PAIRS: Share information with your partner about the advantages and drawbacks of biofuels. Student A's information is on page 255; Student B's information is on page 261. Then take notes on what your partner says.*

B | *PAIRS: Do you think abandoned farmlands should be used to grow staple foods for biofuels? Answer the question using information from your charts.*

STEP 4 EXTENDED PRACTICE

Accuracy Practice *Listen again to Exercises 1 and 2A on page 76. Then record the phrases and words.*

Fluency Practice *Record your answers to the questions.*

1. What staple foods are eaten in your country? What other foods are they eaten with?
2. Have prices for these foods risen because the crops are being sold for biofuels?

16 /s/ s̲ign, /z/ z̲ero, /ʃ/ s̲h̲op, and /ʒ/ televis̲ion

The Consonants

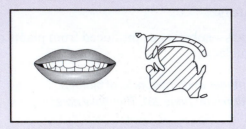

sign **/s/,** z̲ero **/z/**

Keep the tip of your tongue high and in the front of your mouth, behind the top teeth.

/s/ is voiceless.

/z/ is voiced.

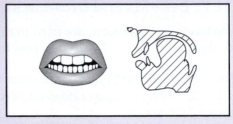

s̲h̲op **/ʃ/,** televis̲ion **/ʒ/**

Pull the tip of your tongue back from the /s/ position.

Round your lips a little.

/ʃ/ is voiceless.

/ʒ/ is voiced. /ʒ/ is a rare sound in English. It does not occur at the beginning of words.

Spellings for /s/	Spellings for /z/	Spellings for /ʃ/	Spellings for /ʒ/

Common
s sister, last
ss boss, address
se house,
   purpose
	Common
	z zoo, zipper
	s (between
	   vowels)
	   reason,
	   present
	se please, rise
		Common
		sh shower, cash
		ti patient,
		   nation
		ci special,
		   physician
		ssi profession,
		   permission
			Common
			si decision,
			   occasion
			ge beige,
			   massage
			su leisure,
			   treasure

Other
sc muscle, scene
ce receive, cent
ci city, acid
sw (silent *w*)
   answer,
   sword
	Other
	ss dessert,
	   possess
		Other
		ss pressure,
		   issue
		su sugar, insure
		si dimension
		ch Chicago, chef
			Other
			ti equation
			zu seizure, azure

EXERCISE 1: Phrases with /ʃ/ and /ʒ/

🎧 Listen and repeat the phrases and sentences.

/ʃ/	/ʒ/
1. I'm not **s**ure.	8. on televi**si**on
2. the Pacific O**c**ean	9. as u**su**al
3. wa**sh**ing ma**ch**ine	10. lei**su**re time
4. T-**sh**irts	11. mea**su**re it
5. an elegant musta**che**	12. it's a plea**su**re
6. I wi**sh** I could.	13. on occa**si**on
7. from **Ch**icago	14. a bei**ge** jacket

EXERCISE 2: Listen for Differences

🎧 **A|** Listen and repeat the words.

1. a. raced	4. a. gashes[1]	7. a. assign
b. raised	b. gasses	b. a shine
2. a. cost	5. a. fierce	8. a. she'd
b. caused	b. fears	b. seed
3. a. bays	6. a. false	9. a. shoes
b. beige	b. falls	b. Sue's

B| PAIRS: Say a word from Part A. Pronounce the consonant carefully so your partner can tell you which word you said.

EXERCISE 3: Spelling and Sound

🎧 Listen to the words. Decide whether the bold letters are pronounced /s/, /z/, /ʃ/, or /ʒ/. Then write each word under the correct column. Compare answers with a partner.

1. di**ss**olve	5. expan**s**ion	9. permi**ss**ion	13. purpo**s**e
2. cla**ss**ic	6. illu**s**ion	10. re**s**ult	14. propo**s**e
3. no**s**e	7. colli**s**ion	11. ca**s**ual	15. era**s**e
4. do**s**e	8. A**s**ia	12. in**s**ure	16. gla**c**ier

/s/	/z/	/ʃ/	/ʒ/
	dissolve		

---

[1] gash: *a long cut*

EXERCISE 4: Sentences Full of Sounds

Listen to the sentences. Then choose a sentence and say it to the class. Pronounce the bold letters carefully.

1. **S**ue **sh**ould per**s**uade the in**s**urance company to **s**weeten the deal before **sh**e in**s**ure**s** her bu**s**ine**ss** with them.

2. **Sh**e **s**ell**s** **s**ea**sh**ells down by the **s**ea**sh**ore.

3. That **s**ign **s**ays, "**S**ue'**s** **Sh**oe **Sh**ine **Sh**op," **s**o I gue**ss** you can get your **sh**oes **sh**ined at **S**ue'**s**.

STEP 3 COMMUNICATION PRACTICE

LEISURE TIME

EXERCISE 5: Leisure or Work?

A | *Listen to the conversation.*

TERESA: I used to love writing. I'd come home from work, sit down in front of the computer, and start writing.*

SAL: But you still write. And now you get paid for it. You're successful, you make a lot of money.

TERESA: I know. But now it's just work. It used to be fun.

SAL: You know, something similar happened to my dad. He was an accountant and couldn't wait to retire. He wanted to learn carpentry and make a table for my mom.

TERESA: What happened?

SAL: Well, he tried carpentry, but he didn't really like it. So he decided to volunteer to help people with their taxes. And now he likes accounting again.

> ***Natural English**
>
> *Used to* + verb and *would* + verb can both be used to describe past, repeated actions. Pronounce *used to* as one word: /yuwstuw/ or /yuwstə/. The *d* is not pronounced.
>
> I *usetə* love writing.
>
> Use the contraction of *would* after pronouns.
>
> *I'd* come home from work and start writing.
>
> *He'd* talk about what he wanted to do.

B | *PAIRS: Practice the conversation. Then answer the questions.*

1. How have Teresa's feelings about writing changed? Why?
2. How did Sal's father's feelings about carpentry and accounting change? Why?

EXERCISE 6: Leisure Time

A | *Listen and repeat. Make sure you understand the words.*

sensual	spare time	quilt(ing)

B | *Read the leisure activities below. Then listen to the recording. Write the needs that the leisure activities fulfill.*

1. Acting and playing baseball _____

2. Fishing and quilting _____

3. Card playing _____

EXERCISE 7: Your Turn

PAIRS: What are your three favorite leisure-time activities? What needs do you think they fulfill? Discuss your answers with a partner.

Activity	Need It Fulfills
_____	_____
_____	_____
_____	_____

STEP 4 EXTENDED PRACTICE

Accuracy Practice *Listen again to Exercises 1 and 2A on page 81. Then record the phrases, sentences, and words.*

Fluency Practice *Record your answers to the questions.*

1. Describe your favorite leisure activities.
2. How much time do you spend a week on these activities?
3. Why do you like doing them?

/tʃ/ <u>ch</u>eck and /dʒ/ <u>j</u>u<u>dge</u>

The Consonants

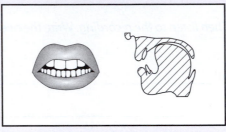

<u>ch</u>eck /tʃ/, <u>j</u>u<u>dge</u> /dʒ/

Keep the tip of your tongue high. Pull it back from the front of the mouth.

Round your lips a little.

/tʃ/ starts with /t/. It's voiceless.

/dʒ/ starts with /d/. It's voiced.

Notes

1. If you pronounce *wat<u>ch</u>* like *wash*, or *ma<u>j</u>or* like *measure*, concentrate on pronouncing the /t/ of /tʃ/ and the /d/ of /dʒ/.

2. If you pronounce *cat<u>ch</u>* like *cats*, or *e<u>dge</u>* like *Ed's*, pull your tongue back and round your lips.

3. If you pronounce *<u>j</u>u<u>dge</u>* like *judgʸ*, don't release the final sound so strongly. Keep it short.

4. If you pronounce *e<u>dge</u>* like *et<u>ch</u>*, concentrate on making a voiced /d/.

5. If you pronounce *zero* like *dzero*, don't let your tongue make firm contact with the top of your mouth (doing this produces the /d/ sound).

Spellings for /tʃ/		Spellings for /dʒ/	
Common		**Common**	
ch	**ch**eck, **ch**ur**ch**	*j*	**j**azz, ma**j**or
tch	wa**tch**, ki**tch**en	*ge, gi*	a**ge**, re**gi**on
Other		**Other**	
tu (inside a word)	na**tu**re, fu**tu**re	*du* (inside a word)	gra**du**al, e**du**cate
ce	**ce**llo		
Exceptions			
ch is pronounced /k/ in these words:			
ar**ch**itecture, **Ch**ristmas			
ch is pronounced /ʃ/ in these words:			
ma**ch**ine, **Ch**icago			

EXERCISE 1: Phrases with /tʃ/ and /dʒ/

🎧 *Listen and repeat the phrases. When /tʃ/ or /dʒ/ ends a word and the next word begins with a consonant, do not release /tʃ/ or /dʒ/ strongly. Say the next word immediately.*

/tʃ/	/dʒ/
1. watch TV	7. judge and jury
2. which one	8. college education
3. nature or nurture[1]	9. a large package
4. How much?	10. gradual changes
5. in the future	11. graduate school
6. latchkey children[2]	12. genetic engineering

EXERCISE 2: Listen for Differences

🎧 **A** | *Listen and repeat the phrases.*

	a.		b.	
1.	a.	two pleasures	b.	two pledgers[3]
2.	a.	Which witch?	b.	Which wish?
3.	a.	cheap land	b.	sheep land
4.	a.	no joking	b.	no choking
5.	a.	cheering crowds	b.	jeering[4] crowds
6.	a.	about the ridge[5]	b.	about the rich

B | *CLASS: Choose a phrase and say it to the class. Your classmates will tell you which phrase you said.*

EXERCISE 3: Differences in Meaning

🎧 **A** | *Listen to the sentences and responses.*

Sentences	Responses
1. a. Why didn't you <u>cash</u> this?	They won't accept checks.
b. Why didn't you <u>catch</u> this?	I hurt my wrist.
2. a. They don't have <u>mush</u>[6] on the menu.	I'll have eggs then.
b. They don't have <u>much</u> on the menu.	Let's go somewhere else then.
3. a. Here's your <u>share</u>.	Are you sure you gave me half?
b. Here's your <u>chair</u>.	You did a nice job fixing the legs.
4. a. <u>AIDS</u> is an important health issue.	Scientists still haven't found a cure.
b. <u>Age</u> is an important health issue.	We need more gerontologists.[7]

---

[1] nature or nurture: *the debate over whether genetics ("nature") or the environment ("nurture") is more responsible for determining a person's character;* [2] latchkey children: *children who come home to empty houses after school because their parents work;* [3] pledgers: *people who pledge or promise to donate something;* [4] jeering: *making fun of;* [5] ridge: *the line of the top of a mountain;* [6] mush: *hot, cooked cereal;* [7] gerontologist: *doctor who cares for the elderly*

B | *PAIRS: Say a sentence. Pronounce the underlined word carefully so your partner can say the correct response.*

STEP 3   COMMUNICATION PRACTICE

COLLEGE REQUIREMENTS

CALCULUS   Introduction to Economics

English Writing 1

PHYSICS 101

SWIMMING

"But I only wanted to be a musician!"

EXERCISE 4: A Well-Rounded Education

A | *Listen to the conversations.*

1. **LUIS:** Do I really have to take all these courses? Can't I just take the courses in my major?*

   ADVISOR: No, you have to take the required courses to gra**du**ate.

   LUIS: But that means another year or two of courses and another year or two of **pay**ing tuition. Colle**ge** is already too expensive.

   ADVISOR: I'm sorry, but that's the way it is. The university's goal is to produce well-rounded, e**du**cated gra**du**ates, not just specialists.

2. **MOTHER:** Don't you have to pass a swimming test before you gra**du**ate?

   LUKA: What? A swimming test?

   MOTHER: Maybe they've gotten rid of that requirement. When I was in colle**ge**, everybody had to pass a swimming test. Nobody could gra**du**ate if they couldn't swim.

   LUKA: I've never heard of that before. You mean, if people couldn't swim, they couldn't gra**du**ate?

   MOTHER: Well, not exactly. If they couldn't swim, they had to take a swimming class.

*Natural English

Notice the meaning of *no* and *yes* answers to negative *yes / no* questions.

  A: Can't I just take courses in my major?

  B: No. (No, you can't just take courses in your major).

  A: Can't I just take courses in my major?

  B: Yes. (Yes, you can just take courses in your major.)

B | *PAIRS: Practice the conversations in Part A. Take turns.*

EXERCISE 5: Your Turn

A | *Read the graduation requirements below. Rate the requirements (**1** = very important,*
*   **2** = important, **3** = least important).*

_____ Technology class

_____ Science class

_____ Math class

_____ Literature class

_____ History class

_____ Fine arts class

_____ Economics class

_____ Swimming test

B | *PAIRS: Compare your answers. Explain why you think some requirements are more important*
than others.

STEP 4   EXTENDED PRACTICE

Accuracy Practice   *Listen again to Exercises 1 and 2A on page 85. Then record the phrases and*
sentences.

Fluency Practice   *Record your answers to the questions.*

1. In your country, what requirements do students have to fulfill to graduate from college?

2. Do you think colleges should require students to take courses outside their major? Why or why not?

18 -s Endings

STEP 1 | PRESENTATION

-*S* endings include the endings for regular plurals, possessives, third person singular present verbs, and contractions.

-*S* endings can be pronounced as a syllable or a final consonant sound.

1. Pronounce the -*s* ending as a new syllable (/əz/ or /ɪz/) when the base word ends in an *s*-like sound (/s, z, ʃ, ʒ, tʃ, dʒ/).

   one rose → two roses

2. Pronounce the -*s* ending as /s/ or /z/ when the base word does not end in an *s*-like sound.

   a. Use /s/ when the base word ends in /p, t, k, θ, f/.

      They work. → He works.

   b. Use /z/ when the base word ends in a vowel sound or /b, d, g, v, m, n, ŋ, r, l/.

      tree → two trees

Notes

1. **Nouns Ending in /f/:** Several common nouns that end in /f/ in their singular form end in /v/ in the plural form. The plural ending is pronounced /z/.

   one leaf → two leaves   one knife → two knives

2. ***TH* Sounds before -*s* Endings:** *TH* sounds before -*s* endings are often simplified or dropped.

   one month → two months /mənts/

EXERCISE 1: Apply the Rule

*PAIRS: Listen and repeat the base words. Should the **-s** ending be pronounced as a new syllable or a final consonant? Check (✔) the correct column. Then practice the words, adding the **-s** endings.*

	/əz/ or /ɪz/	**Final /s/ or /z/**
1. exercise	✔	____
2. wife	____	____
3. ship	____	____
4. bush	____	____
5. bonus	____	____
6. conclusion	____	____
7. amount	____	____
8. salary	____	____
9. judge	____	____

EXERCISE 2: Listen for Differences

A | *Listen to the phrases. Count the syllables in each phrase and write the number in the blank. Compare your answers with a partner.*

1. **a.** some expert advice __5__ **b.** some experts advise __5__

2. **a.** he claps _____ **b.** he collapses _____

3. **a.** describe your folks _____ **b.** describe your focus _____

4. **a.** Liz's Ford _____ **b.** Liz Ford _____

5. **a.** quiet class _____ **b.** quiet classes _____

6. **a.** good grades _____ **b.** good grade _____

7. **a.** hard course _____ **b.** hard courses _____

8. **a.** our hosts _____ **b.** our hostess _____

9. **a.** fiscal condition _____ **b.** physical conditions _____

B | *PAIRS: Choose a phrase and say it to your partner. Pronounce the words carefully so your partner can tell you which phrase you said.*

EXERCISE 3: Phrases and Idioms

Many idioms include verbs that describe physical exercise.

A | *Listen and complete the sentences with the words you hear. Then compare your answers with a partner.*

1. He wasted the whole day **running around in** _____.

2. Stop **beating around the** _____. Just say what you mean.

3. Get the _____ first: **Don't jump to** _____.

4. I've been sitting behind this desk for so long that I'm **climbing the** _____. I've got to get out of the office!

5. I'm **bending over** _____ to make you happy, but nothing I do _____ you.

6. (at a casino) You've won $100 so far. Let's go home. Don't _____ **your luck.**

7. Don't **pass the buck.** These _____ are your responsibility.

8. You're **making** _____ **out of molehills**. Who _____ if she doesn't like your haircut?!

9. Is being a _____ **potato** worse for your body or your mind?

B | *PAIRS: Match the idioms in Part A with the definitions below. Write the number of each idiom in the blank next to its definition.*

_____ **a.** avoid responsibility

_____ **b.** take unnecessary risks

_____ **c.** expend a lot of effort/energy without results

_____ **d.** do everything possible to please someone

_____ **e.** make a problem out of something that isn't a problem

_____ **f.** want badly to be active, to take action

_____ **g.** make decisions/judgments without enough information

_____ **h.** speak indirectly

_____ **i.** a person who spends a lot of time lying on the couch and watching TV

EXERCISE?

EXERCISE 4: Wanted: Professional Couch Potatoes

A | *Listen to the recording and complete the sentences with the words you hear. Then compare your answers with a partner.*

A British newspaper recently wrote an article about a company that _____ to hire
                                                                        1.
couch potatoes. The position involves doing nothing but eating. It _____ pretty
                                                                    2.
well, and the job _____ aren't too tough. The company is testing a weight-loss
                   3.
product they want to sell. Basically, the job will pay some lucky applicants to do exactly what

they already do, but in addition, they have to consume 16 percent more _____ a
                                                                         4.
day. The additional calories must come from _____ that are high in fat, such as
                                              5.
potato _____, fast-food burgers, or pizza. The new _____ will also
        6.   7.
take the weight-loss product once a day. Beyond this, they don't have to do anything but have

their weight and calories monitored by the company. For interested applicants, this could be the

ultimate "work from home" job.

Natural English

In words like *potato* or *tomato*, the letter *o* is unstressed and pronounced /ə/. This vowel does
not have an *o* sound.

pətáto

təmáto

tədáy, təníght, təmórrow (today, tonight, tomorrow)

pəlíce (police)

PAIRS: Answer the questions about the recording in Part A. Use complete sentences and -s endings when necessary.

1. What does the job involve?
2. How does the job pay?
3. What is the company testing?
4. What kinds of foods will workers add to their diets?
5. Does this job sound attractive to you? Why or why not?

EXERCISE 5: Burning Calories

Basal metabolism is the energy required to keep the heart pumping blood and the lungs breathing during rest. Basal metabolism varies according to age, gender, height, and weight. Except for sleeping, everything else we do requires additional calories.

PAIRS: Find out how many calories different activities burn. Each of you has a grid that is partially complete. Don't show your grid to your partner. Take turns asking each other for the missing information. When you finish, compare your grids. They should be the same. Student A's grid is on page 255. Student B's grid is on page 261.

EXERCISE 6: Your Turn

Health professionals recommend that adults get about a half hour of moderate exercise four to five days a week to stay healthy.

A| *Write your answers to the questions in the chart.*

	You	**Your Partner**
Do you like to exercise?		
What kind of exercise do you do?		
How often do you exercise? **a.** regularly (daily, weekly, twice a week) **b.** once in a blue moon (almost never) **c.** never		
Do you feel you get enough exercise?		

B| *PAIRS: Interview your partner and write your partner's answers in the chart.*

C| *CLASS: Report some information about your partner to the class. Use -s endings when necessary.*

STEP 4 EXTENDED PRACTICE

Accuracy Practice   *Listen again to Exercise 2A on page 89. Then record the phrases.*

Fluency Practice   *Record your partner's answers to the questions in Exercise 6A above. Use complete sentences and -s endings when necessary.*

UNIT 19
/y/ yet and /dʒ/ jet;
Joining Vowels with /y/;
Clusters with /y/: regular

STEP 1   PRESENTATION

The Consonants

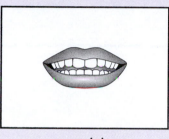

yet /y/

Raise the center of your tongue toward the front of your mouth.

The tip of your tongue rests behind your lower teeth.

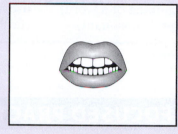

jet /dʒ/

The tip of your tongue is high and pulled back to the center of your mouth.

Your lips are rounded a little.

/dʒ/ starts with /d/. It is voiced.

Joining Vowels with /y/

When vowels ending in /y/ (/iy, ey, ay, oy/) are followed by another vowel, join the two vowels together with /y/. The two vowels are in different syllables. This happens when the vowels are in the same word or in adjacent words. (The letter *y* has been added to show the pronunciation.)

sci^yence   appreci^yate   my uncle   three^y of those

Consonant Clusters with /y/

The sound /y/ occurs in the consonant clusters of some common words. It is usually spelled with the letter *u*.

re**gu**lar /gy/   parti**cu**lar /ky/   po**pu**lar /py/

(continued on next page)

1. If you pronounce *yes* like *Jess*, try this: Say /i/ and slide your tongue forward. Don't let your tongue press against the top of your mouth. Or, try this: Say /i/ twice. Stress the second /i/: *iíes* (*yes*).

2. If you pronounce *year* like *ear*, say /i/ twice. Stress the second *iíear* (*year*).

Spellings for /y/		Spellings for /dʒ/
Common *y* yesterday, beyond		See Unit 18.
Other *u* (beginning of a word) *u* (after a consonant)	**u**se, **u**nit vocab**u**lary, occ**u**pation	

STEP 2 FOCUSED PRACTICE

EXERCISE 1: Listen for Differences

A | *Listen and repeat the words.*

1. **a.** yellow
   b. Jell-O™

2. **a.** year
   b. ear

3. **a.** year
   b. jeer[1]

4. **a.** yolk
   b. joke

5. **a.** yet
   b. jet

6. **a.** yeast[2]
   b. east

7. **a.** mayor
   b. major

8. **a.** the use
   b. the juice

9. **a.** yes
   b. Jess

B | *PAIRS: Say a word. Pronounce the consonants carefully so your partner can tell you which word you said.*

EXERCISE 2: Sounds and Spellings

A | *Complete the sentences with* **a** *or* **an**. *Use* **a** *if the word begins with the consonant sound /y/. Use* **an** *if the word begins with a vowel sound.*

1. He wore __an__ unusual hat.

2. She's a student at _____ university in Ohio.

3. There's going to be _____ union meeting tonight.

4. Take _____ umbrella—it's going to rain.

5. This is _____ unique opportunity to talk with an expert.

---

[1] jeer: *to make fun of someone;* [2] yeast: *bacteria that make bread rise*

6. The book was about _____ utopian community[1] in the future.

7. I'd rather live in _____ urban area than in the country.

8. The candidate's opponents are making _____ united effort to defeat him.

B | PAIRS: *Listen and check your answers. Then practice saying the sentences to each other. Join* an *and the next word.*

EXERCISE 3: Sentences Full of Sounds

Listen to the sentences. Then choose a sentence and say it to the class.

1. Yes, Jess asked if the company's bought a new jet yet.
2. Last year my ear infections were bad.
3. Before he was a mayor, he was a major in the army.
4. Yellow Jell-O™ tastes like lemon, doesn't it?
5. The scientists looked for younger animals in the jungle.
6. The chef is famous for his use of juice in meat dishes.

EXERCISE 4: Words with /y/ Clusters

Listen and repeat the phrases. The bold letters are consonant clusters with /y/.

1. arguing style	5. on a regular basis	9. a million years
2. particular uses	6. computer users	10. vocabulary books
3. particular juices	7. popular music	11. ambulance driver
4. regular checkups	8. human values	12. senior year

EXERCISE 5: Joining Vowels with /y/

A | *Listen to the words. Are the underlined letters pronounced as one vowel sound or two? Write **1** if there is only one vowel sound. Write **2** if there are two vowel sounds.*

1. appreciate	2	6. niece	____	11. theater	____
2. racial	____	7. fiancé	____	12. threaten	____
3. immediately	____	8. denial	____	13. theory	____
4. official	____	9. material	____	14. theoretical	____
5. experience	____	10. sufficient	____	15. geography	____

B | *PAIRS: Practice the words. If the letters are pronounced as two vowel sounds, join the two vowels with /y/.*

---

[1] utopian community: *an imaginary perfect world where everyone is happy*

ARGUING

EXERCISE 6: Stand Up for Yourself

A | *Listen to the conversation.*

EVA: Why didn't you stand up for yourself in the meeting? Everyone thought you were right.*

TOMAS: I don't like to fight. It isn't worth it. Anyway, no one jumped in to defend me.

EVA: That's because they expected you to say something. Arguing isn't fighting, you know.

TOMAS: Well, it's not something I'm comfortable with. The people on this committee don't seem interested in cooperating. They all want to push their own agenda.[1]

EVA: Everyone but you, it seems.

TOMAS: We're supposed to find a solution. That won't happen if we can't work together.

> ***Natural English**
>
> Notice the blending of *you* with a preceding word ending in /t/.
>
> Why didənchew stand up for yourself? (Why didn't you stand up for yourself?)
>
> Everyone thoughtchew were right (Everyone thought you were right.)
>
> Everyone bəchew, it seems. (Everyone but you, it seems.)

B | *PAIRS: Practice the conversation in Part A. Then answer the questions.*

1. What's the difference between arguing and fighting?
2. When shouldn't we push our own agendas?

---

[1] push an agenda: *to argue or work only for your own plan*

EXERCISE 7: Arguing Styles

Arguments are a normal part of relationships. They can lead to growth, or they can damage a relationship. Whether you argue with your father or boyfriend, your neighbor or nephew, your boss or best friend, you probably argue in a generally consistent way.

A | *PAIRS: You and your partner each have eight questions about arguing styles. First answer the questions about yourself. Then take turns asking each other the questions and checking (✓) your partner's answers. How similar are your arguing styles? Student A's questions are on page 256. Student B's questions are on page 261.*

B | *In this recording, you'll hear some advice about arguing effectively. Complete the sentences with the words you hear. When you finish, go back to your answers to the questions in Part A. According to the advice, do you argue effectively? Does your partner?*

1. Don't avoid _____ at all costs. Bottled up _____ will find their way out in one _____ _____ another.

2. Don't _____ in front of third parties.

3. Bringing up old _____ is a bad _____. It's more _____ to stay focused on one _____.

4. Be a good _____. Don't make quick assumptions about what your partner's "real" motives or feelings are.

5. At the end of an argument, make a _____ offering. Tell your partner something you like about him.

6. Be _____ to compromise but don't _____ for things you haven't done or said.

7. Don't let an argument get out of _____ and turn into a shouting _____ where no one listens.

STEP 4 EXTENDED PRACTICE

Accuracy Practice *Listen again to Exercises 1A, 4, and 5A on pages 94 and 95. Then record the words and phrases.*

Fluency Practice *Do you think you argue effectively? Why or why not? Record your answers to the questions.*

UNIT 20 /r/ rate; Consonant Clusters with /r/: growth

STEP 1 PRESENTATION

The Consonants

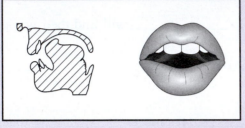

rate /r/

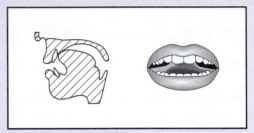

late /l/

Turn the tip of your tongue up and back. Then lower the tip of your tongue.

Do NOT let the tip of your tongue touch the top of your mouth as it uncurls.

Round your lips slightly.

The tip of the tongue touches firmly behind the top teeth.

Clusters with /r/

The consonant /r/ occurs in many consonant clusters. Don't separate the consonants in a cluster:

pray   **tr**ain   **thr**ee   **shr**ink   **scr**atch

Notes

1. *Rate and late*: If you pronounce *rate* like *late*, remember that with /r/, the tip of the tongue does not touch the top of the mouth. With /l/, the tip of the tongue touches the top of the mouth. Look again at the diagrams above.

2. *Red and wed*: If you pronounce *red* like *wed*, make sure that you start with the tip of your tongue turned up and back. Then lower your tongue. If your /r/ still has a *w* sound, don't round your lips at all—keep them flat.

Spellings for /r/	
Common	
r	red, card
rr	sorry, carry
Other	
wr	wrong, wrist

EXERCISE 1: Phrases with /r/

🎧 *Listen and repeat the phrases.*

1. rate of immigration
2. road trips
3. the wrong direction
4. increasing prices
5. transportation problems
6. roughly three-quarters

7. growth in urban areas
8. strict controls
9. foreign-born
10. permanent residents
11. historical trends
12. crowded areas

EXERCISE 2: Listen for Differences

🎧 **A |** *Listen to the words.*

1. **a.** right
   b. light
2. **a.** arrive
   b. alive
3. **a.** crowd
   b. cloud

4. **a.** ride
   b. wide
5. **a.** present
   b. pleasant
6. **a.** correct
   b. collect

7. **a.** fright
   b. fight
8. **a.** prayed
   b. played
9. **a.** crash
   b. cash

🎧 **B |** *Listen again and circle the words you hear.*

C | *PAIRS: Say a word from Part A. Pronounce it carefully so your partner can tell you which word you said.*

EXERCISE 3: Phrases with r and l

🎧 **A |** *Listen and repeat the phrases. Then choose a phrase and say it to the class.*

1. parallel lines
2. religious problems
3. electric rates
4. friendly florist
5. really large salaries
6. celery and carrots

7. brilliant blue bracelet
8. a frightful flight
9. solitary celebrities
10. college library
11. allergic reactions
12. Florida alligators

B | *PAIRS: Read the sentences. Then say a phrase from Part A that describes the sentences.*

1. You don't want to go swimming with these.
2. CEOs earn these.
3. These are good for you.
4. We landed 6 hours late and then the airline couldn't find my bags.
5. These lines never meet.

EXERCISE 4: Differences in Meaning

A | *Listen to the sentences and responses.*

Sentences	Responses

1. a. They <u>erected</u> bridges.   Over what river?
    b. They <u>elected</u> Bridges.   To what office?

2. a. Don't step on that <u>grass</u>!   Did you just plant it?
    b. Don't step on that <u>glass</u>!   Thanks. I might have cut myself.

3. a. Do you have the <u>white</u> books?   No, all my books are green.
    b. Do you have the <u>light</u> books?   No, all my books are heavy.
    c. Do you have the <u>right</u> books?   Yes, these are the right ones.

4. a. Do you like French <u>flies</u>?   No! I hate all insects.
    b. Do you like French <u>fries</u>?   No, I'm allergic to potatoes.

5. a. There's a big <u>cloud</u> over there.   It looks like rain.
    b. There's a big <u>crowd</u> over there.   I wonder what they're looking at.

B | *PAIRS: Say a sentence. Pronounce the underlined word carefully so your partner can say the correct response.*

STEP 3 COMMUNICATION PRACTICE

NEW ARRIVALS

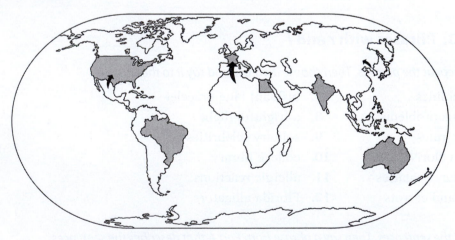

EXERCISE 5: Immigration

PAIRS: Why do people decide to live in another country (temporarily or permanently)? Write your ideas on the lines below.

_____

_____

EXERCISE 6: Human Migrations

PAIRS: Listen to the recording and then answer the questions.

1. How many immigrants worldwide were there in 2010? What's the prediction for 2050?
2. Look at your answers to the questions in Exercise 5. Which of the reasons are "push" factors? Which are "pull" factors?*

---

*Natural English

The vowels in *push* and *pull* are the same as the vowel in *took* (/ʊ/). For this vowel, your lips should be a little rounded (but not tightly rounded). For the vowels in *pool* and *boot*, your lips should be tightly rounded.

Push factors cause people to leave their home countries.

Pull factors attract immigrants to a new country.

EXERCISE 7: Your Turn

A | *To what extent do you think your country should allow people from other countries to come and live? Circle your answer.*

1. Allow many to come and live

2. Allow some

3. Allow a few

4. Allow none

5. Not sure

B | *GROUPS: Share your answers. Do your answers depend on which countries immigrants come from? Do they depend on the socioeconomic or educational background of the immigrants?*

STEP 4 EXTENDED PRACTICE

Accuracy Practice *Listen again to Exercises 2A and 3A on page 99. Then record the words and phrases.*

Fluency Practice *What are some of the problems immigrants face when they come to a new country? Record your answer to the question.*

21
Beginning /l/: light;
Consonant Clusters with /l/: blue;
Contrasts: /l/ and /r/, /l/ and /n/

STEP 1 PRESENTATION

The Consonants

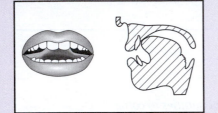

light /l/

Touch the tip of your tongue behind your top teeth.

When you say /l/, there's contact between the tongue and the top of the mouth.

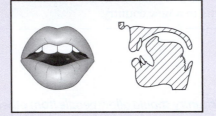

right /r/

Turn the tip of your tongue up and back.

Then lower your tongue without touching the top of the mouth.

There's no contact between the tip of the tongue and the top of the mouth.

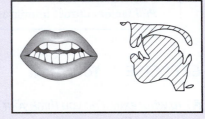

night /n/

The tip of the tongue touches behind the top teeth.
The air passes out through the nose, not through the mouth.

Consonant Clusters with /l/

Don't separate the consonants in the cluster.

Beginning clusters: **cl**imb, **fl**y, **sl**ow, **spl**ash, su**ppl**y

Final clusters: be**lt**, ho**ld**, mi**lk**, fau**lts**

Notes

Night and light: Speakers of some Chinese dialects may substitute beginning /n/ for /l/ and vice versa. When you say /n/ (*night*), the air comes out your nose; touch the tip of your nose when you say these words. When you say /l/ (*light*), the air comes out of your mouth; touch your lower lip when you say these words to remind you of the air flow.

Spellings for /l/
Common
l like, truly
ll yellow, really
Other (*l* is silent)
cou~~l~~d, wou~~l~~d, shou~~l~~d,
wa~~l~~k, ta~~l~~k, cha~~l~~k,
ca~~l~~m, pa~~l~~m, sa~~l~~mon, yo~~l~~k, ha~~l~~f, ca~~l~~f

EXERCISE 1: Phrases with /l/

🎧 *Listen and repeat the phrases.*

1. in love
2. love letters
3. a light lunch
4. a night-light

5. climb up
6. a large allowance
7. longer and longer
8. law and order

9. black clouds
10. clearance sale
11. It looks like rain.
12. eleven o'clock

EXERCISE 2: Listen for Differences

🎧 **A** | *Listen and repeat the words.*

1. a. led
   b. red
   c. Ned

2. a. light
   b. right
   c. night

3. a. lot
   b. rot
   c. not/knot

4. a. collect
   b. correct
   c. connect

5. a. low
   b. row
   c. know/no

6. a. lock
   b. rock
   c. knock

🎧 **B** | *Listen again and circle the words you hear.*

C | *PAIRS: Say a word from Part A. Pronounce it carefully so your partner can tell you which word you said.*

EXERCISE 3: Sentences Full of Sounds

🎧 *Listen to the sentences. Then choose a sentence and say it to the class.*

1. If you buy the right night-light, it will use very little electricity.
2. In your poem, be sure that all nine lines rhyme and have similar rhythm.
3. My connection to the Internet depends on the correction of a large collection of unrelated problems.
4. Late in the year the crime rate climbed a little.
5. Public loyalty to the royal family in Britain has a glorious tradition.
6. Are your relatives really rock and roll celebrities?

EXERCISE 4: Consonant Clusters with /l/

🎧 **A** | *Listen and repeat the words. The first word in the pair starts with a consonant cluster. Don't separate the consonants. The second word starts with a consonant followed by an unstressed vowel.*

1. **a.** claps
   b. collapse

2. **a.** Pluto
   b. polluted

3. **a.** blue
   b. balloon

4. **a.** place
   b. palatial[1]

5. **a.** inclusion
   b. in collusion[2]

6. **a.** clone
   b. cologne

7. **a.** glass
   b. galactic[3]

8. **a.** slew[4]
   b. salute

9. **a.** clam
   b. calamity[5]

B | *PAIRS: Practice saying the words. Take turns.*

STEP 3 COMMUNICATION PRACTICE

LOVE AND MARRIAGE

EXERCISE 5: May–September Marriages

May–September marriages are marriages between a younger person and a much older person. The names of the months are a metaphor for the stages of life.

🎧 **A** | *Listen to the conversation.*

YOUNG: Is that your sister's husband?

SOFIA: No, that's my brother. My sister's married to a guy 17 years older than she is.

YOUNG: Really?! I might have seen her with him last week. I thought he was your father.

SOFIA: Well, her husband's not that old. The man you saw could have been my father.

> **Natural English**
>
> Notice how the verb *have* is reduced in modal perfects.
>
> I mightəv seen her.
>
> The man you saw couldəv been my father.

---

[1] palatial: *adjective for* palace; [2] in collusion: *sharing a secret agreement to do something wrong;*
[3] galactic: *adjective for* galaxy; [4] slew: *the past tense of* slay *(to kill);* [5] calamity: *disaster*

B | PAIRS: Practice the conversation. Then answer the questions.

1. Are May–September marriages common in your country?
2. What problems might May–September couples have?
3. What role does gender play in May–September marriages?

EXERCISE 6: Quotations

A | *Listen to the quotes about love and marriage. Complete the sentences with the words you hear.*

1. The _____ wants what it wants. There's no _____ to those things. (Woody

    Allen)

2. To say that you can love one person all your _____ is just _____ saying

    that one _____ will continue burning as _____ as you _____.

    (Leo Tolstoy)

3. _____ you need is _____. (John Lennon and Paul McCartney)

B | *PAIRS: Read the statements about love. Then match each quote in Part A with a statement below that expresses the same sentiment. Which quotes and statements do you agree with?*

a. Love is not ruled by logic.
b. Love doesn't last.
c. Nothing is more important than love.

EXERCISE 7: The Marriage Project

The Marriage Project conducts research on the state of marriage in the United States. It investigates how social and economic changes affect the meaning and functions of marriage.

A | *The statements below come from research on marriage in the United States. Some statements are supported by research and others are not. Read the statements. Then decide whether they are true or false. Write **T** (True) or **F** (False).*

_____ 1. Men benefit more from marriage than women.

_____ 2. Children bring more stress to a marriage.

_____ 3. The key to a successful marriage is romantic love.

_____ 4. The more highly educated a woman is, the greater her chances of getting married.

_____ 5. Because divorce is more acceptable today, people who stay married have happier

    marriages than in the past when divorce was not an option.

_____ 6. The number of married young adults (aged 25–34) was higher between 2000 and 2009

    than in past decades.

B | PAIRS: Check your answers below. Then correct the false statements from Part A. Discuss whether you think the research reflected in these statements also applies to marriage in your own country.

STEP 4   EXTENDED PRACTICE

Accuracy Practice Listen again to Exercises 1 and 2A on page 103. Then record the phrases and words.

Fluency Practice Record your answer to the question: Have marriage trends in your country changed? Explain.

EXERCISE 7A: 1. *False.* Recent research shows that both men and women benefit, but in different ways. Married men are healthier and live longer lives than unmarried men. Married women are better off financially than unmarried women. **2.** *True.* Many research studies show that the first child pushes the couple apart. **3.** *False.* Most successful couples say the key to a long and happy marriage is commitment and companionship, not romantic love. Couples in happy marriages are friends who share interests with each other. **4.** *True.* In spite of the fact that educated women marry at a later age, they are more likely to be married than less educated women. This is a change from past trends. **5.** *False.* Even though divorce is an option today, research shows that couples who stay married to the same person are somewhat less happy than they were in the past. **6.** *False.* In 2009, there were more young adults who were not married than married.

Final /l/: feel; Contractions of *will*

The Consonants

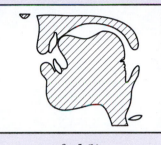

feel /l/

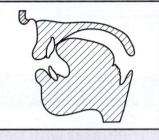

leaf /l/

The tip of the tongue touches behind the top teeth.	The tip of the tongue touches behind the top teeth.
The body of the tongue "bunches up" in the back of the mouth: The back of the tongue rises.	The back of the tongue is not raised.
Final /l/ has a "swallowed" sound: This pronunciation is called a "dark" *l*.	At the beginning of a word or syllable, /l/ is called a "light" *l* or "clear" *l*. Most languages have a "light" *l*.

Endings Pronounced with Dark *l*: -le, -al, -ful, -able, -ible, -ial

little   local   capable

Contractions of *Will*

The contracted forms of *will* are pronounced with a dark *l*.

I'll go.   He'll do it.   You'll like her.

1. When *will* is contracted with a pronoun, the vowel of the pronoun is often reduced to a shorter sound.

    I'll go. (say "all go")

    He'll stay. (say "hill stay")

    We'll go. (say "will go")

    You'll be late. (say "yʊll be late"; *you'll* rhymes with *pull*)

    She'll come. (say "shɪll come"; *she'll* rhymes with *still*)

    They'll do it. (say "thɛll do it"; *they'll* rhymes with *shell*)

2. After a noun, *will* is often reduced to /əl/ and joined to the noun. The full form is usually written and does not reflect the reduced pronunciation. If it is difficult for you to make this reduction and join it to the noun, you can use *will* after nouns.

    The coast will flood. (say "the coastal flood")

(continued on next page)

Silent *l*

The letter *l* is silent in many common words: wa*l*k, ta*l*k, fo*l*k, ha*l*f, wou*l*d, cou*l*d, shou*l*d, cha*l*k, pa*l*m, sa*l*mon, ca*l*m

Notes

If you pronounce *old* like *ode*, or *people* like *peopo*, make sure that the tip of your tongue is firmly touching the top of your mouth.

> ### Spellings for Dark *l*
>
> See Unit 21.

STEP 2 FOCUSED PRACTICE

EXERCISE 1: Phrases with Dark *l*

Listen and repeat the phrases.

1. single people
2. time capsules
3. on the whole
4. double trouble
5. meanwhile
6. old people
7. in a little while
8. healthy children
9. logical results

EXERCISE 2: Endings with Dark *l*

Several adjective endings have dark /l/: *-al, -ial, -ful, -ible, -able*.

*PAIRS: Write the adjective form of the words in the blanks. The last sound of the adjective ending is a **dark l**.*

1. help ____helpful____
2. believe _____
3. president _____
4. magic _____
5. rest _____
6. influence _____
7. office _____
8. reason _____
9. finance _____
10. harm _____
11. sense _____
12. compare _____

EXERCISE 3: Reductions of *will*

*Listen and repeat the sentences. Pronounce **will** as /əl/ and join it to the noun before it. Practice saying the sentences with a partner.*

1. What will the future bring? (say "whaddəl")
2. I think a cure will be found for cancer. (say "curəl")
3. I think population growth will slow down. (say "growthəl")
4. His logic will convince you. (say "logicəl")
5. I think electric cars will replace gas-powered cars. (say "carzəl")
6. The earth will get warmer, and the oceans will rise. (say "earthəl," "oceanzəl")

EXERCISE 4: Sounds Like . . .

Two phrases that sound the same but have different spellings and meanings are called **homophrases**. *Listen and repeat the homophrases. Then work with a partner to think of a homophrase with will. (You can check your answers on page 111.)*

1. royal answer _____*Roy'll answer.*_____

2. the vinyl dye _____

3. The cattle run away. _____

4. your logical persuader _____

5. Alaska fisherman _____

6. the comical joke _____

EXERCISE 5: Quotations with Dark *l*

*PAIRS: Student A has clues to the missing words in quotes 1 and 2 (on page 256). Student B has clues for quotes 3 and 4 (on page 262). Use the clues to help your partner figure out the missing words in the quotes below. Then practice reading the quotes aloud. Most of the missing words contain **dark l**.*

Quote 1: You can (a) _____ (b) _____ the (c) _____ some of the

(d) _____, and some of the (e) _____ (f) _____ the time, but you

cannot (g) _____ (h) _____ the (i) _____ (j) _____ of the

time. (Abraham Lincoln)

Quote 2: That's one (a) _____ step for (b) _____, one giant (c) _____

for mankind. (d) (_____ Armstrong)

(continued on next page)

Quote 3: So many of our dreams at first seem (a) _____, then they seem

(b) _____, and then when we summon the (c) _____, they soon become

(d) _____. (Christopher Reeves)

Quote 4: It is difficult to say what is (a) _____, for the (b) _____ of yesterday is

the hope of today and the (c) _____ of (d) _____. (Robert Goddard)

STEP 3   COMMUNICATION PRACTICE

LOOKING FORWARD AND LOOKING BACK

EXERCISE 6: Time Capsules

Time capsules are collections of objects and information that provide a record of life at a particular time or place. They may be buried in the ground or put in a safe place for future generations. More recently, several time capsules have been shot into space, to provide a record of life on Earth for future space travellers or perhaps aliens.

PAIRS: Listen to the recording and then answer the questions.

1. Describe the 1917 time capsule found in the New York City public school.
2. What did the fifth-graders put in their 2009 time capsule?
3. What 10 things would you put in a time capsule to show what life is like now?

_____

_____

_____

EXERCISE 7: Predictions for 2050

A | *Make predictions about what will happen by 2050. Use* **will/won't** *in your sentences.*

1. Medicine/health _____

2. Environment/the earth _____

3. Technology _____

4. Politics/government _____

5. The family/relationships _____

6. Transportation _____

7. Global population _____

8. Other _____

Natural English

Use *won't* when speaking.

> There *won't* be flying cars by 2050.

> Most couples everywhere *won't* have more than one child.

Uncontracted *will not* has strong meaning. Speakers use *will not* to make strong refusals or strong orders not to do something.

> (Mother to son): You *WILL NOT* watch TV before you do your homework.

B | *GROUPS: Read your predictions to each other. Did you make similar predictions? Is your group optimistic or pessimistic about the future?*

STEP 4 EXTENDED PRACTICE

Accuracy Practice *Listen again to Exercises 1 and 3 on pages 108 and 109. Then record the phrases and sentences.*

Fluency Practice *What will your life be like in 10 years? Will you be married? Will you have children? What will you do for a living? Where will you be living? Record your predictions.*

EXERCISE 4: 1. Roy'll answer. 2. The vine'll die. 3. The cat'll run away. 4. Your logic'll persuade her. 5. I'll ask a fisherman. 6. The comic'll joke.

Final /l/: feel; Contractions of *will*   **111**

/m/ some, /n/ sun, and /ŋ/ sing; Syllabic Nasals: sudden; Glottalized *t* and Syllabic Nasals: cotton

STEP 1 PRESENTATION

Nasal ("Nose") Consonants

so**me** /m/

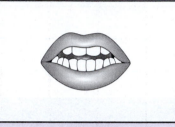

su**n** /n/

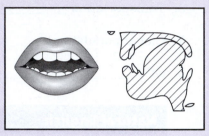

si**ng** /ŋ/

Close your lips firmly.	The tip of your tongue touches behind your top teeth.	Raise the back of your tongue. Keep the tip of your tongue down, behind your bottom teeth.
The air passes out through your nose.	The air passes out through your nose.	The air passes out through your nose.

Final Nasal Consonants

Pronounce nasal consonants clearly at the ends of words. Don't drop them and "nasalize" the preceding vowel.

Pronouncing *ng* Spellings

1. If the letters *ng* end a word, don't pronounce a /g/ sound.

   wro**ng** /ŋ/   you**ng** /ŋ/   bri**ng** /ŋ/   sleepi**ng** /ŋ/

2. Pronounce /g/ in the comparative and superlative of common adjectives that end in *-ng*.

   lo**ng** /ŋ/   lo**ng**er /ŋg/   lo**ng**est /ŋg/

3. Pronounce /g/ in most words with *-ngle* spellings.

   si**ngle** /ŋg/   ju**ngle** /ŋg/   ti**ngle** /ŋg/

Syllabic Nasals

In words like *cotton* and *given*, /n̩/ is long and pronounced without a vowel. It is called a "syllabic nasal" (notation: /n̩/). Listen.

   cotton /n̩/   given /n̩/   lesson /n̩/

Glottal Sounds and Syllabic Nasals

A glottal stop (ʔ) is a quick closing of the vocal cords. It's the sound that separates the two parts of this warning word: *Uh-oh* /ˈʔəˌʔow/. When /t/ follows a stressed vowel and precedes a syllabic nasal, it is pronounced as a glottal stop or a "glottalized *t*" /ˈt/. Listen.

cotton   written   sentence   eaten

If this pronunciation is difficult for you, you can pronounce the words with /t/.

> **Notes**
>
> If you have difficulty pronouncing /ŋ/ by itself, without /g/, concentrate on letting the air pass through your nose throughout the whole sound.

Spellings for /n/		Spellings for /m/		Spellings for /ŋ/	
Common		**Common**		**Common**	
n	**n**o, a**n**other, su**n**	*m*	**m**ore, le**m**on, ha**m**	*ng*	si**ng**, si**ng**er
nn	di**nn**er, su**nn**y	*mm*	su**mm**er, co**mm**on	*n* (before *k*)	ba**n**k, tha**n**ks

STEP 2   FOCUSED PRACTICE

EXERCISE 1: Phrases with Final Nasals

Listen and repeat the phrases. Pronounce the nasal sounds as consonants.

1. something's wrong
2. some time
3. wrong decision
4. someone else
5. mountain climbing
6. written down
7. I'm done
8. a long line
9. a long length
10. strong feelings
11. losing strength
12. young women

EXERCISE 2: Listen for Differences

Listen to the words. Circle the word(s) with a /g/ sound. Then compare your answers with a partner and practice saying the words.

1. anger, hanger, angle
2. long, longer, longest
3. strong, stronger, strongest
4. springing, mingle,[1] stringy
5. single, finger, singer
6. tingle,[2] ringer, jingle[3]

---

[1] mingle: *to mix with people, chat;* [2] tingle: *a stinging sensation, as from cold;* [3] jingle: *a ringing sound, as from bells*

/m/ so**m**e, /n/ su**n**, and /ŋ/ si**ng**; Syllabic Nasals: sudde**n**; Glottalized *t* and Syllabic Nasals: co**tt**on   **113**

EXERCISE 3: Silent Letters

🎧 *Listen to the words. Cross out the underlined letters that are silent.*

1. si**g**n
2. si**g**nal
3. autum**n**
4. ton**gue**
5. paradi**gm**[1]

6. paradi**g**matic
7. colum**n**ar
8. colum**n**
9. an**g**le
10. han**g**er

11. ri**n**ging
12. stro**n**gly
13. stro**n**ger
14. plum**b**er
15. hum**b**le[2]

EXERCISE 4: Jingle Bells

🎧 *Many words that describe clear, musical sounds include /ŋ/. Complete the sentences with the words you hear. Then check your answers on page 117.*

1. Bells and phones _____.

2. But small bells _____.

3. Radar screens _____.

4. And cold fingers _____.

5. Stars _____.

6. But water _____.

EXERCISE 5: Phrases and Idioms

🎧 **A |** *Listen and repeat the idioms in column A. Pronounce the bold letters as syllabic nasals (long n).*

	A		B
_c_	1. writt**en** in the sand	a.	dishonest (as in money or power)
___	2. a hidd**en** agenda	b.	I don't care at all.
___	3. hard-bitt**en**	c̸.	temporary
___	4. writt**en** in stone	d.	clean up
___	5. beat**en** up	e.	a secret plan or purpose
___	6. ill-gott**en**	f.	old and damaged
___	7. straight**en** up	g.	unchangeable (a law, act, or decision)
___	8. I could**n**'t care less.	h.	tough from experience (describing a person)

B | *PAIRS: Match the idioms and expressions in column A with the definitions in column B. Then practice saying the phrases.*

---

[1] paradigm: *an example that serves as a pattern or model;* [2] humble: *modest, not proud*

SHARING YOUR SPACE

EXERCISE 6: Finding a Roommate

A | *Listen to the recording and complete the sentences with the words you hear. Then compare your answers with a partner.*

Finding a roommate can be _____. And _____ to share your

_____ space can be difficult. Lifestyle _____ turn out to be the source of
     3.   **4.**

most roommate _____. It's _____ to find out as much as you can about
                     5.   **6.**

a _____ roommate so you don't make the _____ _____.
      7.   **8.**   **9.**

B | *Complete the Lifestyle Survey. Circle your answers. Then compare your answers with classmates to see whose answers best match your own. Do you think this person would make a good roommate?*

LIFESTYLE SURVEY

1. How would you feel if your roommate invited out-of-town visitors to stay overnight in your room/apartment?

    a. I wouldn't like it at all.

    b. It depends on the length of stay, how many visitors, etc.

    c. I couldn't care less.*

> ### *Natural English
>
> The idiom *I couldn't care less* means the speaker doesn't care at all. In this idiom, the final /t/ is not pronounced. Some speakers use *I could care less* to mean exactly the same thing.
>
> I couldən care less if people borrow my things—they're all old and beaten up.
>
> I couldən care less if my roommate has guests—I like people.

(continued on next page)

/m/ so**m**e, /n/ su**n**, and /ŋ/ si**ng**; Syllabic Nasals: sudd**en**; Glottalized *t* and Syllabic Nasals: co**tt**on   **115**

2. How often do you throw away uneaten food you've left in the refrigerator?

   a. My food never makes it into the refrigerator—I eat it all.

   b. About once a week.

   c. Maybe once, when I move out.

   d. Every day or two.

3. Where do you like to socialize?

   a. I have a few close friends who come to my home from time to time.

   b. I almost always go out when I socialize.

   c. My door is always open—people are always coming and going.

4. How much TV do you watch?

   a. As much as I can.

   b. An hour or two a night.

   c. Two or three shows a week.

   d. I almost never watch TV.

5. What is your attitude toward money?

   a. I keep very careful track of my money—down to the penny.

   b. I sometimes lose track of when bills are due and have to pay a late fee.

   c. I'm pretty good at keeping track of what I owe and paying things on time.

6. How often do you straighten up your room?

   a. Always. I'm very neat.

   b. Every few days.

   c. Messes don't bother me, and I'm not a very neat person.

7. How do you feel when other people borrow your things?

   a. I couldn't care less—everything I own is old and beaten up.

   b. I don't like to lend clothing or personal items, but I don't mind lending things like books or music.

   c. My things are my own, and I don't want anyone else to use them.

EXERCISE 7: Your Turn

A *Read the situations that require sharing space. What are the advantages and disadvantages of each? Write your answers on the lines.*

	Advantages	Disadvantages
Sharing a bedroom with a sibling	_____	_____
Having a roommate	_____	_____
Being married	_____	_____
Staying at a hostel or being a backpacker	_____	_____

STEP 4 | EXTENDED PRACTICE

Accuracy Practice *Listen again to Exercises 1 and 2 on page 113. Then record the phrases and words.*

Fluency Practice *Review your answers to the Lifestyle Survey in Exercise 6B. Then record your answers to the questions.*

1. What type of person could you get along with easily?

2. Have you ever had a roommate? Did/Do you get along with your roommate?

EXERCISE 4: 1. ring **2.** jingle **3.** ping **4.** tingle **5.** twinkle **6.** sprinkles

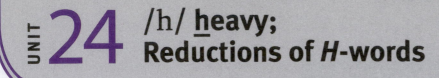

UNIT 24 /h/ heavy; Reductions of H-words

STEP 1 PRESENTATION

The Consonant

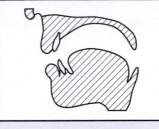

heavy /h/

/h/ is a soft sound, like deep breathing. It's produced by air going through the vocal cords.

/h/ should not sound "noisy." It's not pronounced at the back of the mouth.

Spelling and Pronunciation of /h/

In some words the letter *h* is never pronounced; in others it's always pronounced. These rules will help you decide when to pronounce /h/.

1. The *h* is never pronounced in these words. Most of the words came into English from French:

hour   honor   heir   honest   vehement   exhibition

2. The letter *h* is pronounced in most other words.

heavy   heart   humorous   however

3. *Wh* is pronounced /h/ in these words:

whole   wholly   who   whom   whose

H in Pronouns and Auxiliary Verbs

1. *H* is often dropped in pronouns and auxiliary verbs when these words occur inside a sentence. The pronoun or auxiliary verb joins closely with the preceding word.

What did he do?   (say "what diddy do?")

What's her name?   (say "whatsər name?")

Where has he gone?   (say "wherəziy gone")

If it's difficult for you to join the words together, you can pronounce /h/ in pronouns and auxiliary verbs.

2. Pronounce *h* in pronouns and auxiliary verbs when they begin a sentence or occur before a pause.

He's there.   Her name is Marty.

/h/   /h/

STEP 2 FOCUSED PRACTICE

EXERCISE 1: Phrases with /h/

🎧 *Listen and repeat the phrases. Pronounce /h/ as a soft, breathy sound.*

1. What happened?
2. a huge inheritance
3. Who is it?
4. a healthy heart
5. go ahead
6. a harmful habit
7. hot and humid
8. holding hands
9. a helpful hint

EXERCISE 2: Silent Letters

🎧 *Listen and repeat the words. Cross out **h** when it's silent.*

1. vehicle
2. vehicular
3. inhibit
4. inhibition
5. behind
6. behavior
7. dishonest
8. unhealthy
9. rehearsal
10. adulthood
11. inherit
12. exhibit

EXERCISE 3: Articles before /h/

🎧 **A** | *Listen and write the article in the blank. Cross out silent **h**. Then underline the joining between* an *and the vowel following* **h**.

1. __an__ hour ago
2. _____ herb garden
3. _____ holy site
4. _____ harmful substance
5. _____ honest mistake
6. _____ habitable area
7. _____ hospital bed
8. _____ heterogeneous population
9. _____ hero's welcome
10. _____ honorable agreement
11. _____ hazardous chemical
12. _____ wholesome meal
13. _____ heiress to a fortune
14. _____ history lesson

B | *PAIRS: Practice saying the phrases. Join **an** to the following word.*

EXERCISE 4: Reduced /h/ Words

A | *Listen to the sentences. The underlined words in each sentence are pronounced the same or nearly the same.*

1. Would ̷he ride with Woody Ride?
2. I bought ̷him the present at the bottom of his list.
3. Don't wash ̷her good dishes in the dishwasher.
4. Our church ̷has asked for help from other churches.
5. I know she wants to practice boxing, but don't let ̷her box the letter box.
6. Will ̷he invite Willy?
7. Oliver Tripp paid for all of ̷her trip.
8. The paint ̷had dried on the half-painted wall.

B | *PAIRS: Practice the sentences. Take turns.*

STEP 3 COMMUNICATION PRACTICE

UPBRINGING OR HEREDITY?

EXERCISE 6: A Hard Act to Follow

A | *Check (✓) the names of those people who have or had a famous parent or child. Guess if you're not sure. (You can check your answers on page 121.)*

_____ 1. Angelina Jolie (actress)

_____ 2. Tiger Woods (golfer)

_____ 3. George W. Bush (president)

_____ 4. Rachel Carson (biologist and conservationist)

_____ 5. Francis Ford Coppola (director)

_____ 6. Indira Gandhi (president)

_____ 7. Johann Sebastian Bach (composer and musician)

_____ 8. Laila Ali (boxer)

> **Natural English**
>
> A prepositional phrase with *of* joins closely to the preceding and following nouns.
>
> daughter of an actor
>
> son of a president
>
> father of a musician

B | *PAIRS: Do you think the talents of the famous people in Part A are inherited, learned, or both? Explain.*

EXERCISE 7: Genetic Versus Environmental Traits

Some traits, such as blood type, are almost entirely determined by genetic inheritance. Other traits, such as native language, are entirely the result of upbringing or environment. Many traits, such as athleticism, may be genetic, environmental, or both.

A | *Listen to the people talk about the ways in which they're like their parents. Write each trait they mention.*

G/U/B	Trait	G/U/B	Trait
___	_____	___	_____
___	_____	___	_____
___	_____	___	_____
___	_____	___	_____
___	_____	___	_____
___	_____	___	_____

B | *PAIRS: Discuss the traits: Are they inherited genetically, learned through upbringing, or likely both? For each trait, write **G** for genetic, **U** for upbringing, or **B** for both in the blank. Put a question mark (?) in the blank if you aren't sure.*

STEP 4 EXTENDED PRACTICE

Accuracy Practice *Listen again to Exercises 1 and 2 on page 119. Then record the phrases and words.*

Fluency Practice *Record your answers to the questions.*

1. How much of who you are comes from your parents?

2. Are you more like your father or your mother? Do you think these characteristics are genetic or come from your upbringing?

EXERCISE 6B: 1. Angelina Jolie is the daughter of actor John Voight. John Voight won many awards, including an Oscar award and a Golden Globe award for best actor. **2.** Tiger Woods's father, Earl Woods, was both a college baseball player and writer, and later a golf pro; but he was best known as Tiger's father and trainer. **3.** Former president George W. Bush is the son of former president George H.W. Bush. **4.** Rachel Carson's parents were small farmers. **5.** Francis Ford Coppola's daughter, Sofia Coppola, won an Oscar for best director. **6.** Former Indian prime minister Indira Gandhi was not related to Mahatma Gandhi. **7.** Johann Sebastian Bach was the father of two musicians, both well-known in their time: Carl Philipp Emmanuel Bach and Wilhelm Friedemann. **8.** Laila Ali is the daughter of Mohammed Ali, considered the best boxer ever by many. In 2010, Laila was considered the best female boxer ever, with a record of 24 wins and no losses.

Beginning Consonant Clusters

STEP 1   PRESENTATION

Beginning Consonant Clusters

Consonant clusters are groups of consonant sounds. Clusters at the beginning of words and syllables may contain two or three consonants.

flight   **str**ess   con**fl**ict   re**str**ain

1. **Clusters with /r/ and/l/**

   brain   **cr**ash   **fl**ood   a**ddr**ess   a**ppl**aud

2. **Clusters with /s/**

   stop   **spl**ash   **spr**ing   de**sp**ite   **squ**are /skw/

3. **Clusters with /w/**

   be**tw**een   **qu**iet

   The /w/ sound is sometimes spelled *u:* lan**gu**age /gw/.

   The most common cluster, /kw/, is usually spelled *qu:* **qu**iet.

4. **Clusters with /y/**

   /y/ is usually spelled *u* in clusters.

   cute   re**gu**lar   po**pu**lar   voca**bu**lary   on**i**on

5. **Rare Clusters**

   shrink /ʃr/   **sph**ere /sf/   **thw**art /θw/

Notes

Don't separate the consonants in a cluster with a vowel sound or add a vowel to the beginning of the word. Adding a vowel could create a different word.

Consonant Cluster	Separating the Cluster with a Vowel	Adding a Vowel at the Beginning
dress	duress	address
sport	support	a sport

EXERCISE 1: Phrases with Beginning Consonant Clusters

🎧 *Listen and repeat the phrases. Don't separate the consonants in the bold clusters.*

1. **bl**ood **pr**essure
2. **chr**onic **pr**oblems
3. **tr**ibal **gr**oups
4. **cl**ear **thr**eat

5. **str**ess and **str**ain
6. **sn**ow**st**orm
7. e**st**abli**sh** **str**ategies
8. **sl**ow **st**eps

9. **tw**elve **qu**estions
10. collo**qu**ial lan**gu**age
11. po**p**ular **vi**ews
12. re**gu**lar voca**bu**lary

EXERCISE 2: Listen for Differences

🎧 **A |** *Listen to the words and underline the syllables.*

	A	B			A	B
1.	sport	support		5.	strange	estrange[2]
2.	drive	derive		6.	clone	cologne
3.	steam	esteem		7.	sleep	asleep
4.	plight[1]	polite		8.	blow	below

B | *PAIRS: Say a word. Your partner will tell you which word you said.*

EXERCISE 3: Sentences Full of Sounds

🎧 *Listen to the sentences. Then choose one of the sentences to say to the class. Pronounce the consonant clusters carefully.*

1. The steep stone steps lead from school straight to the stream.
2. I have no esteem for the state because its estate taxes are sky-high.
3. We prayed the parade would please the police.
4. The twelve twins screamed tricky questions across the quiet quadrangle in an unknown language.
5. We've got shrimp, flounder, crabs, clams, crawfish, lobster, squid, and trout.
6. Drive straight to the store without stopping and don't go astray.

---

[1]plight: *difficult situation;* [2] estrange: *to make hostile, alienate*

EXERCISE 4: Spoonerisms

"Spoonerisms" are mistakes that happen when the speaker accidentally switches the first sounds of two words. For example, *bone footh* is a spoonerism for *phone booth*. Consonant clusters are often involved in spoonerisms.

PAIRS: In the spoonerisms below, the underlined words have switched beginning sounds. Decide what the speaker intended to say and write it in the blank. You may need to adjust spelling. (You can check your answers on page 126.)

1. snovel the show ___shovel the snow___

2. It crawls through the fax. _____

3. I was chipping the flannels on the TV. _____

4. fighting a liar _____

5. a blushing crow _____

6. drain bamage _____

7. chilled grease _____

8. teepy slime _____

STEP 3 COMMUNICATION PRACTICE

STRESSED OUT

EXERCISE 5: Types of Stress

A | *Listen. Complete the sentences with the words you hear.*

1. *Acute stress* is short-term, or temporary stress. It is defined as the "fight or

    _____" _____ to an immediate _____.

2. People with episodic acute stress are stressed so _____ that their lives always

    seem to be in _____.

3. Ongoing _____ situations _____ chronic _____.

The "fight or flight" response must be suppressed.

B | *Listen and repeat the conversation.*

LING: I'm so stressed out over work. I really need a vacation.

JOHN: I hear a siren. Pull over!

LING: How can I pull over? We're in bumper-to-bumper traffic!

JOHN: What? I can't hear you!

Natural English

Stressed óut is a phrasal adjective. *Pull óver* is a phrasal verb. In phrasal adjectives or verbs, the preposition functions as an adverb and is usually stressed.

I'm always stressed óut at work.

Pull óver!

Turn that óff.

C | *PAIRS: Reread the definitions of stress in Part A and the conversation in Part B. Besides Ling's work, what is another cause of stress? Do Ling's stressors cause acute stress or chronic stress?*

EXERCISE 6: Stress Studies

Stress and its effects have been studied a great deal because they're so much a part of modern life. They've been linked to problems ranging from high blood pressure to obesity to suicide.

A | *PAIRS: Read and discuss the statements. Write **T** (True) or **F** (False) next to each statement. (You can check your answers on page 126).*

_____ **1.** Adolescent boys and girls experience equal amounts of stress.

_____ **2.** Stress is more likely to result in depression in boys than in girls.

_____ **3.** These are both examples of situations that result in acute stress:

    (a) narrowly escaping being hit by a car as you cross the street

    (b) ongoing problems in your relationship with your spouse

_____ **4.** Persistent financial worries and pressure at work are examples of situations that cause chronic stress.

_____ **5.** Virtually every system and organ in the human body is involved in the response to a stressful situation.

_____ **6.** The effects of stress are negative.

_____ **7.** Older people have higher levels of stress hormones than younger people.

_____ **8.** Women are more vulnerable to the effects of stress than men.

EXERCISE 4: 1. Shovel the snow. **2.** It falls through the cracks (an idiom meaning "something that never gets done"). **3.** I was flipping the channels on the TV. **4.** our dear old queen, **5.** lighting a fire, **6.** a crushing blow, **7.** brain damage, **8.** grilled cheese, **9.** sleepy time

EXERCISE 6A: 1. *False*. Overall, adolescent girls experience more stress than boys. **2.** *False*. Stress is more likely to result in depression in girls. **3.** *False*. Chronic problems with relationships result in long-term stress. **4.** *True*. **5.** *True*. **6.** *False*. The body's response in acute stress situations may be positive: For example, acute stress may give people an advantage during a sports contest, or at a presentation for an important meeting. The effects of chronic stress on the body are negative. **7.** *True*. Higher levels of stress hormones affect the part of the brain that forms new memories and may explain memory loss in older people. **8.** *False*. Newer research suggests that men are more likely than women to develop stress-related disorders like high blood pressure.

B | PAIRS: We're all exposed to stressful situations. Some are short-term situations, such as trying to get information from an automated answering system. Others are long term situations, such as caring for an elderly parent. Write the situations that cause you short-term and long-term stress.

Short-term Stress	Long-term Stress
_____	_____
_____	_____
_____	_____
_____	_____
_____	_____
_____	_____
_____	_____

C | PAIRS: Compare your answers. Then discuss what you do to relieve the stress in your life.

STEP 4 EXTENDED PRACTICE

Accuracy Practice Listen again to Exercises 1 and 2A on page 123. Then record the phrases and words.

Fluency Practice When do you feel stress? How do you deal with it? Record your answers to the questions.

Final Consonant Clusters; Joining Final Consonants

STEP 1 PRESENTATION

Consonant clusters are groups of consonant sounds. They occur at the ends of many words and syllables in English. When you speak, pay attention to the ends of words: Final consonants are an important part of clear, fluent speech.

wo**rk**	be**lt**	mi**x**
/rk/	/lt/	/ks/

Grammatical endings can create large consonant clusters. Be sure that you pronounce grammatical endings: Grammatical endings are never dropped or simplified.

wo**rked**	be**lts**	mi**xed**
/rkt/	/lts/	/kst/

Joining Final Consonants to Following Words

The pronunciation of final consonants depends on the sound that follows. Review the rules.

1. **Final consonant + vowel:** Join the final consonant clearly to the vowel.

   worked out   ask a question

2. **Final consonant + same consonant:** Pronounce one long consonant.

   music class   help people   both theaters

3. **Final consonant + different consonant:** Don't pronounce the final consonant strongly. Say the next word immediately.

   blackᐟ van   wivesᐟ club   He livesᐟ there.

STEP 2 FOCUSED PRACTICE

EXERCISE 1: Hearing Final Consonants

A | *Listen to the word pairs.*

1. **a.** bells
   b. belts

2. **a.** peas
   b. peace

3. **a.** fees
   b. feast

4. **a.** relax
   b. relaxed

5. **a.** works
   b. worse

6. **a.** clap
   b. clapped

7. **a.** kick
   b. kicked

8. **a.** finish
   b. finished

9. **a.** abandon
   b. abandoned

10. **a.** word
    b. world

B | *Listen again to Part A and circle the words you hear.*

C | *PAIRS: Say a word from Part A. Your partner will tell you which word you said.*

EXERCISE 2: Joining Words Together

Listen and repeat the phrases.

Consonant + Vowel	Consonant + Same Consonant	Consonant + Consonant
1. music awards	5. big girl	9. fast) food
2. a heart attack	6. help people	10. He takes) charge.
3. a hard article	7. the fourth thing	11. a wish) list
4. scrambled eggs	8. hum music	12. life) goals

EXERCISE 3: Listen for Differences

A | *Listen and repeat the phrases.*

1. **a.** lab broom   **b.** lab room
2. **a.** talk fast   **b.** talked fast
3. **a.** big eyes   **b.** big guys
4. **a.** golf fan's course   **b.** golf Ann's course
5. **a.** my contact's lenses   **b.** my contact lenses
6. **a.** logged in   **b.** log in
7. **a.** locked out   **b.** logged out

B | *PAIRS: Say a phrase. Pronounce the final consonants carefully so your partner can tell you which phrase you said.*

C | *Listen and complete the sentences with the words you hear.*

1. Did you say "_____ _____" or "_____ _____"?

2. I think I dropped _____ _____ _____.

3. I _____ _____ before I was _____ _____.

4. They _____ _____ on the phone.

5. In the painting, there's a girl with _____ _____ and _____

      _____.

EXERCISE 4: Differences in Meaning

A | *In the a sentences below, the bold consonants in the underlined phrases end a word. They're not strongly pronounced. In the b sentences, the bold consonants begin a word or syllable. They're more strongly pronounced. Listen to the sentences and responses.*

Sentences	Responses
1. a. They have special <u>nigh**t** rates</u>.	Then let's park here.
b. They have special <u>ni**t**rates</u>.	I don't want any chemicals.
2. a. The movie's about a <u>grea**t** rout</u>.[1]	You've always liked military history.
b. The movie's about a <u>gray **t**rout</u>.	I've never heard of a movie about a fish.
3. a. He denied all <u>migh**t** rust</u>.[2]	The tools are probably not made of iron.
b. He denied all <u>my **t**rust</u>.	I'm very sorry.
4. a. There are <u>for**k** racks</u> on the table.	You should fill them with forks.
b. There are <u>four **c**racks</u> on the table.	It's still a very strong table.

B | *PAIRS: Say a sentence. Pronounce the underlined phrase carefully so your partner can say the correct response.*

STEP 3 COMMUNICATION PRACTICE

THE BUCKET LIST

EXERCISE 5: Wish Lists

A | *Listen to the conversation.*

ANA: I'd like to see the pyramids in Egypt someday.

JORGE: I'd like to learn to sail someday.

ANA: I know—I can teach you how to sail.

JORGE: And I can take you to the pyramids!

B | *PAIRS: Practice the conversation. Take turns.*

---

[1] rout: *a complete defeat in a battle or competition.*

[2] rust: *to oxidize; when iron turns red, it has rusted.*

Natural English

Use the contraction *I'd like* rather than the full form *I would like*. Pronounce the /d/ of *I'd like*, but keep it short. Then say *like* immediately.

I'd like to see the pyramids.

I'd like to learn to sail.

Notice the difference between *I'd like* and *I like*.

I'd like to sail. (I want to sail.)

I like to sail. (I enjoy sailing.)

EXERCISE 6: New Orleans Dreams

A | *Listen and repeat. Make sure you understand the words.*

New Orleans
Gulf of Mexico

1. vibrant city
2. infrastructure
3. rebounded
4. passersby
5. installation
6. cartwheel

B | *Listen to the recording. Then answer the questions.*

1. Why are abandoned homes so common in New Orleans?
2. What did Candy Chang do with the abandoned home in her neighborhood? Why?
3. Why was the art installation taken down?
4. Write three dreams that passersby wrote on the walls.

   a. Before I die, I _____ .

   b. Before I die, I _____ .

   c. Before I die, I _____ .

C | *GROUPS: Compare your answers. Who do you think wrote the dreams in question 4?*

EXERCISE 7: Life Goals

A | *A bucket list is a list of things you'd like to do or achieve before you "kick the bucket," or die. Read the list below. Circle the goals on the list that you'd include on your own bucket list. Then add three more goals to your list.*

MY BUCKET LIST

I'd like to . . .

1. start my own business.
2. become a millionaire.
3. travel the world.
4. form a band.
5. learn to fly an airplane.
6. get a tattoo.
7. have a family.
8. _____
9. _____
10. _____

B | *PAIRS: Read your lists aloud. How similar are they?*

STEP 4 EXTENDED PRACTICE

Accuracy Practice *Listen again to Exercises 1A and 2 on pages 127 and 128. Then record the words and phrases.*

Fluency Practice *If money were not an issue, what would you include on your bucket list? Record your answer to the question.*

SYLLABLES AND STRESS WITHIN WORDS

27 Syllables and Stress in Words: Overview

STEP 1 PRESENTATION

Syllables

A syllable is a "beat" of a word. The center of a syllable is usually a vowel, which can be preceded or followed by consonants. In the words below, the syllables are underlined. Use your finger to tap the beats (syllables) of these words:

   face   approve   important   operation   organization

The Stressed Syllable (´)

One syllable has primary or heavy stress. This is the most important syllable in the word because listeners use the stressed syllable to identify words.

The vowel in the stressed syllable is longer than vowels in other syllables. The stressed vowel may also be louder or pronounced on a higher pitch (note). Focus on lengthening the stressed vowel.

   tráffic   adápt   photógrapher

Unstressed Syllables

Unstressed syllables are short. The vowel in an unstressed syllable is usually reduced to /ə/, regardless of how it's spelled. The alternation of long stressed syllables and shorter unstressed syllables is a key to natural-sounding English.

   jéaləs (jealous)   əwárenəs (awareness)   əváiləbəl (available)

Secondary Stress (`) and Compound Nouns

Some words have secondary stress in addition to primary (heavy) stress. Vowels with secondary stress are not reduced to /ə/. They're pronounced on a lower pitch than vowels with primary stress and may also be shorter in length. Compound nouns (noun + noun units) have primary stress and high pitch on the first noun, and secondary stress and low pitch on the second noun.

   páss   shóe
      pòrt   bòx

STEP 2 | FOCUSED PRACTICE

EXERCISE 1: Syllables

A | *Listen to the words. Underline the syllables and then write the number of syllables in the blank.*

1. occur __2__
2. match ____
3. pleased ____
4. management ____

5. clothes ____
6. exhilarating ____
7. liked ____
8. surgeon ____

9. idea ____
10. negotiation ____
11. artificial ____
12. crash ____

B | *PAIRS: Say the words, tapping the syllables with your finger.*

EXERCISE 2: Stressed Syllables

Listen to the words. Place a stress mark (′) over the syllable with heavy stress. Then practice saying the words with a partner. Imagine that you're stretching a rubber band as you say the stressed vowel. This will help you lengthen the vowel.

1. photográphic
2. government
3. approval

4. freedom
5. honeymoon
6. disappointed

7. repeat
8. tomato
9. foundation

10. nationality
11. historical
12. piano

EXERCISE 3: Unstressed Syllables

A | *The words below have been "respelled" to show how the unstressed vowels are pronounced. Listen and repeat the words.*

1. əbándənd
   abandoned

2. réasənəbəl
   _____

3. kəntról
   _____

4. pəlícemən
   _____

5. Áugəst
   _____

6. kənsídərd
   _____

7. Cánədə
   _____

8. fáshənəbəl
   _____

9. cənténtəd
   _____

B | *PAIRS: Write the correct spellings of the words in the blanks. Then practice saying the words. Use /ə/ for unstressed vowels.*

EXERCISE 4: Listen for Differences

🎧 **A |** *Listen to the words. Put a stress mark (´) over stressed syllables.*

1. **a.** pérsonal   **b.** personnél

2. **a.** decade   **b.** decayed

3. **a.** desert   **b.** dessert

4. **a.** secret   **b.** secrete[1]

5. **a.** a rebel   **b.** to rebel

6. **a.** sever[2]   **b.** severe

7. **a.** despot[3]   **b.** despite

8. **a.** attic[4]   **b.** attack

B | *PAIRS: Say a word. Exaggerate the stressed syllable so your partner can tell you which word you said.*

EXERCISE 5: Differences in Meaning

🎧 **A |** *Listen to the sentences and responses.*

Sentences	Responses
1. **a.** What's the <u>desert</u> like?	It's hot, dry, and desolate.
b. What's the <u>dessert</u> like?	It's rich and chocolaty.
2. **a.** How do you spell *despot*?	D-E-S-P-O-T.
b. How do you spell *despite*?	D-E-S-P-I-T-E.
3. **a.** What are you going to do in the <u>attack</u>?	Defeat the enemy.
b. What are you going to do in the <u>attic</u>?	Clean out some old boxes.
4. **a.** I need some <u>personal</u> information.	I'm single but I'm dating someone.
b. I need some <u>personnel</u> information.	Here's a list of our employees.

B | *PAIRS: Say a sentence. Pronounce the underlined word carefully, lengthening the stressed syllable. Your partner will say the correct response.*

---

[1] secrete: *to separate a substance from another by emitting it; to hide;* [2] sever: *to cut;* [3] despot: *tyrant, dictator;* [4] attic: *space between the roof and ceiling*

CULTURE SHOCK

EXERCISE 6: Back from Hanoi

Sonia Rakic and Young Park are classmates in California. They've both returned from a summer in Hanoi.

A | *Listen to the conversation.*

> **YOUNG:** I heard you spent the summer in Vietnam. You were doing an internship at a museum, right?
>
> **SONIA:** Yes, and fortunately my co-workers spoke English. Even though I was living with a Vietnamese family, my Vietnamese is really weak. Three months isn't much time to learn a language.
>
> **YOUNG:** That's true, but you're lucky you got to live with a family. It's a good way to get to know the culture. I was in a dormitory and hung out mostly with students from other countries.
>
> **SONIA:** I really liked my family and learned a lot from them. But I wonder how much we understood each other.
>
> **YOUNG:** What do you mean?
>
> **SONIA:** Well, I got up really early every morning to run because it was coolest then. And I'm also a vegetarian. My family thought I was worried about gaining weight. The grandmother kept dropping pieces of fish and meat into my rice bowl when I wasn't looking. So after a month, I gave up being a vegetarian. My Vietnamese just wasn't good enough to explain my real reasons.

B | *What challenges do people face when they move to a new country?*

_____

_____

_____

_____

EXERCISE 7: Reverse Culture Shock

A | *Make a list of problems that people face when they return to their home country after living in another country. Use the lines below.*

_____

_____

_____

_____

B | *Read about reverse culture shock. Then listen to the recording and complete the sentences.*

Students and others who live abroad for an extended time may experience "reverse culture shock" when they return home. The first stage is the "honeymoon stage," when they're happy to be back home among friends, family, and familiar surroundings. After this stage, they often go through a difficult period that experts call "reverse culture shock" or "re-entry shock." Here are some common complaints from students going through reverse culture shock:

1. Being home is _____.

2. No one is really _____ in hearing about my experiences abroad.

3. It's hard for me to _____ my experiences to others.

4. I feel _____ for my host culture.

5. My old _____ aren't the same as they were before I left.

6. When I follow _____ from my host culture, my friends misinterpret my behavior.

7. I see my friends, family, and country with more _____ eyes.

8. I find it hard to _____ the new skills and knowledge I learned abroad.

9. I'm afraid of losing the experience; I'm afraid it will become nothing more than a

   _____ full of old pictures.

Natural English

The letter *x* is pronounced /ks/ when a consonant follows *x*, when *x* follows a stressed vowel, or when *x* is at the end of a word.

   ekspériences (expériences)

   Méksico (México)

   reláks (reláx)

The letter *x* is pronounced /gz/ when it precedes a stressed vowel.

   egzámple (exámple)

   egzám (exám)

The word *éxit* is an exception. It can be pronounced "eksit" or "egzit."

C | GROUPS: Compare your lists from Exercise 6B and Exercise 7A. How are the challenges of culture shock and reverse culture shock different? How are they the same? What are your own experiences with culture shock (or reverse culture shock)?

STEP 4 EXTENDED PRACTICE

Accuracy Practice *Listen again to Exercises 2 and 4A on pages 133 and 134. Then record the words.*

Fluency Practice *Record your answers to the questions.*

1. What are three challenges a person faces when moving to a new culture? Explain.

2. Do you think that culture shock is less severe for people who know their stay in the new country is temporary? Explain.

STEP 1 PRESENTATION

Syllables have one of three levels of stress: primary stress, no stress (unstressed), or secondary stress.

Level of Stress	Vowel Quality	Vowel Length	Vowel Loudness	Pitch
Primary Stress: *políte* The stressed syllable is the most important syllable in a word. Listeners use this syllable to identify the word.	Full vowel	Longest	Loudest	High
Unstressed: *ago*	Reduced to /ə/or /ɪ/	Short	Not loud	Low

Secondary Stress: *áirplàne*
 Written (ˋ)
 Secondary stress occurs
 1. on the second noun of a compound:
     ráilròad
 2. two syllables back from primary stress in some words:
     còrporátion   *ìnstitútion*
 3. on some suffixes: *-ìze, -àte*
     (as a verb ending):
     apólogìze   *éducàte*
	Full vowel	Long	Loud	Low

1. Pronouncing Unstressed Syllables

Although unstressed syllables are not prominent, in most words they must be pronounced. Be especially careful to pronounce unstressed -*y* endings, unstressed *er*, and unstressed *i* or *e* inside a word.

- Pronounce unstressed *y:* Did you say "the party" or "the part"?
- Pronounce unstressed *er:* Don't excise[1] the *er* of *exercise.*
- Pronounce unstressed *i* and *e:* Say "evidence"—not "ev'dence."

---

[1] excise: *to cut out*

2. Movable Stress

Primary and secondary stress sometimes "exchange" syllables in a word to create a more regular-sounding rhythm.

Movable Stress in *-teen* Numbers
• Stress *-teen* when a pause follows the number. This will make it easier for your listener to hear *nineteen* rather than *ninety*.   I'm ninetéen.

• Stress the first syllable of a *-teen* word when the next word begins with a stressed syllable (stress "moves back" to avoid two heavily stressed syllables in a row).
    1999 (nínetèen nínety níne)
    18 Main Street (éighteèn Máin Street)

Movable Stress in Words Ending in a Stressed Syllable
• If the last syllable of a word has primary stress and a preceding syllable has secondary stress, the two stresses may change places to avoid two primary stresses in a row.   She's Jàpanése.   but   She's a Jápanèse cítizen. *Jápanèse cítizen* has a more regular-sounding rhythm than *Japanése cítizen*.

STEP 2 FOCUSED PRACTICE

EXERCISE 1: Secondary Stress

A | *Listen to the words and phrases. In each word pair, secondary stress occurs two syllables before primary stress. This creates a rhythmic alternation of stressed (full) vowels and unstressed (reduced) vowels.*

1. scìentífic, èconómic: scientific and economic evidence
2. òpportúnity, crèatívity: an opportunity to show creativity
3. àdmirátion, rèstorátion: There's admiration for the restoration.
4. pùnctuálity, relìabílity: We appreciate your punctuality and reliability.
5. ènginéer, vòluntéer: We need an engineer to volunteer.

B | *PAIRS: Take turns reading the words and phrases. Concentrate on creating a regular-sounding rhythm when you speak.*

EXERCISE 2: Unstressed Syllables

Listen and repeat the phrases. Join words together smoothly and make sure to pronounce all the syllables.

1. vígorous éxercise
2. stúdying económics
3. véry expérienced
4. technológical understánding
5. eleméntal énergy
6. clássical árchitecture
7. búsy institútions
8. univérsity applicátion

EXERCISE 3: Dropped Syllables

🎧 **A |** *Listen to the words and draw a line through the unpronounced vowel.*

1. int~e~resting
2. separate (adjective)
3. favorite
4. federal
5. miserable

6. different
7. practically
8. vegetable
9. general
10. evening

> ### Natural English
>
> Native speakers "drop" syllables in some common words.
>
> > my *famly* (family)
> >
> > an *intresting* book (interesting)

🎧 **B |** *Listen and write the words you hear. Draw a line through a syllable if it is not pronounced.*

1. The _____ is unusually cold for May.

2. I'm allergic to _____.

3. I have to study _____ day to pass this test.

4. My boss has invited _____ of us to dinner at his house.

EXERCISE 4: Movable Stress

🎧 **A |** *Listen to the conversations. Mark the syllables with heavy stress (′) in the underlined words.*

1. **A:** What does he like to do?

   B: <u>Volunteer</u>. He's a <u>volunteer</u> firefighter.

2. **A:** How much was it?

   B: <u>Fourteen</u>.

   A: Exactly how much?

   B: <u>Fourteen</u>-fifty ($14.50).

3. **A:** What courses are you taking?

   B: <u>Chinese</u>. And <u>Chinese</u> history.

B | *PAIRS: Compare your answers. Then practice the conversations.*

SCREENING JOB APPLICANTS

EXERCISE 5: Sizing Up the Field

To prepare for a job interview, applicants should check out the company's website to make sure they have some intelligent questions to ask the interviewer. They should also update their resumes, iron a professional-looking outfit to wear for the interview, and rehearse answers to possible questions such as, "Why did it take you seven years to complete a four-year college degree?"

But how do employers make their hiring decisions? How do they size up the field of applicants and then narrow it down to one or two choices? Hiring a new employee is a major investment for a company, and the employer wants to do everything it can to make sure it's found the right employee.

A | *Listen to the words. Place a stress mark (') over the stressed syllable. Then match the words and definitions. Compare your answers with the class.*

	Words		Definitions
_____	1. distracted	a.	unacceptable
_____	2. foolproof	b.	honesty, loyalty
_____	3. recruit	c.	being outgoing, sociable
_____	4. cognitive	d.	impossible to trick, impossible to fail
_____	5. integrity	e.	mental processes such as thinking or perception
_____	6. expertise	f.	carefulness
_____	7. inappropriate	g.	to find new members
_____	8. extraversion	h.	unable to concentrate or pay attention
_____	9. conscientiousness	i.	knowledge in a specific field

B | *Read the types of tests below. Then listen to the recording. Write some information about each of the tests (the information could be a trait or characteristic the test measures, or the purpose of the test).*

1. cognitive abilities tests _____

2. integrity tests _____

3. job knowledge tests _____

4. personality tests _____

5. interviews _____

EXERCISE 6: Your Turn

A | *In addition to tests, employers consider other types of information when they make hiring decisions. For example, the reputation of the applicant's school might be an important factor. Complete the chart below for a job in your field. In the left column, check (✓) the factors that employers in your country consider important. In the right column, rank their importance to employers. Then add other factors to the chart.*

Factors Considered in Hiring Decisions	Importance in Hiring Decisions (*1*=very important, *2*=somewhat important, *3*=not very important)
Job tests (cognitive, integrity, personality, job knowledge, etc.) _____	
Reputation of the applicant's school _____	
Applicant's school record _____	
Connections (family, friends) _____	

B | *GROUPS: Compare your charts.*

STEP 4 EXTENDED PRACTICE

Accuracy Practice *Listen again to Exercises 1A and 2 on page 139. Then record the words, phrases, and sentences.*

Fluency Practice *Record your answer to the question: In your country, what selection criteria do employers use to make hiring decisions in your field?*

Predicting Stress: Parts of Speech and Suffixes

STEP 1 PRESENTATION

When you learn a new word, always learn which syllable is stressed. The stressed syllable is used by listeners to identify the word. Here are some rules to help you predict the stressed syllable.

Stress and Parts of Speech

1. Two-Syllable Nouns

Stress the first syllable.

    fúnction   ségment   clímate

2. Two-Syllable Verbs and Adjectives

Stress the "root" of the word (the part that carries the meaning, without prefixes or suffixes). The root syllable is often spelled with more letters than prefixes or suffixes.

    First syllable is the root: óffer   públish   jéalous
    Second syllable is the root: concéal   repéat   políte

Stress and Prefixes

1. Short Prefixes Used to Form Verbs (*re-, dis-, in-, un-,* etc.)

Do not stress the prefix.

    remémber   disqúalify   uncóver

2. Longer Prefixes and Prefixes that Are Also Words (*inter-, over-, under-, out-*)

When used as nouns, stress the prefix.

    an óvercoat   an óutlaw   an ínterchange

When used as verbs, stress the verb or root; the prefix has secondary stress.

    to òversée   to òutrún   to ìnteráct

(continued on next page)

Stress and Suffixes

1. Primary stress usually falls on these suffixes: -eer, -ier, -ese, -ette, -esque, -ique, -ee.

    voluntéer   Chinése   cigarétte   uníque

    Exceptions: *-ee:* commíttee

2. Primary stress falls on the syllable in front of these suffixes: -ial, -ual, -ian, -ion, -ient, -eous, -ious, -uous, -ic(s), -ical, -ity, -ify, -itive, -itude, -logy, -graphy.

    fináncial   politícian   creátion   relígious   publícity   áttitude

    Exceptions: -ic: Árabic, aríthmetic, pólitics

                  -ion: télevision

3. Primary stress falls two syllables before these suffixes: -ize, -ary, -ate.

    críticize   sécretary   vocábulary   óperate   délicate

    Exceptions: *-ize:* náturalize, cháracterize

                  -ary: documéntary, eleméntary

4. Other Suffixes and Prefixes

When other suffixes and prefixes are added to words, the new word has the same stressed syllable as the basic word.

háppy + ness	háppiness	púnish + ment	púnishment
offícial + ly	offícially	góvern + or	góvernor
advíse + able	advísable	proféssion + al	proféssional

    Exception: *-able:* cómparable

STEP 2 FOCUSED PRACTICE

EXERCISE 1: Hearing Differences in Stress

A | *The words and phrases in the pairs below have similar sounds but different stressed syllables. Listen and repeat the words and phrases. Then place a stress mark over the stressed syllable (´).*

    1. a. massage   **b.** message

    2. a. eligible   **b.** illegible

    3. a. desert (noun)   **b.** dessert

    4. a. refuse (verb)   **b.** refuse[1] (noun)

    5. a. (a) clean-up (noun)   **b.** clean up (verb)

    6. a. present (verb)   **b.** present (noun)

    7. a. invalid[2] (noun)   **b.** invalid (adjective)

---

[1] refuse (noun): *garbage;* [2] invalid (noun): *a disabled person*

144 UNIT 29

B | PAIRS: Complete each sentence with the correct word in parentheses. Then practice the conversations.

1. **A:** Here's a _____ from the spa about your _____. (message/massage)

   B: I can't read this. It's _____. (eligible/illegible)

2. **A:** Did the dormitory _____ to let you in your room after you showed your ID card? (réfuse/refúse)

   B: Yes, maybe my card was _____. Do you have to get your ID card renewed every semester? (ínvalid/inválid)

EXERCISE 2: Stress with Suffixes

**A | Listen and repeat the words.

-ion	-ic(s)	-ical	-ious/eous/uous
1. contribution	7. genetics	13. technological	19. superstitious
2. cooperation	8. problematic	14. physical	20. ambitious
3. imagination	9. scientific	15. cyclical	21. mysterious
_____	_____	_____	_____
_____	_____	_____	_____
_____	_____	_____	_____

-graphy	-logy	-ian	-ity
4. biography	10. biology	16. beautician	22. publicity
5. photography	11. astrology	17. physician	23. audacity
6. orthography	12. archeology	18. Indonesian	24. eccentricity
_____	_____	_____	_____
_____	_____	_____	_____
_____	_____	_____	_____

B | PAIRS: Think of more words for each pattern and add them to the columns. Then read all the words in a column to your partner. Stress the syllable before the ending.

EXERCISE 3: Apply the Rule

PAIRS: Say the word in column A. Then mark primary stress on the words in column B (use the rules in the Presentation to help you).

A	B
1. philósophy	philosopher, philosophical, philosophize
2. negótiate	negotiation, negotiable, negotiator, negotiability
3. apólogy	apologize, apologetic, apologetically
4. phótograph	photography, photographic, photographer
5. prófit	profiteer, profitable, profitability
6. compáre	comparison, comparability, comparative
7. clímate	acclimatize, climatology, climatic

EXERCISE 4: Conversations

PAIRS: Use words from Exercise 3 to answer the questions below. Then practice the conversations.

1. **A:** What do you call a person who takes photographs?

   B: A _____.

   A: What courses should you take if you want to learn how to take photographs?

   B: _____ courses.

2. **B:** What do you do if you want to tell someone you're sorry?

   A: _____.

   B: How do you feel if you're sorry about something you've done?

   A: _____.

3. **A:** When two nations disagree and don't want to go to war, what do they do?

   B: They _____.

   A: If both sides agree to negotiate, how would you describe their demands?

   B: Their demands are _____.

EXERCISE 5: Words Ending in -ate

A | *With nouns or adjectives, the suffix* **-ate** *is unstressed and pronounced /ət/. With verbs,* **-ate** *has secondary stress and is pronounced /eyt/. Listen and repeat the words and phrases.*

		Adjective/Noun		Verb
1.	**a.**	graduate school	**b.**	to graduate
2.	**a.**	a duplicate copy	**b.**	to duplicate
3.	**a.**	an associate	**b.**	to associate
4.	**a.**	an estimate	**b.**	to estimate
5.	**a.**	climate	**b.**	to acclimate[1]
6.	**a.**	separate stories	**b.**	to separate

B | *PAIRS: Decide how the underlined words are pronounced. Then practice reading the sentences to each other.*

1. His delicate health makes it hard for him to acclimate to extreme climates.

2. I can't estimate the cost of fixing the roof, so a carpenter is coming by today to give me an estimate.

3. I won't associate with your associates until they earn their certificates.

4. It's fortunate they can duplicate my duplicate copy.

Natural English

The verb prefix *re-* can be pronounced /riy/, /rɪ/ or /rə/.

The prefix often has the long pronunciation, /riy/, when the root of the verb is a verb by itself (for example, in *reuse*).

   recýcle, replánt, relíve

The prefix usually has the shorter, more reduced pronunciations, /rɪ/ or /rə/, when the root is not a verb (for example, in *recyclable*).

   refér, remémber, recéive

---

[1] acclimate: *to become accustomed to a new environment*

PLASTICS

EXERCISE 6: Properties of Plastics

A | *The adjectives below describe properties of plastics. Listen and place a stress mark over the stressed syllables. Make sure you understand the words.*

1. shatter-resistent
2. synthetic
3. durable
4. lightweight
5. non-porous
6. versatile
7. recyclable

B | *Write each adjective from Part A next to the sentence below that describes the same property.*

1. Plastics are used in everything from car parts to doll parts. _____

2. You can lift a gallon (approximately 4 liters) of milk in a plastic container without hurting

   your back. _____

3. If you drop a plastic water bottle on the floor, it won't break. _____

4. Plastic wrap keeps food fresh, by keeping air out. _____

5. Park benches made of plastic last longer than wooden benches. _____

6. Although some plastics like rubber and asphalt are natural, most are man-made.

   _____

7. Many types of plastic can be processed after use and made into new products.

   _____

EXERCISE 7: Junk Boat

 A | *Listen and repeat. Make sure you understand the words.*

raft	crew	gyre	rotates
afloat	patch	currents	debris

B | *Listen to the recording and then answer the questions about the junk raft.*

1. What was the junk raft's cabin made from? _____

2. How was the raft kept afloat? _____

3. Where did the raft go? _____

4. What was the raft's mission? _____

C | *GROUPS: Compare your answers. Emphasize stressed syllables.*

STEP 4 EXTENDED PRACTICE

Accuracy Practice *Listen again to Exercise 2A on page 145. Then record the words.*

Fluency Practice *The disadvantages of plastic are well known. What are some advantages of plastic? Record your answer.*

UNIT 30 Compound Nouns; Stress in Numbers

STEP 1 PRESENTATION

Compound nouns are two nouns used together as a meaningful unit.

railroad   eyesight

Compound Stress-Pitch Pattern

The first word of a compound has primary stress and is pronounced on a high pitch. The second word has secondary stress and a lower pitch.

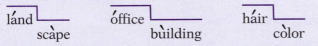

land scape   office building   hair color

The compound stress-pitch pattern is used when other two-word sequence units are used as nouns.

1. Adjective-Noun Sequences

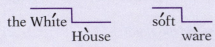

the White House   soft ware

Sequences of adjectives and nouns that don't function as units can have a different stress-pitch pattern.

We live near the gréen hóuse.   (green color; the noun is *house*)

We live near the gréenhòuse.   (an indoor area for plants; the noun is *greenhouse*)

Sequences of adjectives and nouns can be pronounced like compounds when the speaker emphasizes the meaning of the adjective.

A: Is your house the white one?

B: No, I live in the gréen hòuse.

2. Verb-Preposition and Preposition-Verb Sequences Used as Nouns

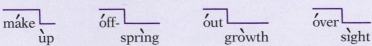

máke ùp   óff- sprìng   óut gròwth   óver sìght

Stress in Numbers

1. Numbers Endings in -*ty*

Stress the number (the root).

síxty   fífty

The *t* in these numbers is pronounced as a flap (a "fast D"; see Unit 16).

sixDy   fifDy

150   UNIT 30

2. Numbers Ending in -teen

Stress *-teen* when a pause follows the word.

> She's sixtéen.

Stress the first syllable of *-teen* numbers in the names of years.

> 1960: "níneteen síxty"

Stress the first syllable of *-teen* numbers when the next word begins with a stressed syllable (see Unit 28, "Movable Stress").

> She's 16. (sixtéen)   *but*   She lives at 16 Oak Street. (síxteen Óak Street)

Stress the first syllable when counting.

> thírteen, fóurteen, fífteen, síxteen

STEP 2   FOCUSED PRACTICE

EXERCISE 1: Compounds

Listen to the recording and complete the sentences with the words you hear. Then practice the sentences with a partner. Use the correct stress-pitch pattern with the compounds.

1. The _____ is so bright we don't need a _____.

2. I know the _____ of your _____: He won't mind if you get another
   _____.

3. I bought _____, _____, and _____ at the
   _____.

4. The _____ for getting the announcement in the _____ is tomorrow.

5. The baby started life in a _____.

6. Who has records of your _____ and _____?

EXERCISE 2: Hearing Compounds

A | *Listen to the phrases and repeat them. Circle the phrases with compound stress.*

1. **a.** girl friend
   b. good friend

2. **a.** exercise equipment
   b. excellent equipment

3. **a.** growing industries
   b. growth industries

4. **a.** popular trend
   b. population trend

5. **a.** swimming pool
   b. swimming fish

6. **a.** the finished product
   b. the finish line

B | *PAIRS: Check your answers. Then practice the phrases.*

EXERCISE 3: Differences in Meaning

PAIRS: Each phrase in the box has two meanings, depending on whether it's used as a compound or as two separate words. Read a question to your partner. Your partner should answer it with a phrase from the box, pronounced with the correct stress-pitch pattern.

light + weights	black + board	green + house
checking + accounts	cheap + skates	dark + room

1. What do you call a house that's painted green?
2. What do you call the slate panel used in classrooms (you write on it with chalk)?
3. What do you call boxers weighing between 127 and 135 pounds?
4. How would you describe a pair of ice skates that didn't cost very much?
5. Describe the weights you should use when you first start weight lifting.
6. What do you call an indoor space used to grow plants?
7. What kinds of bank accounts allow you to write checks?
8. What kind of room does a photographer use to develop photographs?
9. Describe a flat piece of wood that has been painted black.
10. When an accountant is working for a client, what is he or she probably doing?
11. What do you call people who are stingy (who don't like to spend money)?
12. How would you describe a room that doesn't get much light?

EXERCISE 4: Stress in Numbers

A | *Listen to the recording and complete the sentences with the numbers you hear.*

1. It's an important birthday for her—she's _____.

2. Does the flight leave at _____ or _____?

3. This sweater is on sale for _____.

4. There are a lot of kids in my family, and there's a big age range. I have a sister who's

   _____ and a brother who's _____.

5. My clock stopped at _____.

6. You didn't give me enough—I asked for _____.

B | *PAIRS: Say a sentence, using any -teen or -ty number. Use the correct stress-pitch pattern so your partner can tell you which number you said.*

EXERCISE 5: Milestone Birthdays

A | *PAIRS: Choose a year and say it to your partner. Your partner will describe the significance of that birthday.*

Birthday	Significance
13th	You're finally in your teens!
30th	You're not in your twenties anymore.
14th	You're probably in the 7th or 8th grade at school.
40th	Is this the first decade of middle age?
15th	This is a special birthday year for girls in Latin America.
50th	You've lived half a century!
16th	This is a special birthday for some girls in the United States
60th	You're definitely middle-aged.
17th	In one more year, you'll graduate from high school.
70th	A lot of people have retired by this age.
18th	By this age, you can get a driver's license in all U.S. states.
80th	You're now an octogenarian. You should celebrate!
19th	This is your last year as a teenager.
90th	Ten more to go and you'll be a century old!

B | *What are some milestone birthdays in your country? On the lines below, make a list of the birthdays and describe their significance. Share the information with the class.*

Birthday	Significance
_____	_____
_____	_____
_____	_____
_____	_____

SCIENCE AND FICTION

EXERCISE 6: Science Fiction Predictions

Science fiction writers imagine the future. Sometimes, they imagine devices long before they're ever invented or developed. Other times, they imagine how existing devices might develop.

A | *Listen to the phrases in column A. Circle the underlined phrases that have compound stress-pitch pattern.*

	A		B
1.	escalator	**a.**	In 1932, George Orwell wrote about a future world. In that world, people were no longer born naturally, but from a machine that could perfect their genes.
2.	office cubicle	**b.**	In 1899, H.G. Wells wrote that two men, instead of leaving a room through a doorway, walked up to an apparently solid wall, which then rolled up, allowed them to pass, and rolled down again.
3.	tablet computer	**c.**	In 1968, Arthur C. Clarke wrote *2001: A Space Odyssey*. In it, a space traveller had a small, hand-held device he could plug into the main computer to scan reports from Earth.
4.	automatic doors	**d.**	In 1911, Hugo Gernback wrote about the Actinoscope. It could detect wave signals from distant objects and estimate their distance.
5.	surveillance satellites	**e.**	Robert Heinlein (1907–1988) imagined a world where people rode moving staircases.
6.	test-tube babies	**f.**	In 1869, Jules Verne wrote a novel about the adventures of a crew aboard an underwater boat.
7.	radar	**g.**	In 1899, H.G. Wells imagined a world where everyone was constantly being watched.
8.	submarine	**h.**	In 1909, E.M. Forster imagined a world where people worked in small isolated spaces, without windows.

B | *PAIRS: Match the devices in column A with their descriptions in column B. Guess which devices were imagined by science fiction writers before they were invented or developed. (You can check your answers on page 155.)*

EXERCISE 7: Designer Genes

A | *Listen and repeat. Make sure you understand the words.*

1. lustrous   2. life span   3. bald

B | *Read the traits below. Then listen to the recording and check (✓) the traits you hear.*

Sex _____

Appearance	Abilities	Health	Personality
Eye color _____	IQ* _____	Lifespan _____	Outgoing _____
Hair color _____	Athletics _____	Heart disease _____	(Non)violent _____
Body type _____	Music _____	Diabetes _____	Addictive _____
Skin color _____	Art _____	Epilepsy _____	Friendly _____
Height _____		Breast cancer _____	Hardworking _____
Baldness _____			Ambitious _____

---

*Natural English

Stress abbreviations on the last letter.

IQ́

DNÁ

GMÓs (genetically modified organisms)

C | *GROUPS: If you were a parent in a world where genetic engineering was readily available, would you select any of your children's traits, or would you leave everything to chance? Explain.*

STEP 4   EXTENDED PRACTICE

Accuracy Practice *Listen again to Exercise 1 on page 151. Then record the sentences.*

Fluency Practice *Record your answers to the question in Exercise 7C.*

EXERCISE 6B: 1. e, 2. h, 3. c, 4. b, 5. g, 6. a, 7. d, 8. f
Except for the escalator, which was patented in 1898, and the submarine, which was used before 1869, all of the devices were imagined by science fiction writers before they were invented.

STEP 1   PRESENTATION

Words Used As Nouns or Verbs

Some two-syllable words are nouns when stressed on the first syllable and verbs when stressed on the second syllable.

Noun: They keep good récords.   Verb: They recórd their expenses.

Here are some other words with this pattern:

addict	convert	increase²	produce	suspect
convict	insult	conflict	defect	project
refuse	contract	desert	permit	protest⁴
subject	contrast¹	finance³	present	rebel

Words with Prepositional Prefixes

Prepositional prefixes include *out-, over-, under-, up-, for(e)-*.

1. Verbs

The verb has primary stress; the prefix has secondary stress.

òutdó   òverlóok   ùnderstánd   ùpstáge   fòresée

2. Nouns

The prefix has primary stress; the noun has secondary stress.

óversìght   únderdòg   óutràge   úpstàrt

---

¹⁻⁴ *Some speakers stress the first syllable of these words as nouns and verbs.*

EXERCISE 1: Stress Patterns for Nouns and Verbs

A | *Listen and repeat the words.*

Noun		Verb	
1.	a. cónduct	b.	condúct
2.	a. rébel	b.	rebél
3.	a. óbject	b.	objéct
4.	a. prógress	b.	progréss
5.	a. súspect	b.	suspéct
6.	a. prótest	b.	protést
7.	a. próduce	b.	prodúce
8.	a. pérmit	b.	permít
9.	a. óverflow	b.	overflów

B | *PAIRS: Say a word and pronounce it carefully so your partner can say whether it is a noun or a verb.*

EXERCISE 2: Apply the Rule

Complete the sentences with the correct form of the word in parentheses. Put a stress mark (′) over the stressed syllable. Then practice the sentences with a partner.

1. A learner's _____ _____ you to drive when there's a licensed driver in the car.

   (permit)

2. Although the police consider him a _____, I _____ he's innocent. (suspect)

3. A religious _____ is someone who has _____ from one religion to another.

   (convert)

4. The farm _____ a wide variety of _____. (produce)

5. There are _____ opinions about the _____. (conflict)

6. I _____ to the large ugly _____ you've put there. Please move it. (object)

EXERCISE 3: Stress with Nouns and Verbs

Listen to the sentences. Place a stress mark (') over the stressed syllable in the underlined words. Then choose a sentence and say it to the class.

1. You had the <u>foresight</u> to <u>foresee</u> the <u>outrage</u> we <u>overlooked</u>.

2. The farmhands <u>produced</u> <u>record</u> amounts of <u>produce</u>.

3. There were <u>conflicting</u> reports about the <u>conflict</u>.

4. The researchers <u>subjected</u> the <u>subject's</u> <u>forearms</u> to a series of tests.

5. They say that <u>forewarned</u> is <u>forearmed</u>.

6. The soldier decided to <u>desert</u> in the <u>desert</u>.

EXERCISE 4: Prepositional Prefixes

A | *Listen and repeat. Make sure you understand the words.*

outcome	outdistance	overjoyed	overtake	underrate
foresee	tortoise	underdog	uproar	

B | *Listen to the recording and complete the sentences with the words you hear.*

The tortoise and the hare decided to race. The tortoise, of course, was the _____.
                                                   1.

None of the forest creatures in the audience _____ for a moment that the tortoise
                                           2.

might _____ the hare and win. But no one could _____ the
       3.   **4.**

_____ of the race. And, as we all know, the hare _____ the tortoise.
  5.   **6.**

When the race began, the hare easily _____ the tortoise and was soon out of sight.
                                7.

But the tortoise _____ to quit. With such a great lead, the hare _____
             8.   **9.**

himself to take a rest, which soon turned into a nap, and then, into a deep sleep. All the while, the

tortoise was creeping along the course, making slow but steady _____. Well, you
                                       10.

know the story. The tortoise eventually _____ the sleeping hare and won the race.
                                11.

There was a joyous _____ from the forest animals during the minute or so it took
                      12.

the tortoise to cross the finish line. The entire audience was _____ to see the
                                           13.

arrogant hare finally get his comeuppance.[1]

---

[1] comeuppance: *a deserved rebuke or penalty*

HABITS AND ADDICTIONS

EXERCISE 5: Kicking the Habit

A | *Listen to the conversation.*

STAN: Stop that. Stop biting your nails.

VICKI: I don't even know when I'm doing it. I wish I could stop.

STAN: Get a manicure so they look nice. Then you won't want to bite them.*

VICKI: I've tried. But when I think about something else, I start biting them again.

STAN: You've got to do something to break the habit. You stopped smoking five years ago. If you can do that, you can stop biting your fingernails.

VICKI: Easy for you to say. When I stopped smoking, I started biting my fingernails.

---

*Natural English

Use different vowels in the words *won't* and *want*. The vowel in *won't* is /ow/, the same as the vowel in *go*. The vowel in *want* is /ɑ/, the same as the vowel in *father*.

You *won't want* to bite your fingernails.

I know I *won't want* to go.

B | *PAIRS: Practice the conversation.*

EXERCISE 6: Your Turn

A | *Read the dictionary definitions of* **addiction** *and* **habit**.

An *addiction* refers to the inability to stop the repetition of an excessive behavior that has harmful consequences. A *habit* is an act that you do regularly and usually without thinking.

B | *Read the words. Make sure you understand the meanings.*

overdose	overeat	overdo	overwork	overwhelm	foresee
outcome	addict	conduct	produce	refuse	permit

C | *GROUPS: Use the words from Part B to discuss the excessive behaviors below. Are they addictions or habits or both? How serious are the consequences of these behaviors?*

Excessive Behaviors

1. biting your (finger)nails
2. gambling
3. overeating
4. drinking (alcohol)
5. smoking (tobacco)
6. taking prescription drugs
7. vigorous exercise
8. playing video games
9. the Internet
10. shopping
11. working
12. other

STEP 4 EXTENDED PRACTICE

Accuracy Practice *Listen again to Exercise 3 on page 158. Then record the sentences.*

Fluency Practice *Record your answers to the questions.*

1. What bad habits have you had in the past?
2. Were you able to break the habits? Explain.

RHYTHM

STEP 1 PRESENTATION

Rhythm is the "drum" section of language; rhythm includes the patterning of strong (stressed) syllables and weak (unstressed) syllables in phrases and sentences, and the timing and grouping of words.

Stress-Timed Languages and Syllable-Timed Languages

English is a *stress-timed* language. In stress-timed languages, syllables do not have equal "weight." Stressed syllables are long, loud, and prominent. Unstressed syllables are short and less clear. The rhythm of English syllables is similar to the trees in the natural tree line.

Natural tree line

Japanese and Spanish are examples of *syllable-timed* languages. In syllable-timed languages, most syllables are approximately equal in length. The rhythm of syllable-timed languages is similar to the trees in the apple orchard below. Describe the difference in height, size, and spacing of the two tree lines to a partner.

Apple orchard

Content and Function Words

Content words have clear meanings and are stressed. Function words have grammatical meanings and are unstressed.

Content Words (Stressed)

Nouns (*table, man*)

Verbs (*walk, eat*)

Adjectives (*beautiful, tall*)

Adverbs (*quickly, very*)

Question words (*What? How?*)

Demonstratives (*that, those*)

Negatives, negative contractions (*not, doesn't*)

Function Words (Unstressed)

Articles (*a, an, the*)

Auxiliary verbs (*am, is, are, have,* etc.)

Personal pronouns (*I, you, him,* etc.)

Conjunctions (*and, or, when, if,* etc.)

Relative pronouns (*who, which, that*)

Prepositions (*to, at, in, on,* etc.)

Reductions of Function Words

Many function words have reduced pronunciations. In *rock 'n roll* (rock and roll), the spelling *'n* reflects the way *and* is usually pronounced.

Reduced words join closely to surrounding words. If it's difficult for you to join words together smoothly, you can use full pronunciations when you speak.

Thought Groups

Thought groups are meaningful phrases within a sentence. They help the listener identify units of information. The words in a thought group are pronounced together.

1. Grouping Words

There are no fixed rules for deciding which words to include in a thought group. Usually, meaning and sentence length determine the words that belong together. Look at two ways to group the words in the sentences below.

We're going to stay at a hotel in Miami.

We're going to stay at a hotel in Miami.

2. Joining Thought Groups

When you join thought groups together, pause or lengthen the end of a thought group briefly before saying the next group.

I made a reservation for tonight.

lengthen briefly

STEP 2 FOCUSED PRACTICE

EXERCISE 1: Conversations

🎧 *Listen to the conversations. The stressed words are underlined. Then practice the conversations with a partner.*

1. **OFFICER:** May I <u>see</u> your <u>license</u>?

   STEFAN: <u>What's</u> the <u>problem</u>, <u>Officer</u>?

   OFFICER: Do you <u>know</u> you <u>went</u> through a <u>red</u> <u>light</u> at the <u>intersection</u>?

   STEFAN: It was <u>yellow</u>—I'm <u>sure</u> it was <u>yellow</u>.

2. **SPOKESPERSON:** Miss <u>Ritter</u> is going to <u>make</u> a <u>statement</u> at this <u>time</u>. She <u>vigorously</u> <u>maintains</u> her <u>innocence</u>.

   MISS RITTER: My <u>arrest</u> has been a <u>mistake</u>. I was only <u>pretending</u> to be <u>shoplifting</u>. I'm <u>preparing</u> for a <u>role</u> in a <u>movie</u>—where I <u>play</u> a <u>shoplifter</u>.

   SPOKESPERSON: Of <u>course</u> she was going to <u>return</u> the <u>merchandise</u>. <u>This</u> has <u>all</u> been a <u>big</u> <u>misunderstanding</u>.

EXERCISE 2: Reductions of Function Words

🎧 *Listen to the word list and reduced pronunciations. Notice the differences.*

Word List	Normal Reduced Pronunciations
1. and	black and white (sounds like "blacken white")
2. or	black or white (sounds like "blacker white")
3. to	back to school (sounds like "back tə school")
4. can	Your cooking can tempt[1] anyone. (sounds like "contempt")
5. he	Did he go? (sounds like "Diddy go?")

EXERCISE 3: Noticing Reductions

🎧 *Listen and repeat the sentences. The pairs of underlined words have the same or nearly the same pronunciation. Then choose a sentence and say it to the class.*

1. He's <u>fallen</u> behind this <u>fall and</u> winter.

2. <u>Bea can light</u> the <u>beacon light</u>.

3. I don't know how much <u>fun he</u> had in his <u>funny</u> hat.

4. My son's going <u>to day</u> school <u>today</u>.

5. The <u>fortunate</u> old woman made a <u>fortune at</u> Bingo.

---

[1] tempt: *to be attractive, make someone want to do something*

EXERCISE 4: Thought Groups

Listen to the sentences and underline thought groups. Then practice the sentences with a partner.

1. Last summer, we decided to drive across the country.

2. We started in New York and planned to take the northern route, all the way to Seattle.

3. Coming from the east, the Rockies looked spectacular.

4. They rose like a wall from the flat plains, running north and south as far as the eye could see.

STEP 3 COMMUNICATION PRACTICE

WORLD TREASURES

EXERCISE 5: World Heritage Sites

A | Listen to the recording. Complete the sentences with the unstressed function words you hear.

_____ mission _____ the World
    1.   2.

Heritage Program is _____ catalog
                  3.

_____ protect places _____ have
   4.   5.

"outstanding universal value." World Heritage Sites have special

cultural _____ natural significance. The
         6.

Coliseum _____ Rome, used _____
         7.   8.

gladiator fights and other public spectacles, is

_____ example. So is Iguazú National Park, a spectacular semicircular waterfall
   9.

_____ the boundary of Argentina and Brazil. In 2010, _____
  10.   11.

_____ 911 sites found in 151 countries. Italy _____ the country that
  12.   13.

had the largest number _____ sites, 45.
              14.

Natural English

The words *site*, *sight*, and *cite* have the same pronunciation.

There were 911 World Heritage *sites* in 2010.

The town was empty. There was no one in *sight*.

When you write an essay, be sure to *cite* your sources.

B | *In the space below, write the names of places in your country that you feel are "treasures." Then describe the places to your classmates.*

_____

_____

_____

EXERCISE 6: Preservation or Progress?

A | *Listen and repeat. Make sure you understand the words.*

1. Aswan Dam	**3.** modernity	**5.** drought	**7.** launch
2. Nile River	**4.** reservoir	**6.** submerge	**8.** archaeological

B | *Listen to the recording. Then match phrases from the three columns to make sentences that summarize the information.*

1	2	3
Egypt's decision	were buried	and provides electricity.
The Aswan Dam	was able to save	wasn't easy.
An international rescue effort	controls flooding	below the dam's reservoir.
Some treasures	to build the Aswan Dam	many treasures.

C | *PAIRS: Practice the sentences you made. Pronounce the words in each column as a group. Can you think of other examples where there is or was a conflict between progress and preservation?*

STEP 4 EXTENDED PRACTICE

Accuracy Practice *Listen again to Exercises 3 and 4 on pages 164 and 165. Then record the sentences.*

Fluency Practice *Record a description of a place that has great cultural or natural significance for your country.*

STEP 1 PRESENTATION

Just as stressed and unstressed syllables make up words, stressed and unstressed words make up phrases and sentences. The alternation between stressed and unstressed words is a key part of natural English rhythm.

Words in a sentence are either content words or function words. Content words are usually stressed. They're words with clear meaning, such as *computer* or *freedom*. Function words are unstressed. They're words that have grammatical meaning, such as *to* or *an*.

Content Words (Stressed)

Nouns	*computer*
Verbs	*walked*
Adjectives	*intelligent*
Adverbs	*quickly*
Demonstrative pronouns and adjectives	*this*
Interrogative (*wh*) words	*Who? Why? Where?*
Negatives	*no, doesn't*

Function Words (Unstressed)

Articles	*a, an, the*
Short prepositions	*to, at, in, on,* etc.
Conjunctions	*and, or, if, that,* etc.
Auxiliary verbs	*am, is, are, have, has, can, will,* etc.
Personal pronouns	*I, me, you, her,* etc.
Possessive pronouns and adjectives	*his, my, their,* etc.
Relative pronouns	*who(m), whose, that,* etc.

Highlighted Words

In many sentences, one content word expresses the most important information. This word is highlighted by pronouncing it with the heaviest stress and (usually) the highest pitch.

Here are the keys.

Stress/Rhythm Patterns

Stress/rhythm patterns of words and phrases can be the same (′ represents a stressed syllable; ∪ represents an unstressed syllable):

Stress pattern ′∪∪:	Óliver	áll of her
Stress pattern ∪′∪:	arríval	a ríval

EXERCISE 1: Stress Patterns

🎧 *Listen and repeat the phrases and sentences. The phrases and sentences in each column have the same rhythm pattern as the underlined word. Concentrate on keeping the rhythm of the phrases and sentences in a column the same.*

1. voluntéer

    Who was here?
    Take a break.
    That's my car.

2. abándon

    a garden
    I bought it.
    They ate them.

3. idèntificátion

    We met at the station.
    I went to the concert.
    We needed to take it.

4. dèmonstrátion

    John's a doctor.
    What's the matter?
    That's a classic.

5. càpabílity

    Who was calling you?
    That's illogical.
    This is half of it.

6. photógrapher

    a Mexican
    I answered it.
    He's listening.

EXERCISE 2: Rhyme

🎧 *Listen and repeat the rhyme. Put a stress mark (´) over the stressed words in lines 2–5. Then practice reading the rhyme with a partner. Lengthen the stressed syllables.*

The móvie was óver at tén.

I laughed 'til I cried with my friend.

The music was great,

The acting first-rate.

We both want to see it again.

EXERCISE 3: Rhythm Patterns

🎧 *Listen and repeat. The underlined words and phrases have the same stress/rhythm pattern. Then choose one of the sentences and say it to the class.*

1. can táke-contáiners: You <u>can táke</u> these <u>contáiners</u>.

2. forgét-for Káte: Don't <u>forgét</u> to buy the book <u>for Káte</u>.

3. Téll her-téller: <u>Téll her</u> that the <u>téller</u> is busy.

4. admíred-at níght: They <u>admíred</u> the city lights <u>at níght</u>.

5. sómeone-cóme when: Did <u>sómeone</u> <u>cóme when</u> you called?

6. to cláss-todáy: I went <u>to cláss</u> <u>todáy</u>.

7. unáble-an áble: I'm <u>unáble</u> to find <u>an áble</u> person for the job.

EXERCISE 4: Sounds Like . . .

Two phrases that sound the same but have different spellings and meanings are called **homophrases.** *Listen to the homophrases. Then work with a partner to think of a homophrase using a reduced function word. (You can check your answers on page 171.)*

1. girls' locket _____*Girls lock it.*_____

2. Willy Picket? _____

3. Senior class schedule? _____

4. The writer left. _____

5. savior stories _____

6. They conserve water. _____

7. the dresses in the closet _____

8. annoys _____

<table>
<tr><td>STEP 3</td><td>COMMUNICATION PRACTICE</td></tr>
</table>

AWARDS AND MOVIES

EXERCISE 5: Awards Trivia

A | *What do you know about movies and awards? Take this trivia quiz and then compare your answers with a partner. (You can check your answers on page 171.)*

1. The Clios are awards for
   a. restaurants
   b. theater performances
   c. advertisements
   d. gymnasts

2. Nollywood movies are movies made in
   a. Nigeria
   b. Nicaragua
   c. Nepal
   d. New Zealand

3. The Nobel Prize is NOT awarded for achievements in
   a. peace
   b. anthropology
   c. literature
   d. chemistry

4. Pulitzer Prizes are awarded for
   a. music
   b. television
   c. writing
   d. medicine

5. The first Academy Awards was in
   a. 1929
   b. 1927
   c. 1941
   d. 1933

6. Which person has received more Oscar nominations than any other?
   a. Steven Spielberg
   b. Tom Hanks
   c. Walt Disney
   d. Meryl Streep

7. The Emmy Awards are given for
   a. music
   b. movies
   c. television
   d. theater

8. Which awards are not given for movies?
   a. the Grammies
   b. the Golden Globe awards
   c. the People's Choice Awards
   d. the Cannes Festival Awards

B | *Listen to the recording and complete the sentences with the unstressed function words you hear.*

KATY: Why are Indian movies called Bollywood Movies? I don't understand _____ the *B* comes from.

RICARDO: _____ Bombay. Bombay's now known _____ Mumbai. _____ the center of the Indian film industry.

KATY: I like _____ music and dancing _____ Bollywood movies. I really enjoyed *Slumdog Millionnaire.*[1]

RICARDO: That was actually _____ Hollywood-Bollywood collaboration. _____ _____ you want to see Bollywood movies, there's a small theater downtown.

> ### Natural English
>
> The verb *are* joins closely to preceding question words. It's pronounced like an *-er* ending on the question word.
>
> "Wire" Indian movies called Bollywood movies? (Why are Indian movies called Bollywood movies?)
>
> "Wearer" Nollywood movies from? (Where are Nollywood movies from?)

---

[1] *Slumdog Millionnaire won the Academy Award for Best Film in 2008.*

EXERCISE 6: Your Turn

A | *Read the list of movie genres below. Check (✓) the types of movies you enjoy watching.*

Genre
_____ Action/Adventure
_____ Comedies
_____ Dramas
_____ Romance
_____ Science fiction
_____ Horror
_____ Animations
_____ Musicals
_____ Mysteries

B | *GROUPS: Compare your choices. Explain why you like the movie genres you checked.*

STEP 4   EXTENDED PRACTICE

Accuracy Practice   *Listen again to Exercise 1 on page 168. Then record the sentences and phrases.*

Fluency Practice   *Imagine you've won an Oscar for best actor or actress. What would you say? Whom would you thank? Record a brief acceptance speech for your award.*

EXERCISE 5A: 1. c, 2. a, 3. b, 4. c, 5. a, 6. c, 7. c, 8. a

EXERCISE 4: 1. Girls lock it. 2. Will he pick it? 3. Seen your class schedule? 4. the right or left 5. Save your stories. 6. They can serve water. 7. The dress is in the closet. 8. a noise

Highlighting

Highlight the word that expresses the most important information in a sentence by pronouncing it with heavy stress and high pitch.

What do you do on the WEEKend?

I get together with FRIENDS.

1. Beginning a Conversation

When you begin a conversation with a question, you often highlight the last content word.

What did you do on the WEEKend?

2. Highlighting New Information

New information is often presented in the last content word of a sentence.

(What did you do on the WEEKend?) I went DANcing.

3. Highlighting Contrasts and Corrections

Highlight information that presents a contrast or corrects a statement. Sentences with contrasts and corrections may have more than one highlighted word.

The mayor's going to RAISE taxes and CUT spending.

The ELEPHANT isn't the largest animal in the world—the WHALE is.

4. Highlighting in Sentences with *there is/are*

The noun after *is/are* is usually highlighted.

There's some important NEWS on tonight.

5. Highlighting Auxiliary Verbs

Highlight auxiliary verbs (*is, are, have, has*) to show agreement.

A: This has been a GOOD experience.

B: It HAS been a good experience.

6. Highlighting Function Words

Function words are normally unstressed. They can be highlighted if the speaker wants to emphasize their meaning.

(Would you like soup or salad?)   I'd like soup AND salad.

STEP 2   FOCUSED PRACTICE

EXERCISE 1: Conversations

A | *Listen and repeat the conversations. Circle the highlighted words.*

1. **A:** I want to pick up my jacket. Here's the ticket.
   B: It's not ready yet. Come back tomorrow.
   A: They said it would be ready today.
   B: I didn't say that. Come back tomorrow.

2. **A:** Why do you like skydiving?
   B: I like the thrill, the rush.
   A: What about fear? Don't you feel afraid?
   B: Sure. But that's part of it. I like the fear.

B | *PAIRS: Compare your answers. Then practice the conversations.*

EXERCISE 2: Emphasis and Contrast

A | *Read all of the sentences in each set below. Then listen to the sentences and circle the highlighted words.*

1. A saying about friendship:
   a. Everyone hears what you say.
   b. Friends listen to what you say.
   c. Best friends listen to what you don't say.

2. Who makes the decisions? The Patels own a small electronics store. Mr. Patel, his wife, and his three children live above the store, and everyone except the baby spends time working in the store. The sentences describe each of the Patels' roles in making decisions about the business.
   a. Mrs. Patel is the real decision maker.
   b. Mr. Patel thinks he makes the decisions.
   c. Jana Patel thinks she ought to make the decisions.
   d. Al Patel doesn't care who makes the decisions.
   e. The baby doesn't even know there's a business.

B | *Listen again and repeat the sentences.*

EXERCISE 3: Why Is It?

PAIRS: Read the questions below and circle the words that contrast. (The questions are rhetorical, making fun of the logic of English.) Then practice reading the sentences to each other, using heavy stress and high pitch on the contrasting words.

1. Why does the sun lighten our hair but darken our skin?

2. Why is a boxing ring square?

3. Why is the time of day with the slowest traffic called rush hour?

4. Why isn't there mouse-flavored cat food?

5. Why is the third hand on a clock called the second hand?

6. Why do we drive on parkways and park on driveways?

EXERCISE 4: Agreeing

PAIRS: Create short conversations. Student B shows agreement with Student A's statement by repeating it and highlighting the auxiliary verb.

EXAMPLE:

STUDENT A: You drive too slowly.

STUDENT B: { Yes
                   Right.   } I DO drive too slowly.
                   I agree. }

1. Susana should win the prize.

2. The essay was well written.

3. Rafael looks a lot like his brother.

4. The final exam will cover a lot of material.

5. They've been gone a long time.

6. That new student's really cute.

LIVING ON THE EDGE

EXERCISE 5: Thrill Seekers

A | *Listen and repeat. Make sure you understand the words and phrases.*

(to) pound	butterflies in your stomach	adrenaline rush	
palms	crave	roller coaster	hair-raising

B | *Listen to the recording and complete the sentences with the words you hear.*

Everyone knows what it's like to feel _____ scared. Your _____
                                        1.   **2.**

pounds, you _____ faster, your _____ sweat, you get
                3.   **4.**

_____ in your stomach.
        5.

Psychologist Frank Farley has studied people who like to live life "on the edge." He coined the

term *type T* to describe their personalities: They're _____ seekers. They crave the
                                                              6.

_____ and _____ of activities that _____ of us
        7.   **8.**   **9.**

consider _____ terrifying or dangerous. They enjoy the _____
                  10.   **11.**

sensations that accompany _____—the adrenaline rush and the racing heart.
                                      12.

According to Farley, type T's have high levels of _____ and self-esteem. They
                                                              13.

believe their fate is in _____ hands and that life is not worth living if they are not
                              14.

being _____.
              15.

C | PAIRS: *Read the sentences and decide which words should be highlighted. Then practice the sentences.*

1. Many people enjoy the thrill of safe fear, but others need more.
2. Type T personalities crave both the mental intensity and physical sensations of fear.
3. Roller coasters are hair-raising rides; merry-go-rounds are tame.
4. Hiking is a relatively safe sport; rock climbing is more dangerous; walking on a high-wire is even more dangerous.
5. Jumping off a diving board is fun; bungee-jumping off a bridge is crazy.
6. If you're skydiving, your fate isn't in your hands; it's in your parachute.

> **Natural English**
>
> Hyphenated phrases such as *hair-raising*, *merry-go-round*, and *bungee-jumping* are usually stressed on the first word of the phrase. This word is also pronounced on a higher pitch (note).
>
> háir-raising rides
>
> mérry-go-rounds
>
> hígh-wire artists

EXERCISE 6: Your Turn

Read the activities in the chart. Check (✓) the ones you've done or would like to try. Then interview two other classmates to see which of these activities they enjoy or would like to try. Share your results with the class. Are there any type T's among you?

	You	Student's Name _____	Student's Name _____
Watching horror movies			
Bungee-jumping			
Skydiving			
Downhill skiing			
Snowboarding			
Rock climbing			
Mountain biking			
Riding roller coasters/scary rides			
Surfing			

STEP 4 EXTENDED PRACTICE

Accuracy Practice *Listen again to Exercise 2A on page 173. Then record the sentences.*

Fluency Practice *Review the activities in Exercise 6. Choose four and record your opinion of them. Have you ever tried them? Would you ever? Why or why not?*

Thought Groups

Pronounce words in meaningful phrases, or *thought groups*. Thought groups help the listener identify the parts of a sentence. They help the speaker by breaking the sentence into shorter parts.

I don't understand the new rules.

1. Length of Thought Groups

There are no fixed rules for deciding what the thought groups of a sentence are. Look at the two ways the words in this sentence can be grouped together.

If you want to get ahead, dress for success.

If you want to get ahead, dress for success.

When you're learning a language, it's better to use shorter thought groups because they give you more time to plan what you want to say.

2. Thought Groups and Intonation

There is usually a small rise or fall in pitch at the end of a thought group inside a sentence. The change in pitch isn't as great as it is at the end of a sentence.

If you want to get ahead, dress for success.

If you wear a suit, you'll look stuffy.

3. Joining Thought Groups Together

Lengthen the sound that ends a thought group before you begin the next group. The lengthening tells the listener that one group has ended and another is about to begin.

I didn't get the job because of my tattoo.   That cashier wears a nose ring.
           ↑   ↑
    lengthen   lengthen

4. Thought Groups and Grammatical Phrases

Thought groups often correspond to grammatical phrases.

Prepositional Phrases	in a minute	at the airport
Verb + Pronoun	buy them	bring it
Determiner + Noun	my uncle	the park
Short Clauses	When you leave, call me.	

STEP 2   FOCUSED PRACTICE

EXERCISE 1: Rhyme

Listen and repeat the rhyme. Use the lines to group words together.

A mouse in her room woke Miss Dowd.

She was frightened and screamed very loud.

Then a happy thought hit her

To scare off the critter[1]—

She sat up in bed and meowed.

EXERCISE 2: Advice Letters

A | *Listen and repeat the phrases and sentences. Use the lines to group words together.*

1. a job interview

2. an important job interview

3. with a business

4. a youthful image

5. a casual, youthful image

6. with a business that has a casual, youthful image

7. I'm preparing for a job interview

8. I'm preparing for an important job interview with a business that has a casual, youthful image.

---

[1] critter: *slang for creature, living thing; here, the mouse*

Dear MJ,

I'm preparing for an important job interview with a business that has a casual, youthful image. Should I wear something traditional, like a suit? Or should I go with something more trendy? I don't want to appear "stuffy," but I don't want them to think that I think I already have the job.

Standing in Front of My Closet

Dear Standing,

Go with the suit. Traditional business clothes symbolize competence and dedication. If you get the job, you can adopt whatever style the business has. Plus, the interview may be the last time you can wear your suit.

MJ

EXERCISE 3: Differences in Meaning

The way you group words can affect the meaning of a sentence.

🎧 **A** | *Listen and repeat the sentences. Group words to show the different meanings in the sentence pairs.*

1. **a.** "Max," replied Susan, "why don't you wear a suit?"

   b. Max replied, "Susan, why don't you wear a suit?"

2. **a.** There are five, year-old bottles of wine in the basement.

   b. There are five-year-old bottles of wine in the basement.

3. **a.** Stanley asked Stella, "How long is your sister going to stay?"

   b. "Stanley," asked Stella, "how long is your sister going to stay?"

4. **a.** Why are you going to leave Bob?

   b. Why are you going to leave, Bob?

5. **a.** The teacher said we'd have two, hour-long tests.

   b. The teacher said we'd have two-hour-long tests.

6. **a.** My sister, who lives in Boston, is coming tomorrow.

   b. My sister who lives in Boston is coming tomorrow.

🎧 **B** | *Listen again and circle the letter of the sentence you hear.*

C | *PAIRS: Say a sentence from Part A. Group words clearly so your partner can tell you which sentence you said.*

DRESS FOR SUCCESS

EXERCISE 4: Dressing Down or Dressing Up?

Read the paragraphs. Underline the thought groups in the second paragraph. Then compare your answers with a partner (the groupings don't have to be the same). Practice reading the paragraphs to each other, grouping words as you marked them.

After two decades of more casual attire in the workplace, some businesses are returning to a more conservative, formal style of dressing, especially for meetings and visits with clients. Those businesses say a more formal dress code has improved the quality of meetings and discussions. In a survey of 1,000 companies, over 40 percent reported that more relaxed dress codes were accompanied by an increase in employee lateness and absenteeism.

Still, the business casual dress code remains the norm for most businesses in Western countries. Websites define business casual as dressing professionally but looking relaxed. For men, this means wearing a shirt with a collar and casual pants, such as khakis. For women, this means pants or a skirt and a shirt.

Natural English

The verbs *wear* and *dress* have similar meanings but different uses. *Wear* usually requires a direct object, an article of clothing.

> Men should wear a shirt with a collar.

When *dress* means "put your clothes on," it's intransitive and cannot be followed by a direct object.

> You should dress in a suit.

> You should dress professionally.

EXERCISE 5: Business Dress Codes

A | Listen and repeat. Make sure you understand the words and phrases.

tattoos	body piercing	(to) sport a nose ring
come under fire	ban	Sikh
dreadlocks	Rastafarian	infringe upon someone's rights

B | Listen to the recording. Then connect the phrases to make sentences that summarize the information in the recording. Read your sentences to a partner.

A	B	C
A Sikh job applicant	at a Safeway store	has tattoos all over his arms.
A typical student	at Ideal Market	had to cover his tattoo.
A health care worker	at any college in the country	has tattoos and body piercings.
A popular cashier	at a California facility	wasn't hired because he wouldn't shave his beard.
A Rastafarian worker	at Lexmart International	doesn't have to cut his dreadlocks.
A computer worker	at Domino's Pizza	wears a nose ring.

EXERCISE 6: Your Turn

Appropriate appearance in the workplace depends on a variety of factors and is different in different countries. Think about dress codes in your country. Which items in the chart would be appropriate for bank employees, athletes, students, and food service workers in your country? Talk about your answers as a class or in small groups.

	Bank Employees	Athletes	Students	Food Service Workers
Body art				
Tattoos				
Pierced ears (multiple holes/ear)				
Nose rings				
Eyebrow rings				
Clothing				
Jeans				
T-Shirts				
Bermuda shorts[1]				
Sneakers				

(continued on next page)

[1] Bermuda shorts: *shorts for men or women that come down to the knee; the fabric is usually patterned.*

	Bank Employees	Athletes	Students	Food Service Workers
Sandals				
Khakis				
Polo shirts				
Tight pants				
Tight tops				
Suits and ties (men)				
Suits, dresses/skirts (women)				
Uniforms				

STEP 4 EXTENDED PRACTICE

Accuracy Practice *Listen again to Exercise 1 on page 178. Then record the rhyme.*

Fluency Practice *If you were an employer, what kind of dress code would you require of your employees? Record your answer and include information about the type of business you're describing.*

Rhythm Patterns and Personal Pronouns

Pronouns are usually unstressed.

Subject Pronouns

Reductions of Subject Pronouns

Before contractions of *will* (*'ll*) and *are* (*'re*), the vowels in pronouns may be reduced.

<u>I'll</u> dó it. (sounds like *all*)

<u>She'll</u> dó it. (rhymes with *still*)

<u>We're</u> hére. (/wɪr/, /wər/)

<u>They're</u> góne. (sounds like *there*)

Object Pronouns

Object pronouns are pronounced like endings on the preceding verb.

Ópen it.   Réad them.

Pronouns Beginning with *h*

The /h/ in pronouns like *he*, *her*, and *him* is usually dropped when the pronoun is inside a sentence. The reduced pronoun joins closely to the verb. If this is difficult, you can pronounce /h/ in pronouns, but don't stress the pronouns.

call ɦim ("callim")

What did ɦe do? (What "diddy" do?)

This is ɦer office. (This "izzer" office.)

Fast Speech Reductions

The reductions described above are common to all styles of English. Native speakers also make other reductions to pronouns in informal speech. You should be aware of these reductions.

🎧 *Listen to the reductions.*

1. *You* in Common Expressions

you **after /t, d/**

Where "didjə" go? "Wherja" go?

(Where did you go?)

I won't "letchə" go.

(I won't let you go.)

you **after other sounds**

"Seeyə" later.

(See you later.)

I'll "callyə" tonight.

(I'll call you tonight.)

2. *Them* **Reduction:** /əm/

Did you "findəm" at the store?

(Did you find them at the store?)

STEP 2   FOCUSED PRACTICE

EXERCISE 1: Reduced *h* Words

🎧 *Listen and repeat the conversations. Then practice them with a partner.*

1. **A:** Why ̶has she sold ̶her house?

   B: She's moving back home to stay with ̶her mother.

2. **A:** Would you tell Professor Sommers I'll bring ̶him my paper tomorrow?

   B: Why me? Why don't you tell ̶him yourself?

3. **A:** The lawyer said to meet ̶him at ̶his office tomorrow with the papers.

   B: What does ̶he want us to bring?

4. **A:** Please tell Mr. Blake there's a call for ̶him.

   B: I don't know if ̶he's in or out.

EXERCISE 2: Text Messages

Text messages and instant messages make use of abbreviations and often omit function words and punctuation.

PAIRS: Read the messages below. Write unabbreviated sentences, using normal spellings. Add words when necessary. (You can check your answers on page 187.)

NIGHTGLOOM: Palerider u there? _____

PALERIDER: Sup? _____

NIGHTGLOOM: talked 2 sue 2day. She likes u. me 2.

_____

PALERIDER: i like u2. Sue said she likes me?

_____

NIGHTGLOOM: y _____

PALERIDER: working. gtg[1] _____

NIGHTGLOOM: ok Cya tmw _____

PALERIDER: Cya. bye. _____

EXERCISE 3: Hearing Reduced Pronouns

Listen and repeat the sentences. The underlined words and phrases have the same or nearly the same pronunciation. Then choose a sentence and say it to the class.

1. Oliver Hart recorded "All of Her Heart."

2. Put the books I bought him on the bottom shelf.

3. Would he like to meet Woody Harrelson?

4. The sailor agreed to sail her boat in the race.

5. Lee's seen your senior prom[2] pictures.

6. The old concrete wall is too porous[3] so the builder is going to pour us a new wall.

---

[1] gtg: *abbreviation for* got to go

[2] prom: *a dance for seniors in high school;* [3] porous: *allowing substances to pass through*

EXTRATERRESTRIALS

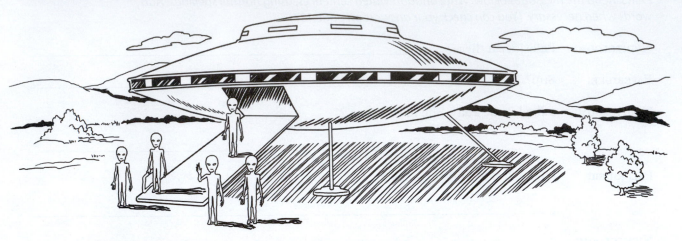

EXERCISE 4: War of the Worlds

On Halloween 1938, a group of actors performed a radio play based on H.G. Wells's novel *The War of the Worlds*, which described an invasion of the earth by aliens from Mars. The radio play was written like a news broadcast, and many listeners believed it was real and panicked.

Seven million Americans heard the radio broadcast of *War of the Worlds*. One million believed that the United States was actually being invaded by Martians. Sociologist Hadley Cantril studied this case of mass panic and interviewed many people. The sentences below are quotations from some of the Americans whom Hadley interviewed.

A | *Read the quotations and complete the sentences with pronouns.*

1. My husband tried to calm _____ *me* _____ and said, "If this were so, _____ *it* _____ would be

   on all the stations."

2. When I heard that poison gas was in the streets of Newark, I called my brother and his wife

   and told _____ to come right over.

3. My son came home during the excitement, and I sent _____ out to see what

   _____ was all about.

4. I couldn't stand _____, so I turned _____ off.

5. I was writing a history paper. The girl from upstairs came and made _____ go up to

   her place.

6. When I got home, my husband wasn't there, so I rushed to the neighbors to tell

   _____ the world was coming to an end.

7. I heard the announcer say that _____ saw a Martian standing in the middle of

Times Square. . . . That's all I had to hear—I knew _____ had to be a play.

8. It was so real. . . . But I turned to [another radio station] to see if they had the same thing on.

They didn't, so I knew _____ must be a fake.

B | GROUPS: *Compare your answers. Then discuss how you think the public would react today if an alien attack were convincingly portrayed as a news report on television.*

EXERCISE 5: Game Changers

A | *Listen. Make sure you understand the words.*

> forecaster   quarrelling   conquer   convert

B | *Listen to the recording.*

Natural English

In quantity phrases like *a third of us*, the pronoun has more stress than *of*. When the next word begins with a vowel, *of* is pronounced /əv/. When the next word begins with a consonant, *of* is usually pronounced /ə/.

a third əv us
the rest əv us
some əv it

half ə them
one ə you

C | *PAIRS: Discuss your answers to these questions.*
1. Why does Saffo describe us (humans) as a lonely species?
2. What's humorous about what he says?
3. Paraphrase what Saffo says at the end: How much will the discovery of non-human intelligence change us?

STEP 4   EXTENDED PRACTICE

Accuracy Practice *Listen again to Exercise 3 on page 185. Then record the sentences.*

Fluency Practice *Do you think the people of 1938 were more gullible, or easily fooled, than people of today? Explain. Record your answer.*

EXERCISE 2: N: Palerider. (are) you there? **P:** What's up? **N:** (I) talked to Sue today. She likes you. **Me too. P: I** like you too. Sue said she likes me? **N:** Yes. **P:** (I'm) working. (I've) got to go. **N:** OK. (I'll) see you tomorrow. **P:** (I'll) see you. Bye.

Rhythm Patterns: Articles

Articles (*a*, *an*, or *the*) are unstressed. They're grouped with the following noun.

a mán   an ónion   the wéather

1. *The*

The is often pronounced /ðiy/ before a vowel. The /y/ of /ðiy/ joins to the following vowel. Be sure to pronounce the *th* of *the* correctly.

the aír   the ócean

/ðiy ɛr/   /ðiy owʃən/

The is pronounced /ðə/ before a consonant.

the bóok   the pláce

/ðə/ book   /ðə/ place

2. *A, An*

Reduce the vowel of *a/an* to /ə/. *An* joins closely to the following word.

a peninsula   an island

/ə/   /ən/

Be careful with words that begin with the letter *u*. In words like *union* and *useful*, the first sound is the consonant /y/ so the article is *a*.

a union member   a useful tool

EXERCISE 1: Joining Words

Listen and repeat the sentences. Use the lines to help you join words.

1. A noise annoys an oyster.

2. This is an answerable question; the others are unanswerable.

3. We're unable to find an able employee.

4. Even though we think of the very rich as unapproachable, she's an approachable rich person.

5. This is an accented word, but the others are unaccented.

6. Is she an interested student or an uninterested student?

7. This is an accurate answer, but that one's inaccurate.

8. An intended consequence is an increase in the food supply; but there are always unintended consequences.

EXERCISE 2: *The*

*Listen and repeat the sentences. Pronounce the **th** of **the** correctly.*

1. I met the^y author.
2. Canada is the biggest country in North America.
3. What's the^y answer?
4. Did you use the method in the book?
5. When did the United States become a country?
6. I didn't understand the^y explanation in the unit on articles.

EXERCISE 3: Apply the Rule

A | *Write **a** or **an** in each blank. Then practice saying the phrases with a partner. Join words together and reduce the vowel of a/an to /ə/.*

1. __an__ announcement
2. _____ utopia
3. _____ continent
4. _____ peninsula
5. _____ island

6. _____ harbor
7. _____ honest man
8. _____ universal truth
9. _____ mountain range
10. _____ university town

B | *PAIRS: Make sentences matching the words on the left to the definitions. Introduce the words with the article **a/an**. Add a verb if necessary.*

Words	Definitions
1. island	a. a protected place where boats can tie up
2. honest person	b. surrounded by water on all sides
3. utopia	c. tells the truth
4. harbor	d. an ideal place or community

EXERCISE 4: Sound Like . . .

🎧 *Two phrases that sound the same (or nearly the same) but have different spellings and meanings are called* **homophrases**. *Listen to the homophrases. Then work with a partner to think of a homophrase that includes an article. (You can check your answers on page 192.)*

1. announce ___*an ounce*_____

2. arrested suspect _____

3. arrival city _____

4. attention _____

5. apparent reasons _____

6. unattractive style _____

EXERCISE 5: The Place Name Game

Play this game in two teams. Team A asks questions of Team B, and vice versa. The questions are about places. Each group decides whether to use the *with the place name in the question and answer. (Guidelines for using* the *with place names are given in the box.) The team that's answering questions receives a point for each correct answer, correctly pronounced. Team A's questions are on page 256. Team B's questions are on page 262.*

Using *the* with Place Names	
Use *the* with	**Do not use *the* with**
• country names that include words such as *United, States, Republic, Union*	• most country names
• names of buildings	• most city names
• names of mountain ranges	• state names
• names of groups of islands	• names of single mountains
• names of groups of lakes	• names of single islands
• names of bridges	• names of single lakes
• names of oceans, seas, and rivers	• names of continents

Examples:

TEAM A: Where's the White House? Name the city.

TEAM B: In Washington, D.C.

TEAM A: Where's Texas? Name the country.

TEAM B: In the United States.

POPULATION PROBLEMS

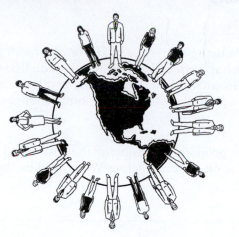

EXERCISE 6: Population Growth and Hunger

A | *The United Nations estimates that nearly a billion people in the world are hungry or suffer from malnutrition. What are some other problems linked with a growing world population? Write your ideas on the lines. Then share them with a partner.*

_____

_____

_____

B | *PAIRS: Read the statements about hunger. Write* **T** *if you think a statement is true; write* **F** *if you think it's false.*

_____ **1.** We don't produce enough food to feed everyone in the world.*

_____ **2.** There's enough grain to provide adequate calories for every man, woman, and child in the world.

_____ **3.** In countries where land is scarce and population density is high, food shortages and famines occur.

> ***Natural English**
>
> If *world* is difficult for you to pronounce, pronounce it as a two-syllable word, stressing the first syllable: "wə́rəld."
>
> wə́rəld population (world population)
>
> every person in the wə́rəld (world)

_____ **4.** The "green revolution," the modernization of farming techniques, will solve the problem of world hunger.

_____ **5.** Small farmers are less productive than large agribusinesses.

_____ **6.** Solving the problem of hunger will mean more pesticide use and more deforestation.

_____ **7.** To solve the problem of hunger, we must increase food aid to hungry nations.

C| *PAIRS: Listen to the recording and check your answers in Part B. Do any of the facts surprise you? Why or why not?*

EXERCISE 7: Aging Populations

A| *Read the paragraph.*

By 2050, the number of people living to the age of 100 or older will be 15 times greater than it is today. On the one hand, this has been called "a triumph of civilization," the result of smaller families, lower death rates, and improved health care. On the other hand, this achievement will require profound and sometimes painful social and economic changes.

B| *GROUPS: Discuss the questions.*

1. Raising retirement age is one proposal for reducing the cost of old age benefits. What are some others? Write your ideas on the lines below. Which will be the most difficult politically for countries to implement?

   _____

   _____

   _____

2. Most discussions about population aging deal with the problems. What opportunities could older people create for a society/economy?

3. In your country, is the population as a whole growing? Is the government concerned about population growth/decline in your country?

STEP 4 EXTENDED PRACTICE

Accuracy Practice *Listen again to Exercises 1 and 2 on pages 188 and 189. Then record the sentences.*

Fluency Practice *Record your answers to questions 1 and 3 in Exercise 7B.*

EXERCISE 4: 1. an ounce, 2. a rested suspect, 3. a rival city, 4. a tension, 5. a parent reasons (here, *reason* is a verb), 6. an attractive style

STEP 1 PRESENTATION

Prepositions are unstressed. Blended pronunciations of prepositions occur with some common verbs, for example, *gonna*.

Unstressed Prepositions

"Short" prepositions (*to, at, in, on, for, of, with, from*) are unstressed and grouped with the following noun. The preposition has become part of some words: *forever, tomorrow*.

at hóme   to cláss   on tíme

The prepositions *at* and *for* are often reduced to /ət/ and /fər/.

I study at night.   I had eggs for breakfast.
    /ət/   /fər/

Of can be pronounced /əv/ or /ə/ before a consonant. It's usually pronounced /əv/ before a vowel.

a cup of coffee   the end of August

"a cuppə coffee"   "əv August"

To has two pronunciations, depending on the following sound. Before consonants, pronounce *to* as /tə/.

to schóol   to wórk
"tə school"   "tə work"

Before vowels, *to* is often pronounced /tuw/.

to a restaurant
"/tuw/ a restaurant"

Phrasal Verbs

In phrasal verbs, prepositions function as adverbs and are stressed. (See Unit 39 for more on phrasal verbs.)

Come ON.   Pick it UP.   Watch OUT.

Hafta, Gonna, Wanna

1. *Have to/Has to*

Have to/Has to are pronounced as one word: /hæftə, hæstə/.

I "haftə" pay my bills.   She "hastə" work tonight.
  (have to)   (has to)

(continued on next page)

2. Gonna

Gonna is a reduction of the future auxiliary *going to*. The pronunciation is common in informal English.

> This year I'm *gonna* lose weight.

Gonna includes *to*. If you use *gonna,* do NOT add *to*.

> This year I'm gonna ⨉ study more.

Do NOT use *gonna* when *go* is the main verb.

> We're going to Cleveland. (not "gonna")

3. Wanna

Wanna is a fast speech reduction of *want to* or *want a*. The pronunciation is common in informal English.

> Do you *wanna* go shopping?   Do you *wanna* sandwich?
>   (want to)   (want a)

STEP 2   FOCUSED PRACTICE

EXERCISE 1: Prepositions

Complete the sentences with prepositions. Then listen to the recording and check your answers.

1. **a.** I spent $143 _____on_____ a date last night.

   b. I paid $85 _____ dinner _____ a restaurant and $8 _____ a valet

   _____ park my car.

   c. Afterwards, _____ a nightclub, I spent another $44 _____ two rounds

   _____ drinks and another $6 _____ valet parking.

   d. I put everything _____ my credit card, except _____ the valet parking. I

   paid _____ that _____ cash.

2. **a.** I was going _____ go _____ the doctor's _____ two o'clock

   today.

   b. My appointment was cancelled because the doctor had _____ be _____

   the hospital _____ a patient.

   c. So I decided _____ go _____ the mall _____ celebrate the

   cancellation.

   d. I saw some shoes I liked _____ a shoe store, but they weren't _____ sale.

EXERCISE 2: Hearing Reductions

🎧 *The underlined words have similar or identical pronunciations. Listen and repeat the sentences. Then choose a sentence and say it to the class.*

1. I brought <u>tamales</u>[1] <u>to Molly's</u>.

2. You have to take this letter to the deputy <u>consul at</u> the <u>consulate</u>.

3. I keep <u>forgetting</u> to thank you <u>for getting</u> the party supplies.

4. You were <u>considerate</u> to deliver the plans we'll <u>consider at</u> work.

5. The officer who performed the <u>act of</u> courage is on <u>active</u> duty in Atlanta.

6. She has the ability to explain <u>indelicate</u> matters <u>in delicate</u> language.

EXERCISE 3: Sounds Like . . .

🎧 *Two phrases that sound the same but have different spellings and meanings are called* **homophrases**. *Listen and repeat the homophrases. Then work with a partner to think of a homophrase that includes a reduced preposition. (You can check your answers on page 198.)*

1. He saved a fortunate school. <u>*He saved a fortune at school.*</u>

2. They explained these incredible terms. _____

3. That's a divisive technology. _____

4. I don't believe indirect advice. _____

5. The legislation was passed by an active Congress. _____

EXERCISE 4: Full or Reduced?

🎧 *The verbs* **have/has to**, **going to**, *and* **want to/a** *all have reduced pronunciations. Listen to the sentences and write the pronunciation(s) you hear. Some forms are used more than once.*

hafta	hasta	gonna	going to	wanna	want(s) the

1. If you ____*wanna*____ come with us, you'll _____ hurry because we're _____ leave in five minutes.

2. My roommate's _____ make spaghetti, so I'm _____ the store.

3. Do you _____ talk now, or do you _____ wait until later?

4. Maria _____ notes from yesterday's class because she _____ study.

5. Are you _____ the library tonight, or do you _____ go out?

6. My credit card is maxed out.[2] I'm _____ _____ pay it off.

---

[1] tamales: *a Mexican dish made of chopped meat and peppers, wrapped in corn husks (the leaves that cover corn)*

[2] maxed out (slang): *charged to the maximum limit*

MEN, WOMEN, AND SHOPPING

EXERCISE 5: Shopping Trips

A | *Listen to the conversations.*

1. **MEI:** I've got to go to the drugstore. Do you need anything?

   CHANG: We're almost out of toothpaste.

2. **PATRICK:** Let's get out of here. I don't want to waste Saturday in a store.

   ANGELA: Just a few more minutes. I want to look around a little bit more.

3. **FELIX:** I don't want to go in there. The checkout lines are too long.

   SANDRA: I agree. They ought to have more help when the store is so busy.*

---

*Natural English

Blend the words in the phrase *ought to* together.

   They *oughtta* have more help.

B | *PAIRS: Practice the conversations in Part A.*

EXERCISE 6: Hunting and Foraging

A | *PAIRS: Do men and women have different shopping styles? What are the differences? Discuss these questions. Then write your ideas on the lines below.*

Men: _____

Women: _____

B | *Listen to the recording and complete the sentences with the words you hear.*

The differences ___*between*___ male and female shopping styles may date back
              1.

_____ prehistoric times, when women foraged _____ food while
    2.   **3.**

men went out hunting. A scientist who investigates the different shopping styles

_____ men and women says he got interested _____ the subject
    4.   **5.**

_____ a vacation with a group of friends. When the group went to a new place,
    6.

the women wanted to go out and shop. The men couldn't understand why. But the women's

behavior is understandable if you consider the skills needed _____ foraging.
                                                      7.

_____ prehistoric times, women had to spend time exploring their
    8.

surroundings. They had to look carefully over possible plants and be able to recognize small

differences. Life or death could rest _____ being able to notice subtle differences
                                          9.

between two berries, for example, one safe to eat, the other poisonous. Men,

_____ the other hand, hunted. After the hunt, they returned home quickly
    10.

_____ safety.
    11.

C | *PAIRS: Review your answers in Part A. Can the differences you wrote be predicted by the different roles of foragers and hunters? Explain.*

EXERCISE 7: Different Styles

A | *Read the statements in the chart. They reflect the shopping preferences of American women and men. If you think a statement is more typical of women than men, check (✓) the* **Women** *column. If you think a statement is more typical of men, check the* **Men** *column. If you think a statement is true for both women and men, check both columns.*

	Women	Men
1. I don't want to shop there because it's difficult to find parking nearby.		
2. A salesperson ought to be familiar with a lot of merchandise, to help me make the right choice.		
3. There ought to be more salespeople to get customers through checkout quickly.		
4. I don't want to shop there because I can't get a salesperson to help me.		
5. I shop a lot online.		
6. I buy things on impulse.[1]		
7. I go to a store to get something specific, not to look around.		
8. I use shopping to celebrate or feel better.		
9. I sometimes hide my spending.		

B | *GROUPS: Compare your charts. (You can check your answers below).*

STEP 4   EXTENDED PRACTICE

Accuracy Practice *Listen again to Exercise 2 on page 195. Then record the sentences.*

Fluency Practice *Review the chart in Exercise 7A. Then record your answers to these questions.*

1. Are your answers typical of the answers given by American shoppers of your gender? Explain.

2. What advice would you give to retail stores to improve your shopping experience?

---

[1] on impulse: *to do something without thinking about the results*

EXERCISE 7A: 1. men, **2.** women, **3.** men, **4.** both, **5.** both, **6.** women, **7.** women, **8.** men, **9.** both

EXERCISE 3: 1. He saved a fortune at school. **2.** They explained these in credible terms. **3.** That's a device of technology. **4.** I don't believe in direct advice. **5.** The legislation was passed by an act of Congress.

Rhythm Patterns: Phrasal Verbs

STEP 1 PRESENTATION

Phrasal Verbs

Phrasal verbs often have idiomatic meanings: *figure out,* for example, means "solve" or "discover."

In phrasal verbs, the verb is followed by a particle (preposition). The particle is stressed.

Come ón! Let's go.

(*come on* means "hurry up" here)

When the verb and particle are separated by a direct object, both the verb and particle can be stressed.

Lóok the wórd úp.   Thrów thése óut tomórrow.

When the verb and particle are not separated, either the verb or particle has heavy stress, but not both.

I don't want to páy off my loan.

I've just paid óff my loan.

When the particle ends the sentence, it's often stressed more heavily than the verb.

Slow dówn.   Put it óff.   Let's go óut.   Do them óver.

Nouns Formed from Phrasal Verbs

The first word is stressed and pronounced on a higher pitch.

Tákeòff's been delayed an hour.   He had a nervous bréakdòwn.

STEP 2 FOCUSED PRACTICE

EXERCISE 1: Sentences with Phrasal Verbs

Listen and repeat the sentences. Then choose a sentence and say it to the class.

1. Even though we took óff in a storm, the tákeoff was smooth.

2. Hand it ín when you've filled it óut.

3. I'm not going to cléan up the kitchen because I didn't mess it úp.

4. Please call him úp before you go óut.

(continued on next page)

5. Did you find out why they called off the interview?

6. I didn't like the coat when I tried it on.

7. Maria picked out a nice hat for her brother, but she ended up keeping it for herself.

EXERCISE 2: Conversations

Listen to the conversations. Notice the pronunciation of the underlined phrasal verbs. Then practice the conversations with a partner.

1. **A:** I've already picked the application up. Should I fill it out now or drop it off later?

   B: Fill it out now if you have time. Otherwise bring it back by tomorrow.

2. **A:** The rain's clearing up, but it's supposed to get worse later. Let's leave now.

   B: You go on without me. I'll catch up with you later.

3. **A:** It's time to clean up the apartment. I'll take out the garbage and straighten up the living room.

   B: I'll bundle the newspapers up and clean out the refrigerator.

4. **A:** Can you help me with this math problem? I've done it over twice, and I still can't figure it out.

   B: You've written it down wrong. This number should be 4, not 3. Try it again. It'll come out right.

5. **A:** Can you find out when try-outs for the school play are being held?

   B: They're today. I tried out for the main role this morning.

EXERCISE 3: Separable Phrasal Verbs

Complete the conversations with the correct form of the phrasal verbs from the box. Add pronouns when necessary. Some verbs are used more than once or as nouns. Then practice the conversations with a partner.

make up	throw out	put off	call up	bring back	try out

1. **A:** Do you have Anton's number? I need to tell him the schedule has changed.

   B: I've already *called him up*.

2. **A:** I don't want to finish this now. Maybe I'll wait till tomorrow.

   B: You shouldn't _____. You won't have time tomorrow.

3. **A:** Thanks for letting me borrow your book. When will you need it?

   B: Could you _____ tomorrow?

4. **A:** Do you want any of these old papers?

   B: No. Go ahead and _____.

5. **A:** I've decided to _____ for the lead role in the play.

   B: When are the _____s?

6. **A:** When are you going to _____ the test you missed?

   B: I've already _____.

EXERCISE 4: The Gadget Game

A | *Think of a machine or gadget such as a toaster, computer, hair dryer, or can opener. Think of a phrasal verb that describes it or how it works. Here are some possible verbs to use:*

turn up	turn down	turn on	turn off
clean up	throw away (out)	pick up	put down
put in	take off	take out	put on

B | *PAIRS: Describe the gadget you've chosen without using its name and without using your hands. Your partner will guess the gadget.*

EXAMPLE:

STUDENT A: I'm thinking of something that's used for writing. When an old one is *used up*, you *throw it away*.

STUDENT B: Is it a pen?

STUDENT A: Yes, it is!

STEP 3 COMMUNICATION PRACTICE

LET'S PUT IT OFF

Not Today

EXERCISE 5: Procrastination

Listen to the recording and complete the quotations with the words you hear.

1. Procrastination is the art of _____ with yesterday. (Don Marquis)

2. The sooner I fall behind, the more time I have to _____. (Author Unknown)

(continued on next page)

3. There are a million ways to lose a work day, but not even a single way to _____. (Tom DeMarco and Timothy Lister)

4. If you want to make an easy job seem mighty hard, just keep _____ doing it. (Olin Miller)

EXERCISE 6: Put It Off

A | *Listen and repeat the conversation. The phrasal verbs are underlined.*

ABBY: I have to call my mother. I'm always <u>putting it off</u>.

TOMAS: Why? Don't you <u>get along</u>?

ABBY: Yes and no. When I call my parents, we always <u>wind up</u> arguing about something.

TOMAS: I know what you mean. I <u>wound up</u> in an argument with my parents last night.

Natural English
The spellings *wind* and *wound* have several pronunciations.
The verbs *wind-wound-wound* are pronounced like the verbs *find-found-found*.
The noun *wind* is a weather term; it rhymes with *pinned*.
The noun *wound* means "an injury"; it has the vowel in *moon*.

B | *PAIRS: Practice the conversation.*

EXERCISE 7: Your Turn

A | *Are you a procrastinator? What do you put off doing? Make a list on the lines below.*

_____

_____

_____

B | *PAIRS: Compare your lists. What ends up happening when you put different things off?*

STEP 4 EXTENDED PRACTICE

Accuracy Practice *Listen again to Exercises 1 and 2 on pages 199 and 200. Then record the sentences and conversations.*

Fluency Practice *Record your answers to Exercise 7A. Use as many phrasal verbs as you can.*

UNIT 40 Rhythm Patterns: *as, than, if*

STEP 1 PRESENTATION

The conjunctions *as, than,* and *if* are unstressed and join closely to surrounding words.

1. As

> *As* is unstressed and reduced to /əz/. It joins closely to surrounding words.
>
> I've dóne as múch as I cán.
> /əz/ /əz/

2. Than

> *Than* is unstressed and reduced to /ðən/.
>
> Is Énglish hárder than Chinése?
> /ðən/

3. If

> *If* is unstressed. It joins closely to surrounding words.
>
> Cóme if you have tíme.

STEP 2 FOCUSED PRACTICE

EXERCISE 1: Conjunctions

Listen to the sentences. Notice how the underlined words are pronounced. Then choose a sentence and say it to the class.

1. After her mother's death, she felt a sadness <u>as</u> deep <u>as</u> the ocean.
2. The college had more applications last year <u>than</u> ever before.
3. She wondered <u>if</u> he'd ever call again.
4. Do women spend more time on the phone <u>than</u> men?
5. Maybe. But they don't spend <u>as</u> much time watching TV.
6. What lives <u>if</u> you feed it and dies <u>if</u> you water it? (Fire.)

EXERCISE 2: Similes

Writers use similes to show that two things are similar. Similes with *as* + adjective + *as* also occur in expressions to show that something possesses a high degree of the adjective: *I'm as hungry as a bear* means "I'm very hungry."

A | *Listen and repeat the sentences. Join the words in the as . . . as phrases.*

1. Summer barbecues are as American as apple pie.

2. I need some water. My throat feels as dry as a bone.

3. After her long illness, she was as light as a feather.

4. At the party, everybody ignored me. I felt as welcome as a skunk at a garden party.

5. When he goes back to visit his hometown, he's as happy as a duck in water.

B | *Match the adjectives and the nouns below. Write a simile using as . . . as on the lines. Then practice reading the similes with a partner. Reduce as and join it to the surrounding words. (You can check your answers on page 207.)*

Adjectives	Nouns	Simile
_c_ 1. hungry	a. grass	_____
____ 2. good	b. peacock[1]	_____
____ 3. shy/quiet	c. bear	*He's as hungry as a bear.*
____ 4. fat	d. mule	_____
____ 5. sly/clever	e. penny	_____
____ 6. bright	f. gold	_____
____ 7. stubborn	g. mouse	_____
____ 8. proud	h. pig	_____
____ 9. green	i. fox	_____

EXERCISE 3: Conversations

Complete the conversations. Then practice them with a partner.

1. **A:** Karen's been sick so long she's as weak as ___*a kitten*_____.

   B: The doctor doesn't know if _____.

2. **A:** Don't tell Mom, but her cookies taste worse than _____.

   B: Try her cake! It's as dry as _____.

---

[1] peacock: *a large bird with brilliant turquoise colors that spreads its tail feathers like a fan*

3. **A:** The questions on that test were trickier than _____.

    B: And it lasted longer than _____.

4. **A:** A storm's coming. The sky's getting as black as _____.

    B: Let's go in. Your hands are colder than _____.

EXERCISE 4: Riddles

Riddles are word puzzles that ask a question.

PAIRS: Each of you has three riddles that contain unstressed conjunctions. Read a riddle to your partner. Your partner will guess the answer. You can give hints if necessary. Student A's riddles are on page 257. Student B's riddles are on page 262.

EXAMPLE:

STUDENT A: What belongs to you, but others use it more than you do?

STUDENT B: Your name.

EXERCISE 5: What if . . . ?

Listen to the conversations. Then practice them with a partner.

1. **A:** I'm taking the TOEFL tomorrow. I need to do better than last time.

    B: What if you don't? Can you take it again?

2. **A:** The picture isn't as clear as it should be. I've tried adjusting the color, but it doesn't work.

    B: What if you turn it off? That usually works for me.

3. **A:** What if I were smarter than I am?

    B: Then we wouldn't be here, trying to figure out this problem.

4. **A:** It's a beautiful day. I wish I didn't have to go to work.

    B: What if you called in sick? Then we could go to the beach.

Natural English

What if questions can be used to make suggestions or to ask for a result. *What* and *if* join closely together. If the subject of the question is a pronoun, the first three words join very closely together.

What if you don't do better than last time? (*What if you* sounds almost like *what a few*.)

TESTING ABILITY

EXERCISE 6: The Flynn Effect

A | *Check (✓) the statement below that you think is correct. Then listen to the recording. Compare your answers with a partner.*

_____ Average IQ is higher than it was 100 years ago.

_____ Average IQ is the same as it was 100 years ago.

_____ Average IQ is lower than it was 100 years ago.

B | *GROUPS: The Flynn Effect was a surprise to many people. Although psychologists have confirmed that the Flynn Effect is real, they aren't really sure why it's happening. Read three explanations of the Flynn Effect. Which ones do you agree with? Why?*

1. We're not becoming more intelligent. However, the increased availability of information and technological tools has increased our "cultural intelligence."

2. We're not becoming smarter. However, because testing is so widespread, we've become better test-takers.

3. We're becoming smarter. Smaller families mean that parents can spend more time with each child, and each child receives more intellectual stimulation.

EXERCISE 7: Tests

A | *Visual pattern recognition is used in intelligence testing to measure the ability to recognize underlying patterns and relationships. This is an important ability for scientists and mathematicians. Answer the visual pattern questions below.*

1. Circle the letter of the diagram that doesn't fit the pattern.

A   B   C   D   E

2. Choose the word that completes this pattern: hat, bed, little, _____, just.

   a. rang   **b.** money   **c.** get   **d.** kitchen   **e.** summer

B | PAIRS: *Explain your choices to your partner. Use* **as . . . as** *or* **than** *when possible. Do you and your partner agree? (You can check your answers below.)*

C | Complete the sentences with conjunctions. Then practice reading them with a partner.

1. I can get into a good medical school, _____*if*_____ my MCATs are high enough.

2. I can't drive _____ I didn't pass the driving test.

3. The director didn't like my audition, _____ I didn't get the part.

4. The MCAT, the driving test, _____ auditions are examples of high-stakes tests.

   Success or failure rests on one test.

5. Evaluation can also be based on continuous assessment, how well a person does over time.

   Job promotions, for example, are often based on continuous assessment rather

   _____ a single test.

EXERCISE 8: Your Turn

GROUPS: *Complete the chart. Check (✓) the characteristics that you think high-stakes tests and continuous assessment have. Add other characteristics to the last column. Then answer the questions.*

	Efficient	Fair	Objective	Stressful	Other
High-stakes Tests					
Continuous Assessment					

1. What high-stakes tests have you taken?
2. What high-stakes tests will you take in the future? How do you feel about this type of test? Explain your answer.

STEP 4 EXTENDED PRACTICE

Accuracy Practice *Listen again to Exercise 1 on page 203. Then record the sentences.*

Fluency Practice *Record your answers to the questions in Exercise 8.*

EXERCISE 7B: 1. c: The square spiral has one more turn than the other square spirals. **2. b:** The second letter in each word is a vowel; the vowels are in the order they occur in the alphabet (*a, e, i, o, u*).

EXERCISE 2B: 1. c, **2.** f, **3.** g, **4.** h, **5.** i, **6.** i, **7.** d, **8.** b, **9.** a

41 Rhythm Patterns: Conjunction *that*; Intonation and Clauses

STEP 1 PRESENTATION

That

That can be stressed or unstressed, depending on its use.

1. When *that* is a demonstrative pronoun or adjective, it's stressed and pronounced /ðæt/.

Thát's ríght.   Thát mán.   Thát one.   I dón't líke thát.

2. When *that* is a conjunction, it's unstressed and reduced to /ðət/.

Thís méans that I'm ríght.
    /ðət/

The Spánish explórers belíeved that Sóuth América was fúll of góld.
        /ðət/

3. As a conjunction, *that* is usually grouped with words in the following clause.

Is it true that Americans eat only fast food?

Intonation and Clauses

There's usually a change in intonation to mark a boundary between two clauses. Intonation may rise or fall a little at the end of a phrase/clause.

She said that it was important.

He told me a story that I don't believe.

STEP 2 FOCUSED PRACTICE

EXERCISE 1: Reduced *that*

Listen and repeat the sentences. Group words together. Then practice the sentences with a partner.

1. Whích mán? The mán that léft?

2. She insísted that they práctice.

3. I tóld him that I cóuldn't cóme.

4. He sáid that he could cóme.

5. Is it trúe that téa with lémon gets ríd of a cóld?

6. I dón't thínk that it's trúe.

EXERCISE 2: Stressed and Unstressed *that*

🎧 *Listen to the sentences. Put a stress mark (ʹ) over* **that** *if it's used as a demonstrative adjective (that book) or pronoun (That's my brother). Then choose a sentence and say it to the class.*

1. Did you buy thát coat that I showed you?

2. He said that that one wasn't working.

3. That car that that woman drives used to be mine.

4. That's the one that I want.

5. Did you like that movie that you saw?

6. Don't forget that that program is on TV tonight.

EXERCISE 3: *TH* Sounds

Natural English
When *that* is followed by *the*, a difficult sequence of consonants occurs between the two words. Pronounce all of the consonants and don't separate the words with a vowel sound.
Spanish explorers believed <u>that the</u> City of Gold was somewhere in the mountains. /t ð/
People worry <u>that the</u> environment is in danger. /t ð/

🎧 *Listen to the sentences. Then practice them with a partner. Pronounce* th *sounds correctly.*

1. Spanish explorers in the 1500s believed <u>that the</u> "city of gold," El Dorado, lay somewhere in the mountains of South America.

2. Some people say <u>that the</u> Pacific Northwest is the home of Bigfoot, a huge hairy creature that's half man, half beast.

3. In the late 1600s in Salem, Massachusetts, several people were hanged because they refused to say <u>that they</u> were witches.

4. A sailor's superstition says <u>that the</u> albatross, a large bird, is unlucky.

EXERCISE 4: Definitions

PAIRS: Match the phrases in the left column with the definitions in the right column. Then take turns asking questions and giving definitions. Speak smoothly, grouping words together. Follow the example.

EXAMPLE:

STUDENT A: What's a clock?

STUDENT B: A clock is something that tells time.

Phrases	**Definitions**
_b_ **1.** a clock (something)	**a.** has circular winds
____ **2.** a battery (something)	**b.** tells time
____ **3.** a bat (an animal)	**c.** dispenses cash
____ **4.** a glider (a plane)	**d.** combines breakfast and lunch
____ **5.** a mousetrap (something)	**e.** does not have an engine
____ **6.** an ATM (machine)	**f.** "sees" with its ears
____ **7.** a hurricane (a storm)	**g.** catches mice
____ **8.** brunch (a meal)	**h.** stores energy

STEP 3 COMMUNICATION PRACTICE

MISTAKEN BELIEFS

EXERCISE 5: Beliefs

A | *Listen to the sentences. Notice how the conjunction **that** is pronounced with the words that follow.*

1. European geographers used to believe that California was an island.
2. Climatologists used to believe that human settlement in dry areas would cause a permanent increase in rainfall.
3. Metallurgists used to believe that some combination of other metals could produce gold.
4. People used to believe that a pregnant mother's sadness meant her baby would be depressed.

B | *PAIRS: Practice the sentences. Group the conjunction **that** with the words that follow.*

C | PAIRS: Science has changed many of our past beliefs. Each partner has a list of several past beliefs that modern science has disproved or challenged. Read one of the past beliefs to your partner, starting the sentence with **People used to believe that** . . . . Your partner should then state the modern belief. Student A's statements are on page 257. Student B's statements are on page 262.

EXAMPLE:

Belief: Tomatoes are poisonous.
STUDENT A: People used to believe that tomatoes were poisonous.
STUDENT B: Now we know that tomatoes are nutritious.

EXERCISE 6: Stereotypes

A | Listen and repeat. Make sure you understand the words and phrases.

overgeneralizations	a grain of truth	khakis

B | Listen to the recording describing stereotypes about Americans. Write the stereotypes you hear.

_____

_____

_____

_____

_____

_____

_____

_____

C | GROUPS: Discuss the stereotypes you heard. Can you add any others to the list? What's the "grain of truth" in these stereotypes? What makes them false? What stereotypes do people from other countries have about your country? When answering these questions, use expressions like:

People say that . . .

It's true that . . .

It isn't true that . . .

STEP 4 EXTENDED PRACTICE

Accuracy Practice Listen again to Exercises 1 and 2 on pages 208 and 209. Then record the sentences.

Fluency Practice Most cultures and societies have a creation myth or belief—a story about how the world or their nation was created. Record a description of your culture's creation myth. Use sentences with **think that . . . , believe that . . . , say that . . . .** etc.

Contractions and Reductions of Verbs; *Can* and *Can't*

STEP 1 PRESENTATION

Auxiliary verbs (helping verbs) are unstressed; they may be contracted or reduced. You'll understand English better if you're aware of these shortened forms.

Contractions of Verbs

Use contractions after pronouns when you speak. Contractions sound more natural than full forms.

He's late.   We've already seen it.   I'd rather stay home.

Reductions of Verbs

After nouns, auxiliary verbs are often reduced; consonants may not be pronounced and vowels are usually reduced to /ə/. Reductions must be joined closely to surrounding words. If this is difficult for you, use the full forms of auxiliaries, but don't stress them.

1. *Has, Is*

Has and *is* after /s, z, ʃ, ʒ, tʃ, dʒ/ are reduced to /əz/. They sound like the "long plural" ending.

Liz is athletic.   Liz has started college.
"Lizzəz"   "Lizzəz"

2. *Have*

Have is reduced to /əv/. It sounds like *of*.

The men have left.
"menəv"

3. *Had/Would*

Had and *would* are reduced to /əd/. They sound like the "long" past-tense ending.

Ann had seen the movie.   Dominick would rather sleep.
"Annəd"   "Dominickəd"

4. *Will*

Will is reduced to /əl/. It sounds like an *-al* ending.

The fine will be high.
"final"

5. *Are*

Are sounds like an *-er* ending.

Where are my gloves?
"wearer"

Can and Can't

1. Can

Reduce *can* to /kən/ when it occurs inside a sentence. When listeners hear the reduced vowel, they hear *can*. If you use the full vowel /æ/, listeners may hear *can't*.

Plants can produce vaccines for humans.

/kən/

Use the full vowel /æ/ in short answers.

A: Can you deliver?

B: Yes, we can, but there's an extra charge for delivery.

/kæn/

Use the full vowel when no verb follows *can*.

If I can, I'll come at 10:00.

/kæn/

2. Can't

The negative *can't* is always stressed. *Can't* is always pronounced with the full vowel /æ/.

I can't help you tomorrow.

STEP 2   FOCUSED PRACTICE

EXERCISE 1: *Can* and *Can't*

A | *Listen and repeat the phrases and sentences. Stress the pronoun more than* **can**. *Stress* **can't** *more than the pronoun.*

1.	I can	I can check his profile online.
2.	You can	You can ask Tomas if she has a boyfriend.
3.	He can	He can tell you if she's dating someone.
4.	She can	She can set up a meeting.
5.	We can	We can go to the party together.
6.	They can	They can introduce the two of you.
7.	I can't	I can't check his profile online.
8.	You can't	You can't ask Tomas if she has a boyfriend.
9.	He can't	He can't tell you if she's dating someone.
10.	She can't	She can't set up a meeting.
11.	We can't	We can't go to the party together.
12.	They can't	They can't introduce the two of you.

B | *PAIRS: Say a sentence. Your partner will tell you which sentence you said.*

Contractions and Reductions of Verbs; *Can* and *Can't*   **213**

EXERCISE 2: Auxiliary Verbs

Read the conversations. Complete the sentences with auxiliary verbs. Then listen and check your answers.

1. **A:** _____ you ever used an online dating service?

    B: Never, but you know—I _____ _____ thinking about it.

    A: I _____ checked some out, and they seem pretty safe.

    B: So _____ I. But you have to send in a picture. I _____ be embarrassed if anyone I know ever saw my picture.

2. **A:** Who _____ you go out with last night? Your roommate said you _____ gone out.

    B: Yeah. A girl from school. She _____ in a different class.

    A: So who is she? Do I know her?

    B: I don't know. I _____ meeting her here now. Stick around and I _____ introduce you.

EXERCISE 3: Hearing Reductions

Listen to the sentences. The underlined words have the same or nearly the same pronunciation. Then choose a sentence and say it to the class.

1. <u>Bea can light</u> the <u>beacon light</u>.

2. My <u>watch is</u> broken. Who fixes <u>watches</u> around here?
3. Their <u>tenants have</u> joined the <u>tenants of</u> the next building in a rent strike.
4. Your objection is <u>logical</u>, but I don't know if <u>logic will</u> convince them.
5. The <u>ad had</u> cost $800, which <u>added</u> to our total costs.
6. <u>Some have</u> spent <u>some of</u> the profits.
7. <u>Why are</u> there <u>wires</u> sticking out of the wall?
8. Why don't <u>you chew</u> more slowly?
9. <u>Ed had edited</u> it.

EXERCISE 4: Sounds Like . . .

🎧 *PAIRS: Two phrases that sound the same (or nearly the same) but have different spellings and meanings are called* **homophrases.** *Listen and repeat the homophrases. Then work with a partner to think of a homophrase that includes a reduced auxiliary verb. (Hint: An -es ending could be* **has** *or* **is;** *of could be* **have;** *an -er ending could be* **are;** *an -al ending could be* **will.***) (You can check your answers on page 217.)*

1. Alaska hunter   *I'll ask a hunter.*

2. Roses scent the letter. _____

3. the Indians of Painted Towers _____

4. Answer fast. _____

5. The prizes cost a lot. _____

6. the seasonal change _____

7. summer home _____

STEP 3   **COMMUNCATION PRACTICE**

COUPLES

EXERCISE 5: Changes in Marriage Patterns

A | *Read the words and phrases. Make sure you understand the meanings.*

decline	social stigma	reject

🎧 **B** | *Read the statements. Then listen to the recording. Write* **T** *(True) or* **F** *(False) next to each statement.*

_____ 1. Marriage rates are increasing around the world.

_____ 2. It's more acceptable for couples to live together without marrying than it used to be.

_____ 3. Well-educated people are less likely to be married than less educated people.

_____ 4. Married people are generally healthier and better off economically than unmarried people.

C | PAIRS: Compare your answers in Part B. If a statement is false, correct it. Then compare the marriage trends described in the recording with those in your country.

EXERCISE 6: Cyber Romance

A | Read the paragraph and complete the sentences with auxiliary verbs. Then listen and check your answers.

The Internet, including social networking sites, email, and dating services, ___is___ 1.

now the second most common way for couples to meet, after friends and family. Online dating

services _____ proliferated, and the industry as a whole _____ grown 2. 3.

at a healthy rate. For people with little free time, online services offer a private, inexpensive, and

relatively safe way to meet other people and find out about them before going on a date. The

services provide a way to take some of the "blind" out of "blind dates."

Here are some recent facts about online dating services:

- 17% of U.S. couples who got married met on a dating site.

- 1 in 5 singles _____ dated someone they met on a dating site. 4.

- In a survey of 3,000 singles in India, 50 percent had tried online dating.

- The Japanese government _____ offering a free dating service to singles, in 5.

  the hopes of boosting marriage rates and birth rates.

Natural English

Use the preposition *to* (not *with*) after *get married* and *be married*. In *get married*, the verb *get* is rarely stressed.

Bob got márried *to* Marla last month.

My sister's married *to* her high-school sweetheart.

After the verb *marry*, there is no preposition.

My sister married her high-school sweetheart.

B | PAIRS: Compare your answers in Part A. Then answer these questions.

1. Have you ever met someone new online? What was the nature of the relationship (friend, business colleague, possible date)?

2. If you're married or have a boyfriend or girlfriend, how did you meet? How did your parents meet?

EXERCISE 7: Your Turn

A | Compare the advantages and disadvantages of meeting someone new online or through friends/family. Write your ideas in the chart. Use **can** or **can't** when possible.

Advantages/Disadvantages of Online Dating Services	Advantages/Disadvantages of Meeting Someone Through Friends or Family

B | PAIRS: Read your answers to each other. Pronounce **can** and **can't** correctly.

STEP 4   EXTENDED PRACTICE

Accuracy Practice Listen again to Exercises 1 and 3 on pages 213 and 214. Then record the phrases and sentences.

Fluency Practice What information would you include in an online profile of yourself? Record a one-minute description of yourself. Speak smoothly and use contractions/reductions of auxiliary verbs.

EXERCISE 4: 1. I'll ask a hunter. 2. Rose has sent the letter. 3. The Indians have painted towers. 4. Ants are fast. 5. The prize has cost a lot. 6. The season will change. 7. Some are home.

Reduction of Modal Perfects; Reduction of "H-Words"

STEP 1 PRESENTATION

In pronouns and auxiliary verbs that begin with the letter *h*, such as *he, her, have,* and *had,* /h/ is often dropped by native speakers. The reduced function word joins closely to the preceding word.

Modal Perfects: Modal + *have* + Past Participle

The auxiliary *have* is reduced to /əv/ or /ə/ and pronounced like an ending on the preceding modal. *Have* is almost never pronounced in its full form in modal perfects.

That might h̶a̶v̶e̶ happened.   You should h̶a̶v̶e̶ done it.

    "mightəv"   "shoulddə done"

In negative contractions of modal perfects, *have* is reduced to /əv/or /ə/ and joins closely to the negative contraction.

That couldn't h̶a̶v̶e̶ happened.

    "couldəntəv"

H-Word Reductions

Inside a sentence, the beginning *h* of personal pronouns (*he, him, his, her*) and auxiliary verbs (*have, has, had*) is often dropped. The reduced word joins closely to the preceding word. If it's difficult for you to join words together, you can pronounce the /h/, but don't stress the *H*-words.

If h̶e comes, give h̶im the message. The bus h̶ad already left.

"iffy"   "givim"   "bussəd"

Pronounce *h* when there's a pause before the word, when the word is highlighted, in short answers, and in negatives (*hasn't, haven't, hadn't*).

He's réady.   Wé don't care but hé does.

Yes, I háve.   I háven't been to that restaurant before.

STEP 2 FOCUSED PRACTICE

EXERCISE 1: Modal Perfects

🎧 *Listen and repeat the phrases and sentences. Reduce* **have** *and join it to the preceding word. Then choose a sentence and say it to the class.*

1. should h̶a̶v̶e̶ been watching   Oh, I'm sorry. I should h̶a̶v̶e̶ been watching where I was going.

2. should h̶a̶v̶e̶ asked   Don't worry. We can take it back. I should h̶a̶v̶e̶ asked you first.

3. should h̶ave left — I should h̶ave left earlier. I don't know when the next bus will come.

4. should h̶ave looked — I guess I should h̶ave looked in a cookbook.

5. should h̶ave done — I know I should h̶ave done this last night, but I was just too busy.

6. should h̶ave checked — Now I'll have to call a locksmith. I should h̶ave checked my bag before I left.

7. should h̶ave listened — I should h̶ave listened to you and checked the tires at the gas station.

8. shouldn't h̶ave had — Another four pounds. I shouldn't h̶ave had so much.

EXERCISE 2: Guesses with Modal Perfects

PAIRS: Make guesses about why the sentences in Exercise 1 were said. Use the modal perfects in the box and reduce **have**.

Strong guesses (99% sure)	*must (not) have* + Past Participle
Guesses	*might (not) have* + Past Participle
	could have + Past Participle
Impossible	*couldn't have* + Past Participle
Advice	*should(n't) have* + Past Participle

EXAMPLE:

Sentence: I know I shouldn't h̶ave tried to go through that yellow light.

Guesses:

a. The person might h̶ave been speeding.

b. A policeman could h̶ave given her a ticket.

EXERCISE 3: Conversation

A | *Listen to the conversation. Cross out* **h** *in the underlined words if it isn't pronounced.*

A: Something's going on at the office with my boss. He isn't interested in what I have to say.

B: Maybe something's on his mind. Maybe it isn't you. Maybe it's him. Why don't you ask Rachel? She always has her ear to the ground.[1]

A: Yeah. I can trust her. I probably should have talked with her before now. The atmosphere's been difficult for a while.

B: Is your job in danger? Has your boss complained about your work?

A: He hasn't, but I know the manager in the sales department doesn't like me. He always gives me dirty looks.

B: Talk to Rachel. She might have heard something. In the meantime, maybe you'd better dust off[2] your résumé.

---

[1] has (her) ear to the ground: *to know what's going on;* [2] dust off: *get something ready that you haven't used in a while*

B | PAIRS: Practice the conversation in Part A. Speak smoothly.

EXERCISE 4: Twenty Questions

A | Listen and repeat the questions.

1. Is he alive or dead?

2. What does he do?

3. What's her occupation?

4. How old is he?

B | GROUPS: Play the game 20 Questions in small groups. Student A thinks of a person and gives the group the first letter of the person's name (for example, E for Albert Einstein). Choose a person your classmates have heard of. The other players can ask up to 20 questions (total, not per player) to find out who the person is. The player who guesses the person correctly then becomes Student A.

EXAMPLE:

STUDENT A: I'm thinking of a person whose last name begins with *P*.

STUDENT B: Is the person male or female?

STUDENT A: He's male.

STUDENT C: Is he alive or dead?

STEP 3   COMMUNICATION PRACTICE

REGRETS

EXERCISE 5: Woulda, Coulda, Shoulda

A | Listen to the conversation between Joe (a teaching assistant), and Maya (a student).

MAYA: I'm sorry my paper's late, Joe. I would have gotten it to you earlier, but my computer wasn't working.

JOE: But what about the last two late papers? I don't think Professor Watson will accept it.

MAYA: Can't you talk to him? My computer really was broken. I would have turned it in on time.

JOE: Woulda, coulda, shoulda, Maya. Every time you say you're sorry and every time you have an excuse. You're going to have to talk to him this time.

When *have* is the main verb, and in forms of *have to*, the vowel in *have* is not reduced, and *h* is usually pronounced. Remember that *have to/has to* is pronounced as one word.

Every time you have an excuse.
/hæv/

You're going to have to talk to him yourself.
/hæftə/

B | PAIRS: Practice the conversation in Part A. Then write two new excuses for Maya.

1. I would have turned the paper in on time but _____.

2. I know I should have turned the paper in earlier but _____.

EXERCISE 6: It's Not My Problem

A | *Listen to three situations in which the speaker could have done something about what he saw, but chose not to. Take notes on the situations.*

Situation 1: _____

_____

Situation 2: _____

_____

Situation 3: _____

_____

B | *PAIRS: In each of the situations, what should the speaker have done? What would you have done? Use modal perfects. Under what circumstances would you intervene to help a stranger?*

STEP 4 EXTENDED PRACTICE

Accuracy Practice Listen again to Exercise 1 on pages 218 and 219. Then record the phrases and sentences.

Fluency Practice Think of something you did in the past that you now regret. Record what happened and why you now regret it. Use modal perfects to express what you could have done, should have done, etc.

PART V

INTONATION

Intonation Overview

Intonation, the melody of phrases and sentences, is meaningful. In the examples below, intonation makes the difference between a statement and a question.

It's closed.   It's closed?

Intonation refers to the pattern of notes in phrases and sentences. *Pitch* refers to the note on a particular syllable.

Highlighting

In many sentences, one word expresses the most important information. Pitch and stress help to highlight this information for the listener. Features of rhythm such as heavy stress and long length are also used to highlight information (see also Unit 34).

The stressed syllable of a highlighted word is long, heavily stressed and pronounced on a high pitch (very low pitch is sometimes used to highlight information).

   A: What happened to Joe?

   B: He broke his LEG.

Final Intonation

1. Final Falling Intonation

Final falling intonation (also called final rising-falling intonation): Intonation falls from the highlighted word to the end of the sentence. Final falling intonation is common with statements and information questions. Speakers use this pattern to show certainty about what they're saying.

   A: What's the weather going to be?

   B: It's going to rain.

2. Final Rising Intonation

Final rising intonation: Intonation stays high or continues to rise after the highlighted word. Final rising intonation is common with yes-no questions. Speakers use this pattern to indicate uncertainty about what they're saying.

   Is it raining yet?

Pitch Range in English

Pitch range refers to the difference between the highest and lowest notes. English uses a wider range of pitch than some languages, such as Japanese, Spanish, and Dutch. When you speak English, you may need to expand your pitch range in order to avoid sounding "flat." Sounding "flat" can make you seem bored or disinterested to native speakers, who expect to hear a greater pitch range.

EXERCISE 1: Highlighting Information

In column A, the questions ask for specific information. In column B, the words in bold highlight specific information. Listen to the responses in column B. Then match the questions with the responses to make short conversations. Practice the conversations with a partner. Use high pitch and heavy stress to highlight words.

A	B
_____ 1. What did you say? To the football game?	**a.** I want to go to the baseball **game** tomorrow.
_____ 2. Who wants to go?	**b.** I **want** to go to the baseball game tomorrow.
_____ 3. Today, did you say?	**c.** I want to go to the **baseball** game tomorrow.
_____ 4. Do you have to go to the game?	**d.** I want to go to the baseball game **tomorrow**.
_____ 5. What did you say? To the practice?	**e.** **I** want to go to the baseball game tomorrow.

EXERCISE 2: Rising or Falling Intonation?

Listen to the sentences. If intonation rises at the end of a sentence, add a question mark and a rising intonation line (⌣) in the blank. If intonation falls at the end of a sentence, add a period and a falling intonation line (⌒) in the blank.

1. Your car needs new tires .⌒

2. Classes have been cancelled for today _____

3. Felipe's going to Florida for spring break _____

4. Spring break's in mid-March _____

5. Robert's never skied before _____

6. Yuko and Nori went to Washington, D.C., last weekend _____

7. They ran out of gas on the highway _____

EXERCISE 3: Conversations

A | *Listen and repeat the conversations. Pay attention to how the speakers use their voice to express their attitudes. Then practice the conversations with a partner.*

1. **JAIME:** What are you doing for spring break?

   CAROL: I'm going skiing with Susana and Steve. What about you?

   JAIME: I don't have plans yet. I might go somewhere or I might just stay here.

   CAROL: Well, at least you won't have classes.

2. **RACHEL:** I think I need a break from spring break. I'm exhausted!

   JOHN: Did you have a good time? You didn't call, so I assume you did.

   RACHEL: It was great. You know—a lot of parties, dancing, music, food.

   JOHN: I had a pretty good time here. I saw Peter and Melanie a couple of times. It was OK.

B | *PAIRS: How do Jaime and Carol feel about their plans for Spring Break? How do Rachel and John feel about theirs? Discuss.*

STEP 3   COMMUNICATION PRACTICE

REFUSALS

EXERCISE 4: Telemarketers

A | *Listen to the conversations. Notice the intonation of the questions.*

1. **TELEMARKETER:** Hi Jim.

   JIM: Hi. Wait—who is this?

   TELEMARKETER: This is Phillip Watson. I'm conducting a market study and I wondered if . . .

   JIM: I don't know you, and I didn't give you permission to call me by my first name.

   TELEMARKETER: Sorry, Mr. Lukic. I represent XYZ Market Research Group.

   Do you have time to answer some questions?

   JIM: No. I don't have time.

2. **SARA:** You were pretty rude.

 JIM: Oh, and calling me at night isn't rude?

 SARA: I know. I feel uncomfortable with telemarketers.*

 JIM: Uncomfortable? Why uncomfortable?

 SARA: They put you in an awkward situation. You almost have to be rude to get off the phone.

 JIM: I don't think you should feel uncomfortable. I have no problem being rude to them.

---

*Natural English

Pronounce *comfortable* as a three-syllable word: cómf-ter-bel. Pronounce *uncomfortable* as a four-syllable word: un-cómf-ter-bel. The spellings of these words do not match their pronunciations.

I don't feel *cómfterbel* (*comfortable*) talking to telemarketers.

Why do you feel *uncómfterbel* (*uncomfortable*)?

B | *PAIRS: Practice the conversations in Part A. Then answer the questions.*

1. Do you think Jim was rude to the telemarketer?
2. Do you get calls from telemarketers? How do you feel about them?
3. Is it rude to hang up on people? Do you ever do it? Explain.

EXERCISE 5: Interactions

A | *Read the three situations below. The first speaker in each situation is making a request. Refuse each request. Write what you would say on the lines. If you wouldn't say anything, write what you would do.*

1. A homeless man stops you as you're walking down the street.

 Homeless man: Can you spare some change? I'm really hungry.

 You: _____

 _____

2. A coworker asks you to check a draft[1] of a report he's written.

 Coworker: Could you take a look at this draft and suggest changes?

 You: _____

 _____

(continued on next page)

---

[1] draft: *a non-final version of a paper or report*

3. Your younger sister asks you to drive her to her friend's house.

   Sister: Can you drive me to Rachel's?

   You: _____

   _____

B | *PAIRS: Perform the conversations with a partner. Do you and your partner agree on how to refuse the requests?*

EXERCISE 6: How Much Should I Say?

Read the paragraph below. Then review the refusals you wrote in Exercise 5A. Discuss them with a partner. Does the length of your refusal depend on how well you know the person making the request?

A refusal is an example of a difficult social interaction. When you refuse a request, you're saying something that the listener doesn't want to hear. The amount of language people use when they're involved in difficult social interactions depends on how well the speaker and listener know each other. We use less language and shorter explanations when we refuse requests from people we know well or don't know at all. We use more language and longer explanations with acquaintances. With acquaintances there is a relationship, but it's not a clearly defined one. We use more language because we want to make sure we don't offend the other person. With strangers, there's no relationship and therefore little need for words. With close friends and family, the relationship is well-established and, again, there isn't as much need for long explanations.

STEP 4   EXTENDED PRACTICE

Accuracy Practice *Listen again to Exercise 2 on page 225. Then record the sentences.*

Fluency Practice *Record sentences about the spoken interactions below, using **I feel comfortable/uncomfortable.** Then explain your feelings about each interaction.*

1. Asking a stranger for help
2. Refusing the request of an acquaintance
3. Complimenting a friend
4. Inviting someone to do something

STEP 1   PRESENTATION

Final Intonation Patterns

Final intonation refers to intonation that ends a sentence.

1. Final (Rising-) Falling Intonation

Pattern: Intonation rises on the highlighted word (the most important word of the sentence) and then falls to a low pitch to end the sentence.

It's hot in here.

Meaning: Use falling intonation to show that you're certain about what you're saying. This pattern is also used to show that you've finished speaking.

There's a letter for you.

A: What did you do this weekend?

B: Nothing.

Sentence types: Statements, Information questions

2. Final Rising Intonation

Pattern: Intonation rises on the highlighted word and stays high or continues rising to the end of the sentence.

Meaning: Final rising intonation indicates uncertainty. It can also show that the speaker has not finished speaking, although the voice doesn't rise as high as at the end of a *yes / no* question.

Are you staying?

OK?

I think . . . (The speaker hasn't finished the sentence.)

Sentence types: *Yes / no* questions; *wh-* questions asking for a repetition (see Unit 46.)

EXERCISE 1: Minimal Conversation

A | Listen and repeat the conversation. Follow the intonation lines.

A: Problem?

B: Yeah.

A: What?

B: My credit card bill.

A: Wow! Three pages long.

B: Yeah.

A: Is it a mistake?

B: No.

B | PAIRS. Practice the conversation. Then write your own minimal conversation. Here are some suggestions for the first line: **Ready? Finished? Hungry?**

A: _____Ready?_____

B: _____ _____

A: _____ _____

B: _____ _____

A: _____ _____

B: _____ _____

EXERCISE 2: Nothing but Questions

Listen and repeat the conversations. Use rising intonation. Why do the speakers answer each other with questions?

1. **A:** Do you want to come?
   B: Do you want me to?
   A: If I say no, will you be angry?
   B: Do you care if I'm angry?

2. **A:** Does Boris live here?
   B: Are you a friend of his?
   A: Is this his house?
   B: Is he expecting you?

3. **A:** Did you find a brown wallet?

   B: Did you lose one?
   A: Isn't that a wallet over there?
   B: Do you have any identification?

EXERCISE 3: Hearing Intonation

A | Listen to the sentences. If the speaker sounds certain, add a period (.) and a falling intonation line (⌐) in the blank. If the speaker is asking a question, add a question mark (?) and a rising intonation line (⌐) in the blank.

1. The midterm is next week ?⌐

2. They're predicting a snowstorm for tomorrow _____

3. Your credit card company increased your credit line _____

4. The aerobics class is full now _____

5. Maurice was a victim of credit card fraud _____

6. Robert's car is at the mechanic's again _____

7. Martha's going to be moving to Florida _____

8. She's moving out at the end of the month _____

B | PAIRS: *Say a sentence with falling or rising intonation. Your partner will tell you whether you're stating a fact or asking a question.*

STEP 3 COMMUNICATION PRACTICE

PAYING FOR COLLEGE

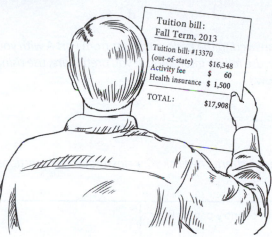

Tuition bill:
Fall Term, 2013

Tuition bill: #13370
(out-of-state) $16,348
Activity fee $ 60
Health insurance $ 1,500

TOTAL: $17,908

EXERCISE 4: The Twenty Under Twenty Fellowship

A | Read the paragraph below.

    Twenty Under Twenty is a fellowship program for young people 17 to 20 years old. Twenty recipients receive $100,000 each over two years to pursue an entrepreneurial dream in science or technology. Recipients who are attending college must drop out to receive the money. The foundation believes that student debt pushes students into high-paying "safe" careers that don't encourage them to think creatively. It also believes that universities have not proven to be effective teachers of the skills needed for innovation and entrepreneurship. The founder of the Twenty Under Twenty program adds that global technological breakthroughs require an intensity of effort that students in school don't have the time to make. The Twenty Under Twenty program has raised controversial questions about education: Is a university education overvalued? Do university courses provide the skills students need to succeed? Is the Twenty Under Twenty program sending the wrong message about college to kids?

B | PAIRS: *Ask and answer the three questions at the end of the paragraph in Part A.*

EXERCISE 5: Trivia

A | *Take the trivia quiz on debt in the United States. Circle the answer you think is correct. Guess if you don't know the answer.*

1. In 2011, what was the average college debt for a graduating American senior?*

   a. $42,000   c. $19,000

   b. $27,000   d. $4,000

2. In 2011, which was greater?

   a. average credit card debt

   b. average student loan debt

3. Assume you charge a $400 coat to your credit card. The interest on your credit card is 18 percent and you make only the minimum payments. How long will it take you to pay off the coat?

   a. 13 months   c. 3.6 years

   b. 2.1 years   d. 5.2 years

4. What percent of Americans spend more than they earn?

   a. 14%   b. 25%   c. 40%   d. 62%

B | *PAIRS: Take turns asking and answering the trivia questions from Part A with your partner. If you're sure about your answer, use falling intonation. If you aren't sure, use rising intonation. (Then check your answers below.)*

EXERCISE 6: Your Turn

GROUPS: Answer the questions in the chart. Then ask your classmates the questions and compare your answers.

How do university students in your country pay for their education?	
What are the biggest purchases families in your country typically make? Is college one of them?	
Is it easy for recent college graduates in your country to find good jobs?	

STEP 4   EXTENDED PRACTICE

Accuracy Practice   *Listen again to Exercise 3A on pages 230 and 231. Then record the sentences, using the intonation on the recording.*

Fluency Practice   *In your country, how do families pay for a big purchase such as a home, car, or college education? Record your answer.*

EXERCISE 5A: 1. b, 2. b (the first time in history average student debt exceeded average credit card debt), 3. d, 4. c

STEP 1 PRESENTATION

Rising intonation is used with words in lists and with question words that ask for a repetition.

Listing Intonation

Words in a list are usually pronounced with "listing intonation": The first words in the list are pronounced with rising intonation. The last word is pronounced with falling intonation.

one, two, three

ambitious, intelligent, and energetic

Intonation Patterns with *or*

1. Choice Questions with *or*

Choice questions ask the listener to choose an alternative. Rising intonation is used on the first choice. Falling intonation is used on the second choice. The two choices are in different thought groups.

A: Do you want this one or that one?

B: That one.

A: Should I use a pencil or a pen?

B: A pen.

2. Open Choice Questions

In open choice questions, the last choice is pronounced with rising intonation to show that the list is not complete: There may be other choices the speaker does not say.

What shall we have for dinner? Do you want fish, chicken, meat, . . . ?

Where shall we go for vacation? To Europe, Canada, Mexico . . . ?

3. *Yes / No* Questions with *or*

Some questions with *or* don't present alternatives: They're true *yes / no* questions and are pronounced with final rising intonation. The words joined by *or* are grouped together.

Do you want to go on Friday or Saturday? (It doesn't matter which day.)

Do you have a cat or dog? (It doesn't matter which: The question is really "Do you have a pet?").

(continued on next page)

Question Words and Rising Intonation

Use rising intonation on a question word (such as *what?*) when you don't understand or when you want a repetition. Use falling intonation when you want an answer to the question.

A: I've got something for you.

B: What?

A: I said, I've got something for you.

B: What?

A: Tickets to the concert.

STEP 2 FOCUSED PRACTICE

EXERCISE 1: Conversations

🎧 *Listen and repeat the conversations. Then practice them with a partner.*

1. **A:** Are you ready to order?

   B: Yes. I'll have coffee, a corn muffin, and orange juice.

2. **A:** What are the Columbia, the Missouri, and the Mississippi?

   B: They're the three largest rivers in the United States.

3. **A:** When you were in Seattle, did you see the Space Needle or the Pike Place Market?

   B: No. I just visited the university and went shopping.

4. **A:** What would you like: A one-bedroom, a studio, a view, close to transportation?

   B: I want a studio that's close to the university, quiet, and furnished.

EXERCISE 2: Lists

🎧 **A** | *Listen to the lists. Write **F** in the blank if the list is finished. Write **U** if the list is unfinished.*

1. 100, 99, 98 _____

2. beef, lamb, chicken _____

3. the Rocky Mountains, the Andes, the Alps _____

4. sunny, quiet, safe _____

5. How do you want your steak: rare, medium, well-done _____

6. March, April, May _____

B | PAIRS: *Choose a phrase from Part A. Decide whether you want to say it as a finished list or an unfinished list. Then say the phrase to your partner. Your partner will tell you whether the list is finished or unfinished.*

EXERCISE 3: Intonation with Question Words

Listen and repeat the conversation. Draw intonation lines (⌣ or ⌐) in the blanks to show the intonation on the question words. Then practice the conversation with a partner.

A: I heard some good gossip.

B: What? _____

A: I said I heard some good gossip.

B: What? _____

A: Maria and Tony are getting married soon.

B: When? _____

A: Soon. I said soon.

B: When? _____

A: I think next month.

EXERCISE 4: What?

A | *Complete the conversations. Each conversation can be completed in two ways, depending on whether Speaker B is asking for a repetition or for more information.*

1. **A:** I heard some interesting news.

   B: What?

   A: _____

2. **A:** I met someone nice today.

   B: Who?

   A: _____

3. **A:** My mother will be arriving next week.

   B: When?

   A: _____

4. **A:** We're going to meet at a restaurant after class.

   B: Where?

   A: _____

B | PAIRS: *Read the conversations with a partner. When you read B's part, use appropriate intonation on the question word to show whether you want a repetition or an answer to the question.*

STEP 3 COMMUNICATION PRACTICE

PLACES

EXERCISE 5: Jeopardy

"Jeopardy" is a game where the answers are known and contestants have to think of the questions. The game below is about places.

A | PAIRS: *You and your partner will take turns being the **host** (the one who has the information) and the **contestant** (the one who must provide the question). Student A's answers are on page 257. Student B's answers are on page 263.*

Here's how to play:

- **Contestant:** Choose an amount (100, 200, 300, 400) to risk in one of the categories. The higher the amount, the greater the difficulty.

- **Host:** Read the information for that amount. Since there are three pieces of information, use listing intonation.

- **Contestant:** Say a question that makes sense for the answer the host just read. If you're sure your question is correct, use falling intonation. If you aren't sure, use rising intonation. If you don't understand the host, ask, *What?*, using rising intonation to show you want a repetition.

- If the question is correct, the contestant earns the number of points assigned to that answer. If the question is incorrect, the contestant loses that amount. Listen to the example.

EXAMPLE:

C (CONTESTANT):	I'll take Bodies of Water for 100 points.
H (HOST):	the Mississippi, the Amazon, and the Thames
C:	What?
H:	the Mississippi, the Amazon, and the Thames
C:	Hmm . . . What are rivers?*
H:	That's correct for 100 points!

> ***Natural English**
>
> Use rising intonation on *wh*-questions when you aren't sure whether your question is correct.
>
> I'm not sure.
>
> *What* are rivers? Is that correct?

B | *PAIRS: Look at the places listed in the Jeopardy game in Part A. Which ones have you visited or seen? Which ones would you like to visit?*

EXERCISE 6: Home Sweet Home

A | *What criteria are important when you choose a place to live? Read the list below and check (✓) the three factors that would most influence your decision to rent/buy a particular house or apartment.*

Price	_____	Size/Space	_____
Neighborhood	_____	Parking	_____
Noise level	_____	Location (close to school/ work/shopping)	_____
Sunlight	_____		
Furnished	_____	Other	_____

B | *GROUPS: Share your criteria, using listing intonation. Do you agree on what criteria are important? Does the place you're living in now meet your criteria?*

STEP 4   EXTENDED PRACTICE

Accuracy Practice *Listen again to Exercise 2A on page 234. Then record the lists, using the intonation you hear.*

Fluency Practice *Record your answer to the question in Exercise 6A. Which three criteria are most important to you? Least important? Explain. Pay attention to intonation.*

Checking Understanding; Low-Rising Intonation with *Yes* / *No* Questions

STEP 1 PRESENTATION

Checking Understanding

Right?

Check understanding by adding *right?* to the end of a sentence. Use rising intonation: *right?*

A: I should wear a suit to the wedding, right?

B: Right.

Notice how to agree with a negative statement followed by *right*. A *no* answer means the speaker agrees with the negative statement.

A: I shouldn't keep my napkin on the table while I'm eating, right?

B: No. (You shouldn't keep your napkin on the table while you're eating.)

Tag Questions

Tag questions, such as *didn't you?*, are added to the ends of sentences. You can use rising or falling intonation on a tag question.

You sent the letter, didn't you?   He can't dance, can he?

1. Rising Intonation:

- **Changes a statement into a question.**

  I paid that money back to you, didn't I? I hope I didn't forget.

- **Makes a command more polite. The tag is usually *would you?***

  Bring that here, would you?

2. Falling Intonation:

- **Asks for confirmation of something the speaker believes is true.**

  Another price increase. Well, prices never go down, do they?

- **Shows agreement with a previous statement. Used this way, tag questions aren't followed by a question mark.**

  A: It's awfully cold today.

  B: Isn't it.

Low-Rising Intonation with *Yes / No* Questions

Speakers sometimes use low intonation to highlight an important word in a *yes/no* question. After the low note, the voice rises to the end of the question. This intonation pattern is often used with strangers to ask for help or information.

Intonation on the highlighted word drops quickly to a low pitch and then rises again.

Do you have the time?   Where can I find a drugstore?

STEP 2 FOCUSED PRACTICE

EXERCISE 1: Conversations

Listen and repeat the conversations. Then practice them with a partner.

1. **CARLA:** 'Scuse me. Where's Hamilton Hall?

   MIKE: Oh. OK. See those stairs over there?

   CARLA: Yes.

   MIKE: Go up the stairs. It's the building at the top of the hill.

   CARLA: Up the stairs, right?

   MIKE: That's right.

2. **SARA:** The dinner tonight's going to be formal. Have you ever been to a formal dinner?

   JOE: Uh, no I don't think so. But I've seen pictures. There are a lot of forks and glasses, right?

   SARA: Stop texting and listen. Do you want me to explain the table setting?

   JOE: No. I just start with the silverware on the outside, right?

   SARA: Yes. And no texting at the table, OK?

   JOE: Of course. No texting at the table.

EXERCISE 2: Tag Questions

Listen to the conversations. Draw the intonation (⌣ or ⌢) you hear over the tag questions.

1. **A:** It's time to go, isn't it?

   B: Yeah. We should get started now.

2. **A:** Oh, no!

   B: You forgot your keys again, didn't you?

3. **A:** You can help me tonight, can't you?

   B: I'm sorry. I just can't do it tonight.

(continued on next page)

4. A: You're not leaving so soon, are you?

   B: No. I'm just going out to make a quick call. I'll be right back.

5. A: They don't have the money, do they?

   B: No. They can't afford to go.

6. A: The bus hasn't left yet, has it?

   B: Not yet. But you'll have to run to make it.

EXERCISE 3: Low-Rising Intonation

🎧 *Listen and repeat the sentences. Which word does the intonation drop on? Circle the word.*

1. Excuse me. Where is the (admissions) office?

2. (to a stranger in a bus) Is this seat taken?

3. (to a stranger) I can't open this—could you give me a hand?

4. (to an airline employee) When is the plane going to leave?

5. (to a stranger next to you in a theater) Is this your coat?

STEP 3   COMMUNICATION PRACTICE

ETIQUETTE AND CUSTOMS

Which fork do I use first?

EXERCISE 4: Etiquette Explanations

🎧 **A |** *Listen. Make sure you understand the words.*

1. chopsticks   3. lap   5. spear

2. elbows   4. utensils   6. the Middle Ages

B | *Read the statements below. Then listen to the recording. Write **T** (True) or **F** (False) next to each statement.*

_____ **1.** The first eating utensil was the spoon.

_____ **2.** During the Middle Ages in Europe, the host of a dinner party didn't provide knives for

the guests.

_____ **3.** The blade of a table knife should point away from other diners.

_____ **4.** When you're served the first course, use the fork closest to the plate.

C | *PAIRS: Compare your answers. Then correct the false statements.*

EXERCISE 5: You Shouldn't Point Your Chopsticks at People, Right?

PAIRS: Learn about table manners in Japan and the United States. Student A will ask questions about table manners in Japan, and Student B will answer with facts. Then Student B will ask questions about table manners in the United States, and Student A will answer with facts. Review the facts before you begin so that you can match them with your partner's questions. Student A's information is on page 258. Student B's information is on page 263.

EXERCISE 6: Don't Forget to Give the Hairdresser a Tip, OK?

Natural English
You can add *OK?* to the end of a request to ask for agreement or approval. Intonation rises on the *K* of *OK?* Don't forget to give a tip, OK? I'll meet you there, OK?

A | *Tipping practices vary a great deal around the world. Read the list of service providers in the chart. Check (✓) the ones you think it's customary to tip in the United States. Then check the ones it's customary to tip in your country.*

	In the United States, tipping is customary for:	**In my country, tipping is customary for:**
Waiters		
Food delivery people (e.g., the person who delivers a pizza to your home)		
Take-out food services (tip jars)		
Babysitters		

(continued on next page)

	In the United States, tipping is customary for:	In my country, tipping is customary for:
Home helpers (cleaners, cooks, dog walkers, newspaper deliverers)		
Mail carriers		
Apartment staff (doormen, superintendent)		
Airport porters (people who carry your bags)		
Teachers		
Taxi drivers		
Plumbers or electricians		
Hair stylists		
Manicurists		
Doctors		

B | GROUPS: *Compare your answers. (You can check below to see which U.S. service providers it's customary to tip.) Then answer the questions.*

1. How do you feel about tipping people?

2. How much should you tip service providers in your country?

STEP 4 EXTENDED PRACTICE

Accuracy Practice *Listen again to Exercise 3 on page 240. Then record the sentences.*

Fluency Practice *Describe the table manners you learned as a child. Record your description.*

EXERCISE 6B: In the United States it's customary to tip most of the service providers in the chart. Some people leave a small tip in the tip jar for people who provide take out food, but others don't. It's not appropriate to tip mail carriers, teachers, professionals like plumbers or electricians, or doctors.

UNIT 48 Contrastive Stress; Non-Final Intonation

STEP 1 PRESENTATION

Contrastive Stress

Use heavy stress on words that contrast or compare information. Pitch is usually high on the contrasted words, to help bring them to the listener's attention.

Put the FORK on the LEFT and the KNIFE on the RIGHT.

I need a FULL-time job, not a PART-time job.

Non-Final Intonation

Intonation rises (or falls) slightly at the end of a clause or thought group, but not as much as it does at the end of a sentence. Non-final intonation changes help mark the parts of the sentence for the listener.

I'll come as soon as possible.   I'll do it if I can.

Unfinished Sentences

Sometimes speakers pause before they've finished speaking. To show that your sentence is unfinished, don't let your intonation drop when you pause.

Turn left at the corner . . . then go straight for five blocks.

STEP 2 FOCUSED PRACTICE

EXERCISE 1: Contrastive Stress

A | *Listen and repeat the jokes about work. The underlined words are pronounced with contrastive stress.*

1. They said my work had been <u>excellent</u>, but I wouldn't get a <u>raise</u>. It was like being told I'd get <u>dessert</u>, but the dessert was <u>onions</u>.

2. We're going to keep having these daily <u>meetings</u> until I find out why no <u>work</u> is getting done.

3. How many government <u>workers</u> does it take to change a light bulb? Twelve. <u>One</u> to change the bulb and <u>eleven</u> to do the paperwork.

4. Machines that break <u>down</u> work <u>perfectly</u> when the repairman comes.

5. Boss: We no longer accept notes from doctors as excuses. If you're able to go to a <u>doctor</u>, you're able to come to <u>work</u>.

B | PAIRS: Read the jokes below. Decide which words are in contrast and underline them. Then practice saying the jokes.

1. Boss: I didn't say it was your fault. I said I was going to blame it on you.

2. Remember not to do your job so well that you're irreplaceable. If you can't be replaced, you can't be promoted.

3. We waste more time by nine o'clock in the morning than other companies do all day.

4. I sleep more at work than at home.

5. Job evaluation report: This employee sets low personal standards and then fails to achieve them.

EXERCISE 2: Differences in Meaning

A | The way in which words are grouped and pronounced together can affect meaning. Listen and repeat the sentences in the left column.

Sentences	Meanings
1. **a.** My brother, who won the lottery, finally got married.	**a.** I have one brother.
b. My brother who won the lottery finally got married.	**b.** I have more than one brother.
2. **a.** "Joe," replied Sam, "is my best friend."	**a.** Sam said Joe was his best friend.
b. Joe replied, "Sam is my best friend."	**b.** Joe said Sam was his best friend.
3. **a.** I promised not to tell, Felipe.	**a.** I told Felipe I would not reveal something.
b. I promised not to tell Felipe.	**b.** I said I would not tell Felipe.
4. **a.** I have three, hundred-year-old coins.	**a.** I have three coins that are 100 years old.
b. I have 300-year-old coins.	**b.** I have some coins that are 300-years old.
5. **a.** The employees, who got pink slips,[1] were devastated.	**a.** All the employees got pink slips.
b. The employees who got pink slips were devastated.	**b.** Some employees got pink slips.

B | Listen again. Circle the meaning in the right column that matches the sentence you hear.

C | PAIRS: Choose a sentence from Part A and say it to your partner. Use intonation and thought groups so your partner knows which meaning you intended.

---

[1] pink slip: *a notice that an employee has been fired*

EXERCISE 3: Finish Your Thought

A | *Listen to the sentences. Write **F** if the speaker is finished with the sentence. Write **U** if the speaker is not finished (unfinished) with the sentence.*

1. I'll start looking for another job ___F___

2. Return the books to the library _____

3. Alex thinks he's going to make a lot of money _____

4. He left work early _____

5. Make sure you bring your ID card _____

6. Lee's boss doesn't ask him for suggestions _____

7. My job became unbearable _____

8. She used to be invited to make suggestions _____

B | *PAIRS: Read a sentence to your partner. Use appropriate intonation so your partner can tell you whether you've finished speaking or plan to say more.*

STEP 3   COMMUNICATION PRACTICE

OUT OF WORK

EXERCISE 4: No Layoff Policy

A | *Listen and repeat. Make sure you understand the words.*

1. welding

2. bonus

3. unorthodox

4. put aside

5. skeptical

6. incentive

B | *Listen to the recording and fill in the blanks.*

1. Describe Lincoln Electric's business practices:

   a. Basis of workers' pay: _____

   b. Hours worked by employees: _____

   c. Evaluation of employees: _____

2. Why are business school professors skeptical of Lincoln's no-layoff policy?

C | *PAIRS: Compare your answers in Part B. Do you think Lincoln Electric's no-layoff policy could work in many industries? Why or why not?*

EXERCISE 5: Leaving a Job

A | *Read this passage. Circle the words in the underlined sentences that contrast.*

In the old work model, employees exchanged job loyalty for job security. Today, that model is out-of-date in many areas of employment. Workers feel less loyalty to their employers, and employers provide less security to their workers. As a result, the chance that you'll work for the same company for your entire work life is getting smaller and smaller.

But changing jobs is difficult. Career counselors say employees shouldn't wait until a work situation has become intolerable. And certainly, they shouldn't wait until they're out of work and desperate. Employees need to recognize the early signs that say it's time to look for another job.

Natural English

Pronounce *out-of-date, out of work, out of luck* as one word: outtədate, outtəwork, outtəluck.

That model is *outtədate*.

Don't wait until you're *outtəwork* and *outtəluck*.

B | *Listen to the recording. Take notes on the eight signs that it's time to look for another job.*

_____

_____

_____

_____

_____

_____

_____

_____

_____

C | PAIRS: Use your notes to paraphrase the signs mentioned in the recording. Use intonation and thought groups to organize the parts of your sentences. Here are some sentence frames to help you paraphrase:

If . . . , it may be time to go.

You should think about another job if/when . . . .

_____

_____

_____

EXERCISE 6: Your Turn

Interview two classmates about past and future jobs. Then share the information with the class.

	Student's Name _____	Student's Name _____
What jobs have you had in the past?		
If you've ever left a job, why did you leave?		
How many jobs do you think you'll have in your lifetime?		
In what field(s) do you want to work?		
Have you ever had two jobs at the same time?		
Do you think you'll continue to get training and education throughout your work life?		
Do most people in your country keep the same job their whole career?		

STEP 4 EXTENDED PRACTICE

Accuracy Practice *Listen again to Exercise 1A on page 243. Then record the sentences.*

Fluency Practice *Record your own answers to the questions in Exercise 6. Answer in complete sentences. Use thought groups and intonation to organize your ideas.*

STEP 1   PRESENTATION

Parentheticals

Parentheticals are expressions that are set apart from a main sentence. They can be at the beginning, in the middle or at the end of a sentence.

> <u>Well</u>, the house looked pretty good after the party.
>
> I was cleaning up, <u>I guess</u>, for an hour.
>
> This is your sister's phone, <u>I think</u>.

In speaking, intonation and thought groups are used to set a parenthetical off from the main sentence. In writing, commas are used.

1. Parentheticals at the end and in the middle of a sentence.

Intonation is low. It can rise a little, fall a little, or stay low at the end of the parenthetical.

> This is your phone, I think.
>
> I was waiting, I guess, for an hour.

2. Parentheticals at the beginning of a sentence.

Intonation can rise on the parenthetical or fall.

> Mary, is this your coat?
>
> You know, this hike looks easy.

Appositives

Appositives are phrases that follow a noun and give more information about the noun.

> I'm sorry, but Latin dancing, <u>the course you signed up for,</u> is full.

In speaking, low intonation and thought groups set the appositive off from the rest of the sentence. Within the appositive, the voice rises a little on important words.

> I'm sorry, but Latin dancing, the course you signed up for, is full.

EXERCISE 1: Telephone Call

Listen to the telephone conversation. Then practice the conversation with a partner. Your intonation should be low on the underlined parentheticals. How does Max feel about the news that Sarah is selling their car?

MAX FREMONT:	Hello?
ROBERT MORSE:	Hello. Is Sarah there?
MAX:	She's at work, <u>I think</u>. May I take a message?
ROBERT:	I'm calling about the car for sale, <u>the Malibu</u>.
MAX:	She's selling the car?
ROBERT :	Uh, yeah. She posted an ad.
MAX:	And you're interested in buying that car, <u>I suppose</u>.
ROBERT:	Yeah. My name's Robert Morse, and my number's 555-0102. Tell her I called, <u>please</u>.
MAX:	I'll give her the message.

EXERCISE 2: Direct Address

Listen to the sentences. Circle the forms of address that are appropriate in English. (Then check your answers on page 252.)

1. **Addressing a Teacher**

   a. Teacher, when is the test?

   b. Professor, when is the test?

   c. Mr. Jones, when is the test?

   d. Bill, when is the test?

   e. Miss Jane, when is the test?

2. **Addressing a Stranger**

   a. Sir, you dropped your gloves.

   b. Mister, you dropped your gloves.

   c. Miss, you dropped your gloves.

   d. Lady, you dropped your gloves.

   e. Ma'am, you dropped your gloves.

   f. Hey you, you dropped your gloves.

   g. Mrs., you dropped your gloves.

EXERCISE 3: Escalation

🎧 *Listen to the conversations. Then practice them with a partner. Use your voice to show how the mood in each conversation changes.*

1. **The Hike**
   SANDRA: This is an easy hike, according to the guidebook. I think we can do it.
   ALEX: Yeah. The trail's in good shape, and the weather's going to be clear all day.
   SANDRA: Alex, what's this? What happened to the trail? Is this the trail?
   ALEX: Don't ask me—this is your hike! Is that rain I feel?
   SANDRA: Forget the rain. How are we going to get up that?
   ALEX: Up? Forget up! Look behind you. How are we going to get down?

2. **Installing a Ceiling Light**
   ALEX: This light will be easy to put in. We can do this.
   SANDRA: Alex, maybe we should get an electrician. Look at all the wires!
   ALEX: I've done this before, you know. You just read the instructions. I'll do the wiring.
   SANDRA: OK. It says match the black wire, the one in the light, to the black wire from the ceiling. Then white to white.
   ALEX: You're on the wrong page, I think. There's nothing black or white here.
   SANDRA: I'm on the ONLY page. This is your project—you read the instructions. I'm making a sandwich.

EXERCISE 4: Hearing Intonation

When you want information, use falling intonation on a *wh-* question. When you want a repetition, use rising intonation. To express disbelief, use high-rising intonation.

🎧 **A** | *Listen to the conversation. Then circle the meaning of the question word.*

JOE: Hi, Mary.

MARY: Hi.

JOE: Did you have a nice weekend?

MARY: What?   *wants information*   *didn't hear*   *disbelief*

JOE: I asked if you'd had a nice weekend.

MARY: Why?   *wants information*   *didn't hear*   *disbelief*

JOE: Why?   *wants information*   *didn't hear*   *disbelief*

MARY: I mean, why do you want to know?

JOE: Want to know what?

MARY: If I had a nice weekend. Why do you want to know?

JOE: Let's just forget the whole thing.

MARY: Forget what?   *wants information*   *didn't hear*   *disbelief*

JOE: What I asked you.

MARY: What did you ask me?

JOE: I've forgotten . . . see you, Mary.

B | *PAIRS: Compare your circled answers. Then practice the conversation.*

THE LIGHTER SIDE OF GENDER WARS

EXERCISE 5: Men Know How to Shop for Groceries

A | *Listen to the recording and complete the sentences with the words you hear. Then compare answers with a partner.*

1. _____, I can shop for groceries.

2. I'm talking about real groceries, _____.

3. I can be relied on to get the basics, _____.

4. But my wife always adds exotic foods, _____.

5. I don't know where those things are, _____.

6. Ask someone, _____.

7. _____, that advice doesn't make sense to me.

8. _____, why would a stranger know where to find something he isn't even looking for?

B | *PAIRS: What kinds of household chores do men do? Women? Explain.*

EXERCISE 6: Courses for Men and Women

Here are some humorous courses that men and women would recommend for the opposite sex. The humor is based on stereotypes that men and women have of each other.

A | *PAIRS: Read the course titles to each other. Highlight the important words with stress and pitch.*

Cooking 101:	How Not to Force Your Diet on Others
Cooking 102:	Beyond Hot Dogs and Beer: You CAN learn to find broccoli in the grocery store.*
Bathroom 101:	How to Change a Roll of Toilet Paper
Bathroom 102:	How to Shower in Five Minutes or Less
Driving 101:	Cars Need Both Gas AND Oil
Driving 102:	Introduction to Asking for Directions
Communication Skills 101:	How to Pretend You Like Dancing
Communication Skills 102:	How to Pretend You Like Sports
Classic Clothing 101:	Wearing Clothes You Already Have
Classic Clothing 102:	Just Because It's Comfortable Doesn't Mean It's Classic

*Natural English

Although function words are usually short and unstressed, you can stress them to emphasize their meaning.

You CAN learn to find broccoli in the grocery store.

Cars need both gas AND oil.

B | *PAIRS: Which courses in Part A would women recommend that men take? Which courses would men recommend that women take? What stereotypes of men and women do the course titles reflect?*

STEP 4 EXTENDED PRACTICE

Accuracy Practice *Listen again to Exercise 5A on page 251. Then record the sentences.*

Fluency Practice *Choose four of the course titles from Exercise 6A. Record the course titles and explain the stereotypes that each course reflects.*

followed by a last name.
1d. Appropriate: only if your teacher has asked you to use his/her first name. **1e.** Inappropriate. *Miss* must be followed by a last name (except with strangers). **2a.** Appropriate. **2b.** Inappropriate. *Mister* must be followed by a last name. **2c.** Appropriate. **2d.** Inappropriate. **2e.** Appropriate. **2f.** Inappropriate. **2g.** Inappropriate. *Mrs.* must be
EXERCISE 2: 1a. Inappropriate. Teacher is not a form of direct address. **1b.** Appropriate. **1c.** Appropriate.

APPENDICES

UNIT 1

Exercise 4, page 4

Don't show your partner your grid. Ask your partner questions to complete your grid: for example, "What's in box A2?" When you have both completed your grids, compare them. They should be the same.

	1	2	3	4
A	waiter			
B		wetter		
C		stuck	stock	
D	main	man	stack	men

UNIT 2

Exercise 5, page 9

Don't show your partner your grid. Ask your partner questions to complete your grid: for example, "What's in box A2?" When you have both completed your grids, compare them. They should be the same.

	1	2	3	4
A	list			steal/steel
B			least	
C	still	better	rich	
D		bitter	reach	

UNIT 4

Exercise 2, page 18

1. If you don't see well, you may need to wear these.
2. What's a word for a "short coat"?
3. What's a word for "money"?
4. What's the past tense of "say"?
5. What do you put in a car to make it go?

6. What's the opposite of "hell"?
7. You can take pictures with this.
8. Dogs and cats have fur covering their bodies. What do birds have?
9. What kind of food does McDonald's sell?
10. What's the opposite of "cheap"?

Answers:

1. glasses
2. jacket
3. cash
4. said
5. gas (gasoline)
6. heaven
7. camera
8. feathers
9. fast food/hamburgers/French fries/sandwiches
10. expensive

UNIT 5

Exercise 6A, page 24

Read these statements to your partner. Your partner will decide which intangible money is being used to buy.

1. I really don't spend much money on anything. I save almost everything I make. You never know what's going to happen. What am I going to do with a bunch of nice clothes if I lose my job?
2. The clothes I wear, the car I drive, the neighborhood I live in—they're all important in my line of work. They're signs that I'm successful. My clients want to know that.
3. Our company contributed heavily to your election campaign, and we expect you to protect our interests in Congress. We want you to support legislation that doesn't hurt this company.

UNIT 6

Exercise 3, page 27

Don't show your partner your grid. Ask your partner questions to complete your grid: for example, "What's in box A2?" When you both complete your grids, compare them. They should be the same.

	1	2	3	4
A	bucks			dock
B			box	
C	deck		nut	backs
D		not	duck	

Exercise 7B, page 29

1. Genetics: False. Genetics appears to play an important role in an individual's baseline happiness, although it is not the only factor.

2. Age research. False. 20-30 year olds and 70-80 year olds are both happier than 40-50 year olds. One explanation is that 40-50 year olds are going through a "mid-life crisis."

4. Marriage: True. Married people seem to be happier than unmarried people, although not all research shows this.

UNIT 7

Exercise 7, page 36

Start as the host. When your partner selects an amount, read the clue for that amount. Your partner must guess the *question*. Pronounce *first* correctly.

100: This man was the first president of the United States in the twenty-first century.

200: According to the Bible, these were the first two people on earth.

300: This man is recognized as the first European to discover the New World.

400: This country was the first to win the World Cup four times.

500: This man was the first person to walk on the moon.

[Who was/is George W. Bush? Who were Adam and Eve? Who was Christopher Columbus? What is Brazil? Who was Neil Armstrong?]

Contestant role: Choose an amount: 100, 200, 300, 400, or 500. When your partner reads you the clue, say the *question* that the clue answers.

UNIT 11

Exercise 4, page 57

Don't show your partner your grid. Ask your partner questions to complete your grid: for example, "What's in box A3?" When you both complete your grids, compare them. They should be the same.

	1	2	3	4
A	sing	thing		
B	past	fast		correct
C				collect
D	fourth	force		

UNIT 14

Exercise 4, page 71

1. In the American Civil War, which side won?
2. What's an adjective that means "two"?
3. What's the name of our planet?
4. What's an instrument that measures temperature?
5. What's 20 + 10?
6. What fraction do you get if you divide 1 by 1,000?
7. What's a word for the front of the neck?
8. What's the part of the news that tells you about rain or snow?
9. What's another word for a robber?
10. What's a word that describes what's between "everything" and "nothing"?
11. Life starts with _____.
12. What's the sound of lightning?
13. These white things in your mouth help you chew.
14. If you're nervous, take a deep _____.

Answers:

1. the North
2. both
3. the earth
4. thermometer
5. 30
6. (one) one-thousandth, a thousandth
7. throat
8. the weather (report)
9. a thief
10. something
11. birth
12. thunder
13. teeth
14. breath

UNIT 15

Exercise 7A, page 79

Advantages of biofuels	Drawbacks of biofuels
Biofuel crops could sta**b**ilize or lower the **p**rice of oil. This will **b**e **b**eneficial to the economies of **p**oor countries.	
Biofuels are renewa**b**le. Although energy is required to con**v**ert **p**lants to fuel, when the **p**lants are growing, they take carbon dioxide out of the air.	
Bio-energy can create jo**b**s in **p**oor countries.	
Biofuel s**p**ills do less damage to the environment than oil s**p**ills.	

UNIT 18

Exercise 5, page 92

Activity (30 minutes long)	Calories (the range depends on the size of the person)
Sports and outdoor activities	
Swimming	
Weight-lifting	
Playing soccer	
Planting a garden	
Walking (at a moderate pace)	
Daily life	
Cleaning house (moderate)	148-204 calories
Computer work	41-61 calories
Standing in line	38-56 calories
Watching TV	28-33 calories
Playing with kids	120-178 calories

Exercise 7A, page 97

	You	Your partner
1. When your partner wants to argue, do you leave or find some way to avoid the argument?	Usually ☐ Sometimes ☐ Rarely ☐	Usually ☐ Sometimes ☐ Rarely ☐
2. If you hurt your partner's feelings in an argument, do you apologize?	Usually ☐ Sometimes ☐ Rarely ☐	Usually ☐ Sometimes ☐ Rarely ☐
3. Do you ask for your partner's side of the story when you argue?	Usually ☐ Sometimes ☐ Rarely ☐	Usually ☐ Sometimes ☐ Rarely ☐
4. When you argue, do you attack your partner where you know it will hurt?	Usually ☐ Sometimes ☐ Rarely ☐	Usually ☐ Sometimes ☐ Rarely ☐
5. Do you believe it's better to fight than to hold in negative feelings?	Usually ☐ Sometimes ☐ Rarely ☐	Usually ☐ Sometimes ☐ Rarely ☐
6. Do you end up fighting about something completely different from the problem you started with?	Usually ☐ Sometimes ☐ Rarely ☐	Usually ☐ Sometimes ☐ Rarely ☐
7. Do you view arguments as an opportunity for growth?	Usually ☐ Sometimes ☐ Rarely ☐	Usually ☐ Sometimes ☐ Rarely ☐
8. Do your arguments solve the problems you fight about?	Usually ☐ Sometimes ☐ Rarely ☐	Usually ☐ Sometimes ☐ Rarely ☐

UNIT 22

Exercise 5, page 109

Quote 1

a. a word that means the opposite of "wise"; a word that means "deceive" or "trick"; a word that rhymes with "tool"

b. a word that means everyone; a word that rhymes with "tall"

c. a word that means "men and women"; a more common way of saying "persons"

d. what the clock tells you; a word that rhymes with "lime"

e. the same as *c*.

f. the same as *b*.

g. the same as *a*.

h. the same as *b*.

i. the same as *c*.

j. the same as *b*.

Quote 2

a. another word for "little"; a word that rhymes with "tall"

b. not a woman but a _____; a word that rhymes with "tan"

c. a word that means "a large step"; a word that rhymes with "keep"

d. a man's first name that rhymes with "meal"; a word that sounds the same as the verb that means "be on your knees"

Answers:

Quote 1

a. fool	**d.** time	**g.** fool	**j.** all
b. all	**e.** people	**h.** all	
c. people	**f.** all		**i.** people

Quote 2

a. small	**c.** leap
b. man	**d.** Neil

UNIT 37

Exercise 5, page 190

1. Andes Mountains (continent)
2. Mississippi River (country)
3. Nile River (continent)
4. Mount Everest (country/countries)
5. Tokyo (country)

6. Hollywood (state)
7. Beijing (country)
8. United Nations headquarters (city)
9. Golden Gate Bridge (city)
10. Taj Mahal (country)

Answers:

1. in South America
2. in the United States
3. in Africa
4. between Nepal and Tibet
5. in Japan
6. in California
7. in China
8. in New York
9. in San Francisco
10. in India

UNIT 40

Exercise 4, page 205

Read the riddles to your partner, speaking smoothly and clearly. If your partner can't guess the answer, give hints.

1. What is better than the best and worse than the worst? Answer: nothing.
2. You want to share it if you have it, but if you share it, you don't have it. What is it? Answer: a secret.
3. Why are 2001 American dollar bills worth more than 1999 American dollar bills? Answer: Because $2,001 is more than $1,999.

UNIT 41

Exercise 5C, page 211

Read these past beliefs to your partner. Introduce the sentence with "People used to believe that . . ." and change the verb in the sentence to the past tense. Your partner will state the current belief.

1. The Earth is the center of the universe.
2. The sun goes around the Earth.
3. The character of a person can be seen in the shape of the head. (This was an early theory of psychology, called *phrenology*.)
4. The first two people on earth were Adam and Eve.

UNIT 46

Exercise 5A, page 236

When you are the contestant, choose a category and an amount. After you hear the clue, ask a question that the clue answers.

Category 1: Bodies of Water (rivers, lakes, oceans, seas)	Category 2: Countries
100	100
200	200
300	300
400	400

When you are the host, read these clues:

Category 3: States	Category 4: Continents
100 Clue: Miami, Disney World, the Everglades (Answer: What is Florida?)	100 Clue: France, Portugal, Austria (Answer: What is Europe?)
200 Clue: San Antonio, the Alamo, Houston (Answer: What is Texas?)	200 Clue: Brazil, Peru, Uruguay (Answer: What is South America?)
300 Clue: Sacramento, Silicon Valley, the Golden Gate Bridge (Answer: What is California?)	300 Clue: the Great Wall, Bangkok, Mongolia (Answer: What is Asia?)
400 Clue: Harvard, Beacon Hill, Cape Cod (Answer: What is Massachusetts?)	400 Clue: Cairo, Lagos, Nairobi (Answer: What is Africa?)

Exercise 5, page 241

Questions about Japanese table etiquette	Facts about U.S. table etiquette.
When you're not using your chopsticks, you should place them in front of you with the tips pointing right, right?	The napkin should be placed on the table to the left of your plate when you leave the table.
You can hold a soup bowl like a cup and drink the liquid from it, right?	Men should never wear hats at the table although women can.
You shouldn't eat everything on your plate, right?	The general rule is that you use the same method to remove food that you used to bring it to your mouth. Fish bones, however, can be removed with your fingers.

UNIT 1

Exercise 4, page 4

Don't show your partner your grid. Ask your partner questions to complete your grid: for example, "What's in box *A1*?" When you have both completed your grids, compare them. They should be the same.

	1	2	3	4
A		filled	field	ten
B	waste		tan	tin
C	west			ton
D				

UNIT 2

Exercise 5, page 9

Don't show your partner your grid. Ask your partner questions to complete your grid: for example, "What's in box *A1*?" When you have both completed your grids, compare them. They should be the same.

	1	2	3	4
A		mill	meal	
B	risen	reason		greed
C				grid
D	cheek			chick

UNIT 4

Exercise 2, page 18

1. What's another word for "slim"?
2. What's a word that means "not present or future"?
3. People who want to lose weight should eat foods low in _____.
4. What word describes food that doesn't have much flavor?
5. Your head sits on this part of your body.
6. What's the past tense of "flee"?
7. What's the opposite of "cried"?
8. Add this color to red and you'll get orange.

9. What's the word for a baby cow?
10. What's the name of a yellow fruit that's long and curved, and white on the inside?

Answers:

1. slender
2. past
3. fat/calories
4. bland
5. neck
6. fled
7. laughed
8. yellow
9. calf
10. banana

UNIT 5

Exercise 6A, page 24

Read these statements to your partner. Your partner will decide which intangible money is being used to buy.

1. I'm good to my employees. I've just upgraded their health insurance, and I help them out whenever I can. I stand by them, and I expect them to stand by me.

2. I take my friends out all the time. I have a good time and I know they do. I like spending my money on people; I know they like it, too. I never have any trouble finding people to do things with.

3. If I win the lottery, I'm going to quit my job. Nobody's ever going to tell me what to do again. I'm going to do whatever I want, whenever I want.

UNIT 6

Exercise 3, page 27

Don't show your grid to your partner. Ask your partner questions to complete your grid; for example, "What's in box *A1*?" When you both complete your grids, compare them. They should be the same.

	1	2	3	4
A		rut	sacks	
B	sex	hem		rot
C		sucks		
D	socks			ham

Exercise 7B, page 29

3. Income research: True. Not surprisingly, poor people report lower levels of happiness. However, once someone earns a comfortable, upper middle class income, additional wealth does not bring additional happiness.

5. Children: The statement is partially true. Married couples with up to three children seem to be happier than other groups of people. Other research shows that children may not be necessary for happiness.

6. Social ties: True. A British study found that happiness tends to spread more consistently through people in close relationships than unhappiness.

UNIT 7

Exercise 7, page 36

Start as the contestant: Choose an amount: 100, 200, 300, 400, or 500. When your partner reads you the clue, say the *question* that the clue answers.

Host role: When your partner selects an amount, read the clue for that amount. Your partner must guess the *question*. Pronounce *first* correctly.

100: These people were the first inhabitants of North America.

200: The first Olympics were in this country.

300: This man was the first president of the United States.

400: This was the first woman to win a Nobel Prize.

500: This country was the first to send a person into space.

[Who are Native Americans/American Indians? What is Greece? Who was George Washington? Who was Marie Curie? What was the Soviet Union?]

UNIT 11

Exercise 4, page 57

Don't show your partner your grid. Ask your partner questions to complete your grid: for example, "What's in box *A1*?" When you both complete your grids, compare them. They should be the same.

	1	2	3	4
A			very	berry
B			rate	
C	west	vest	late	
D			breathe	breeze

UNIT 14

Exercise 4, page 71

1. The word "parents" refers to your _____ and _____
2. What's the opposite of "rough" or "bumpy"?
3. What should you say when someone does something nice for you?
4. What's a word that means "a way (of doing something)"?
5. What's the term for the hide (skin) of a cow that is used to make shoes?
6. Someone who writes a book is an _____.
7. What's the plural of "that"?
8. What preposition do you use with tunnels?
9. When you want to ask about the value of something, you say "How much _____?"
10. What's the name of the science of numbers?
11. What's the name of the day you were born?
12. What's an adverb that means carefully and completely?
13. What's the name of the day that follows Wednesday?
14. What's the name of the upper part of the leg, above the knee?

Answers:

1. mother and father
2. smooth
3. thank you/thanks
4. method
5. leather
6. author
7. those
8. through
9. is it worth
10. math(ematics)
11. birthday
12. thoroughly
13. Thursday
14. thigh

UNIT 15

Exercise 7A, page 79

Advantages of biofuels	Drawbacks of biofuels
	Forests are cut down to plant bio-fuel crops. This is catastrophic for the climate and for wildlife.
	Small farmers are being pushed off the land by large-scale energy companies.
	Land taken out of production for food will worsen food shortages.
	The demand for fuel from corn, sugar, or rice will drive up the prices of these staple foods.

UNIT 18

Exercise 5, page 92

Activity (30 minutes long)	Calories (the range depends on the size of the person)
Sports and outdoor activities	
Swimming	180-266 calories
Weight-lifting	90-133 calories
Playing soccer	210-311 calories
Planting a garden	120-178 calories
Walking (at a moderate pace)	150-222 calories
Daily life and occupations	
Cleaning house (moderate)	
Computer work	
Standing in line	
Watching TV	
Playing with kids	

UNIT 19

Exercise 7A, page 97

	You	Your partner
1. Do you apologize for things you haven't done or said to end an argument?	Usually ☐ Sometimes ☐ Rarely ☐	Usually ☐ Sometimes ☐ Rarely ☐
2. If you realize you were wrong during the course of the argument, do you admit it?	Usually ☐ Sometimes ☐ Rarely ☐	Usually ☐ Sometimes ☐ Rarely ☐
3. Do you prefer to have a friend or relative around when you argue (as a "judge")?	Usually ☐ Sometimes ☐ Rarely ☐	Usually ☐ Sometimes ☐ Rarely ☐
4. When you argue about something current, do you bring up past unresolved issues in your relationship?	Usually ☐ Sometimes ☐ Rarely ☐	Usually ☐ Sometimes ☐ Rarely ☐
5. After you argue, are you left with bitter feelings?	Usually ☐ Sometimes ☐ Rarely ☐	Usually ☐ Sometimes ☐ Rarely ☐
6. Do you tell your partner what you don't like about his/her behavior?	Usually ☐ Sometimes ☐ Rarely ☐	Usually ☐ Sometimes ☐ Rarely ☐
7. Do you ask your partner what he/she doesn't like about your behavior?	Usually ☐ Sometimes ☐ Rarely ☐	Usually ☐ Sometimes ☐ Rarely ☐
8. Do you get so furious during arguments that you can't think clearly?	Usually ☐ Sometimes ☐ Rarely ☐	Usually ☐ Sometimes ☐ Rarely ☐

UNIT 22

Exercise 5, page 109

Quote 3

a. the opposite of "possible"

b. the opposite of "probable"

c. a four letter word for determination; rhymes with "hill"

d. a word that means "certain to happen; unstoppable"

Quote 4

a. a word that means "can't be done"

b. you do this sometimes when you sleep

c. a noun for "real"

d. the day after today

Answers:

Quote 3

a. impossible   c. will

b. improbable   d. inevitable

Quote 4

a. impossible   c. reality

b. dream   d. tomorrow

UNIT 37

Exercise 5, page 190

1. Alps (continent)
2. Eiffel Tower (city)
3. Great Wall of China (continent)
4. Miami (country)
5. Kremlin (city)
6. Sears Tower (city)
7. Hawaiian Islands (ocean)
8. Sahara Desert (continent)
9. Empire State Building (city)
10. Amazon River (continent)

Answers:

1. in Europe   6. in Chicago
2. in Paris   7. in the Pacific Ocean
3. in Asia   8. in Africa
4. in the United States 9. in New York
5. in Moscow   10. in South America

UNIT 40

Exercise 4, page 205

Read the riddles to your partner, speaking smoothly and clearly. If your partner can't guess the answer, give hints.

1. The poor have it; the rich need it, and if you eat it, you'll die. What is it? Answer: nothing.

2. You destroy me if you name me. What am I? Answer: silence.

3. Even if it's starving, an Arctic polar bear will never eat a penguin egg. Why? Answer: Penguins live in Antarctica.

UNIT 41

Exercise 5C, page 211

Your partner will read some past beliefs to you. Tell your partner the current belief.

Then, read these past beliefs to your partner. Introduce the sentence with "People used to believe that . . ." and change the verb in the sentence to the past tense. Your partner will state the current belief.

1. The four basic substances of the universe are earth, air, fire, and water.

2. The spirits of the dead continue to live in animals.

3. The world is flat.

4. The world is held up by Atlas, a very strong man.

Exercise 5A, page 236

When you are the host, read these clues:

Category 1: Bodies of Water	Category 2: Countries
100 Clue: the Pacific, the Atlantic, the Arctic (Answer: What are oceans?)	100 Clue: Toronto, Vancouver, Quebec (Answer: What is Canada?)
200 Clue: the Mediterranean, the Baltic, the Caribbean (Answer: What are seas?)	200 Clue: Kyoto, Tokyo, Hiroshima (Answer: What is Japan?)
300 Clue: the Nile, the Hudson, the Yangtze (Answer: What are rivers?)	300 Clue: Berlin, Frankfurt, Munich (Answer: What is Germany?)
400 Clue: Michigan, Tahoe, Victoria (Answer: What are lakes?)	400 Clue: Sydney, Adelaide, Melbourne (Answer: What is Australia?)

When you are the contestant, choose a category and an amount. After you hear the clue, ask a question that the clue answers.

Category 3: States	Category 4: Continents
100	100
200	200
300	300
400	400

Exercise 5, page 241

Questions about U.S. table etiquette	Facts about Japanese table etiquette
You can wear a hat at the table, right?	When you're not using your chopsticks, the tips should point left.
You can use your hand to remove inedible food like bones from your mouth, right?	In most situations, you should eat everything on your plate.
You should put your napkin on your chair when you leave the table, right?	If you only have chopsticks, you can hold a soup bowl like a cup and drink the liquid from it.

3 RECORDING AND SENDING A SOUND FILE

Windows XP Operating System
Recording
1. Plug in the microphone.
2. Open the START menu and click on the following: ALL PROGRAMS → ACCESSORIES → ENTERTAINMENT → SOUND RECORDER.
3. With the microphone plugged into the computer, click the red RECORD button and speak into the microphone. The recorder will record one minute of speech. Click the red RECORD button again to continue recording.
Saving and Compressing
4. Open the FILE menu and click SAVE AS. Compress the file if it is large: On the SAVE AS window, click the CHANGE button. In the SOUND SELECTION window, under FORMAT, select MPegLayer 3 (MP3). Close the SOUND SELECTION window. Name the file and save it.
Sending
5. The file can now be attached to an email and sent.

Windows VISTA and Windows 7 Operating System
Recording and Saving
1. Plug in the microphone.
2. Open the START menu and click on the following: ALL PROGRAMS → ACCESSORIES → SOUND RECORDER.
3. Click the red START RECORDING button and speak into the microphone.
4. Click the STOP RECORDING button when you finish. A SAVE box will appear. Name the file and save it.
Compressing and Sending
5. Right click on the saved sound file. SEND TO → COMPRESSED (ZIPPED)
6. Attach the compressed file to an email and send it.

MACINTOSH
Recording and Saving
1. Open an existing Sound Recording application on your Mac. If you do not have a Sound Recording application installed, download and install the free version of **Audacity**™ sound recorder (http://audacity.sourceforge.net/download/). It is very easy to use.
2. After installing **Audacity**™, open the application from your desktop and then use the recording tools to Record, Stop, Rewind, Pause, or Fast-forward.
3. To save the recorded file, click on the FILE menu and then click on EXPORT AS MP3.
4. Choose the location to save the file and then click on SAVE.